regional planning in Europe

London Papers in Regional Science

1 Studies in regional science
edited by Allen J Scott

2 Urban and regional planning
edited by A G Wilson

3 Patterns and processes in urban and regional systems
edited by A G Wilson

4 Space-time concepts in urban and regional models
edited by E L Cripps

5 Regional science—new concepts and old problems
edited by E L Cripps

6 Theory and practice in regional science
edited by I Masser

7 Alternative frameworks for analysis
edited by Doreen Massey, P W J Batey

8 Theory and method in urban and regional analysis
edited by P W J Batey

9 Analysis and decision in regional policy
edited by I G Cullen

10 Developments in urban and regional analysis
edited by M J Breheny

p Pion Limited, 207 Brondesbury Park, London NW2 5JN

edited by R.Hudson, J.R.Lewis · London papers in regional science 11 · a pion publication

regional planning in Europe

Pion Limited, 207 Brondesbury Park, London NW2 5JN

Copyright © 1982 by Pion Limited

ISBN 0 85086 097 0

Printed in Great Britain by Page Bros (Norwich) Limited

Preface

This volume is largely based upon papers presented at a session of the Annual Conference of the Regional Science Association (British Section) held in London during September 1980 which we convened. It also contains two papers that, in their present form, reflect the work of the Regional Social Theory Workshop of the British Section.

We would like to record our thanks to the secretarial and technical staff of the Department of Geography of the University of Durham, for their invaluable help in preparing these papers for publication.

R Hudson, J R Lewis
Durham
May 1982

Contributors

L F Alonso Teixidor — *Oficina Municipal del Plan, Alfonso XIII 129, Madrid-16, Spain*

F Arcangeli — *Dipartimento di Analisi Economica e Socologica del Territorio, Istituto Universitario di Architettura di Venezia, Venezia, Italy*

D Bleitrach — *Laboratoire de Sociologie Industrielle, Département de Sociologie et d'Ethnologie, Université de Provence, Aix-en-Provence, France*

P Breathnach — *Department of Geography, St Patrick's College, Maynooth, Co. Kildare, Eire*

A Chenu — *Laboratoire de Sociologie Industrielle, Département de Sociologie et d'Ethnologie, Université de Provence, Aix-en-Provence, France*

P Damesick — *Department of Geography, Birkbeck College, University of London, 7–15 Gresse Street, London W1P 1PA, England*

M Hebbert — *London School of Economics and Political Science, University of London, Houghton Street, London WC2A 2AE, England*

R Hudson — *Department of Geography, University of Durham, Science Laboratories, South Road, Durham DH1 3LE, England*

J R Lewis — *Department of Geography, University of Durham, Science Laboratories, South Road, Durham DH1 3LE, England*

H Toft Jensen — *Institute for Geography, Socioeconomic Analysis, and Computing, Roskilde University Centre, PO Box 260, 4000 Roskilde, Denmark*

H Voogd — *Department of Urban and Regional Planning, Technische Hogeschool Delft, Stevinweg 1, Postbus 5048, 2600 GA Delft, The Netherlands*

C Weaver — *School of Community and Regional Planning, University of British Columbia, 6333 Memorial Road, Vancouver, BC, Canada V6T 1W5*

Contents

⟋ Regional Planning in Europe: Introductory Remarks 1
R Hudson, J R Lewis

Regional Planning in Spain and the Transition to Democracy 7
L F Alonso Teixidor, M Hebbert

The Demise of Growth-centre Policy: The Case of the Republic 35
of Ireland
P Breathnach

Regional and Subregional Planning in Italy: An Evaluation of 57
Current Practice and some Proposals for the Future
F Arcangeli

Strategic Choice and Uncertainty: Regional Planning in Southeast 85
England
P Damesick

Issues and Tendencies in Dutch Regional Planning 112
H Voogd

The Role of the State in Regional Development, Planning, and 127
Implementation: The Case of Denmark
H Toft Jensen

⟋ Regional Planning—Regulation or Deepening of Social 148
Contradictions? The Example of Fos-sur-Mer and the
Marseilles Metropolitan Area
D Bleitrach, A Chenu
The Development of Fos-sur-Mer: A Footnote 179
R Hudson, J R Lewis

The Limits of Economism: Towards a Political Approach to 184
Regional Development and Planning
C Weaver

Regional Planning in Europe:
Introductory Remarks

R HUDSON, J R LEWIS
University of Durham

This volume is based upon a set of papers originally presented to the annual conference of the Regional Science Association (British Section) in London during September 1980. Our aim in organising these papers for the conference was to prompt an evaluation of the experience of regional planning in Western Europe which situated the formulation of planning policies, their implementation, and their effects within their broader economic and political context. This remains our aim in offering the papers—each modified in the light of discussions at the conference—to a wider audience as it has become increasingly apparent that the search for new measures to cope with the problems of uneven regional development in the 1980s requires much more than a simple comparison of the relative efficiency of the different techniques of intervention employed during the 1960s and 1970s. We have sought to advance the debate at the conference as one part of the work of the Regional Social Theory Workshop of the Regional Science Association (British Section) and include here two further papers which, in their present form, were produced within that framework and deal with other national experiences. One, by Toft Jensen, is a paper specially commissioned for this volume; the other, the classic study by Bleitrach and Chenu, was originally presented to the Northwest European Multilingual Regional Science Association meeting at Louvain in 1974 (Bleitrach and Chenu 1975), but has not yet appeared in English.

The papers collected here thus cover a broad range of approaches to the problems of reorganising the distribution of activities within a region, and consider their impacts both at the national and at the regional scale. In addition, there is diversity in the theoretical points of departure of different authors, but all are united in their critical view of the actual impacts of regional planning on the problems that it was intended to address. In the remainder of this introduction we briefly summarise the common features of these regional planning experiences and place the authors' criticisms in the context of broader political and economic changes.

During the latter part of the 1950s and 1960s, regional planning emerged as a specific form of state intervention in many of the countries of Western Europe. The economic and political circumstances of this period were important in helping to shape the character and content of these new planning initiatives. The 1950s and 1960s were generally marked by high rates of national economic growth, by 'economic miracles' and the long postwar boom. Politically, the climate was a more variable one, for although social democratic concerns with progressive reform were visible

through the workings of parliamentary democratic systems over much of
Western Europe, in some countries (such as Spain) this was not so and the
decisive political force remained right-wing authoritarianism (see Scase,
1980). Nevertheless, despite such differences, and so for differing reasons,
national governments of varying political persuasions tended to converge
upon the concept of managing the national space via centrally conceived
and directed regional planning initiatives, identifying balanced regional
growth as the route to faster national growth. This in turn was seen either
as an end in itself or as an expression of broader progressively reformist
programmes, as an element in these programmes that would help attain
their aims both by promoting the development of peripheral regions per se
and, insofar as this enhanced national growth rates, by providing a larger
pool of resources for future redistribution. The creation of some of the
conditions conducive to faster overall growth necessitated the transformation
of the environments of economically peripheral regions, by modernising
them and by creating new settings that were more attractive to private
capital. One important way in which such transformations were to be
accomplished was through increased public expenditure on infrastructure,
on modern road and motorway systems, houses, and industrial estates, for
example. Characteristically, such expenditures were channelled to regions
and coordinated there through the actions of regional branches of central
government departments, sometimes linked to those of local authorities.
    At the same time as fostering more rapid overall growth rates, the
promotion of faster growth in such regions through a combination of
regional planning measures and regional industrial policy (see Yuill et al,
1980) would allow national states to deal with specific, isolated regional
problems, caused by the locationally-concentrated decline of particular
sectors of the economy. In the 1960s, such regions tended to be those of
declining employment in coal mining, which was being cut back in response
to changed energy-market conditions (especially the availability of cheap
oil) and state policies designed to cut unit energy costs.
    In the core regions of national economies, the creation of conditions for
faster overall national growth was seen to require the damping down of
the inflationary, overheated character of development arising from the
tremendous concentration of people and economic activities there and
from the varied problems—economic, environmental, and social—which
arose from this. Typically this was attempted by physical planning
controls on the location of activities, but also in some cases, such as in the
Paris region (Rubenstein, 1978), financial ones.
    Both in core and in peripheral regions, attempts to restore interregional
balance usually involved, as one of their central, fundamental elements,
planned attempts to change the intraregional distribution of economic
activities, employment, and population through settlement policies that
selectively concentrated public sector infrastructure investment into
designated growth areas and points, such as new and expanded towns.

These policies drew upon an ideology of settlement planning that long predates that of regional planning (see, for example, Hudson, 1980). In core regions, such developments involved the decentralisation of economic activities and people away from congested metropolitan areas, whereas in peripheral regions they led to the concentration of public investment and people in locations seen as attractive to private capital and hence conducive to faster regional growth. Such planned alterations in the distribution of jobs and people in countries such as Denmark (Toft Jensen, this volume), Eire (Breathnach, this volume), and France (Bleitrach and Chenu, this volume) were justified both as enhancing national growth rates and as improving living conditions; thus they could be presented as serving a wide variety of diverse, if not competing, interests, and could attract general support and gain legitimacy on that basis.

Policies for managing national spaces in this way both reflected and helped bring about changes in the intranational spatial division of labour that emerged strongly in the 1960s. Lipietz (1980) has suggested the emergence of a threefold typology of regions in terms of their function in providing labour power of various levels of qualification and skill. Although developed specifically within the context of regional industrial change in France, this concept of a new spatial division of labour has also been applied elsewhere (see, for example, Massey, 1979). Overlaying these broad interregional changes was a tendency for moves from large to small urban areas and from urban to rural ones, as the spatial organisation of the economy responded to changes in organisational structure and production technologies within companies. Such changes—for example, as companies sought out reserves of unskilled labour in peripheral regions or in small towns on the peripheries of core regions—often coincided with expressed political objectives of reintegrating such areas into the national growth process, at least for a time. At the same time, the implementation of regional planning (and regional industrial policy) measures to a degree facilitated the making of such changes, and the fact that they *were* made seemed to indicate that policies were attaining some of their intended objectives.

Thus by the early 1970s it is reasonable to talk of an emergent consensus in Western Europe in regional planning theory and practice, which hinged on the perception of the management of growth as constituting the central policy problem. One reflection of this, particularly in those countries with strong economies, was an increasing concern with the deleterious effects of economic growth on environmental quality, and pressures for the incorporation of environmental protection into the goals of regional planning (see Voogd, this volume). This in turn posed fresh methodological problems for regional planning practice. Increasingly in the 1970s and especially after 1973, however, sustained rapid economic growth was replaced by slower growth, stagnation, or even decline. These intra-European changes reflected fundamental ones occurring at the level of the world economy and, associated with the response of capital to profitability crises, marked changes in the international division of labour, especially in manufacturing industry. Tendencies already established in the 1960s, associated with the increasing preeminence of multinational companies, of the relocation of more labour-intensive industries (clothing and textiles especially) and stages of production in other industries (such as the assembly or manufacture of electronic components) from Western Europe to branch plants in parts of the Third World and Mediterranean region, were intensified as companies sought to restore their degree of international competitiveness and restore profitability (see Frobel et al, 1980). Moreover, similar processes of restructuring and locational switches in production were also becoming established in other industries, such as automobile manufacture and bulk iron and steel production (see Balassa, 1981).

The effect of these sectoral changes at the level of the world market, and the increasing reinforcement of the world scale as the decisive one in the organisation of production, was not only to create new macroeconomic management problems for the states of Western Europe, but also to transform radically the problems of regional planning and of managing the national space. Not only did old regional problems deepen and intensify, but new ones also emerged, often in regions that in the preceding two decades had been core regions in the national growth process (the two most notable examples perhaps being the West Midlands in England and, in West Germany, the eastern part of the Ruhr, centred on Dortmund). Moreover, overlaying and intertwined with these regional shifts, urban and, in particular, inner-city problems became more severe in terms both of employment decline and of deteriorating environmental conditions. The severity of these regional and urban problems and the perceived inability of national governments to solve them successfully—not least because of the pursuit of deflationary fiscal and macroeconomic policies intended to curb rising inflation via control of the money supply and public expenditure cuts—led to forms of protest which spilled over from conventional democratic political channels to mass demonstrations and violence on the streets: for example, the urban riots in Britain in 1981 and the protests against steel closures in France in 1978–1979 (Carney et al, 1980), in West Germany in 1980–1981, and in Belgium in 1982.

Thus it was painfully evident by the start of the 1980s that there was an urgent need for a new, radically different methodological and theoretical basis for the practice of regional planning in Western Europe. The consensus established in the 1960s—of the essential problem being that of regional management against a background of national growth— was increasingly and correctly recognised as irrelevant to the challenge posed by the 1980s; likewise, the accompanying theoretical and methodological tool-kit no longer appeared relevant as the nature of the regional planning problems was seen to change. No longer was there a consensus as to the ability of national governments to deal successfully with regional planning on a centralised basis; indeed, they themselves drew back from this task. An important reason for this was the increasing realisation of the limits of the regional planning orthodoxies established in the 1960s, for the implementation of policies of spatially selective public expenditure on infrastructure provided no more than some of the necessary conditions for economic revival in peripheral regions, whereas the effects of regional industrial policy in subsidising companies' fixed capital investment costs served not only to increase external control via the creation of branch plant economies, but also to shorten the stay of these branch plants in such regions by accelerating the hypermobility of capital (Damette, 1980). Moreover, both in core and in peripheral regions, the promotion of new and expanded towns came to be seen as a proximate cause of the emergence of inner-city problems. More generally, the national implications of guiding investment away from central core regions, which the panoply of planning incentives and controls implied, were less acceptable to governments confronted with the problems of recession.

Filling the void left by the retreat of national governments from the regional planning front, and reflecting the emergent analyses of the changing spatial division of labour and the problems this poses for regional planning, a new consensus has begun to emerge centred upon ideas of regional self-management and the decentralisation and devolution of more powers and responsibilities to regions, with a greater degree of autonomy and closure for regional economies (see Weaver, this volume). Often such transfers of powers to regions by central governments have been in response to regionalist or nationalist separatist pressures, as attempts to guarantee the integrity of existing nation states. Such tendencies towards decentralisation and devolution are observable in Belgium, France (Ardagh, 1982, pages 123-206), Italy (Arcangeli, this volume), Portugal, Spain (Alonso Teixidor and Hebbert, this volume), and in the UK (for example, via the establishment of the Scottish and Welsh Development Agencies), as central governments concede more powers for local economic initiatives to regions and create the legislative basis needed to allow this. Is this then to be the new orthodoxy of the 1980s? Will such a strategy of regional economic management (based on intraclass alliances) prove a successful replacement for the failed attempts of central governments to manage their national spaces, given the further major changes in the international division of labour that are already under way [for example, in petrochemicals production; see Hudson, 1983)] and which will make the control and management of regional economies still more problematic? These are questions that only history will be able to answer.

References
Ardagh J, 1982 *France in the 1980's* (Penguin Books, Harmondsworth, Middx)
Balassa B, 1981 *The Newly Industrialising Countries in the World Economy* (Pergamon Press, Oxford)

Bleitrach D, Chenu A, 1975 "L'aménagement: régulation ou approfondissement des contradictions sociales? Un exemple: Fos-sur-mer et l'aire métropolitaine marseillaise" *Environment and Planning A* 7 367-391

Carney J, Hudson R, Lewis J R (Eds), 1980 *Regions in Crisis: New Perspectives in European Regional Theory* (Croom Helm, London)

Damette F, 1980 "The regional framework of monopoly exploitation: new problems and trends" in *Regions in Crisis: New Perspectives in European Regional Theory* Eds J Carney, R Hudson, J Lewis (Croom Helm, London) pp 76-92

Frobel F, Heinrichs J, Kreye O, 1980 *The New International Division of Labour* (Cambridge University Press, Cambridge)

Hudson R, 1980 "New towns and spatial policy: the case of Washington new town" in *Production of the Built Environment: Proceedings of the Bartlett Summer School, 1979* (Bartlett School of Architecture and Planning, University College, London) pp 142-161

Hudson R, 1983 "Capital accumulation and chemicals production in Western Europe in the postwar period, an examination of locational, structural, and technical change" *Environment and Planning A* 15 (forthcoming)

Lipietz A, 1980 "The structuration of space, the problem of land and spatial policy" in *Regions in Crisis: New Perspectives in European Regional Theory* Eds J Carney, R Hudson, J Lewis (Croom Helm, London) pp 60-75

Massey D, 1979 "In what sense a regional problem?" *Regional Studies* 13 233-243

Rubenstein J M, 1978 *The French New Towns* (Johns Hopkins University Press, Baltimore, MD)

Scase R (Ed.), 1980 *The State in Western Europe* (Croom Helm, London)

Yuill D, Allen K, Hull C (Eds), 1980 *Regional Policy in the European Community* (Croom Helm, London)

Regional Planning in Spain and the Transition to Democracy

L F ALONSO TEIXIDOR
Madrid City Council
M HEBBERT
London School of Economics

1 Introduction

So many fundamental changes have occurred since Harry Richardson (1975) published *Regional Development Policy and Planning in Spain*, that we feel the time is ripe for a fresh account in English. Democratization has not only created a very different institutional and political context, but also placed the previous experiences of Francoist planning—described by Richardson—in a new perspective. We therefore begin with a backward look at the expansion of the Spanish economy after 1960, and at the authoritarian political framework within which this took place. Next, we describe the collapse both of the economic boom and of the political framework, and the process of democratic reconstruction which followed, leading to the new Constitution of 1978. The final section is concerned with the reorientation of spatial planning in the past five years under the influence of democratization.

Figure 1. Spain.

2 Economic expansion in the 1960s

The expansion of the Spanish GNP in the 1960s ran at Japanese levels, with an annual maximum of 11·4%, a minimum of 4·5%, and an average of 7·4%.

The industrial sector of the economy multiplied its production almost
three times during the decade 1963–1973. The basic process at work
behind the 'miracle' of new prosperity was the opening up to market
forces, and particularly to foreign capital, of one of the most closed and
stagnant economies in Western Europe. Closure had been a deliberate
policy of the Nationalist government, which had attempted after the civil
war to maximize the self-sufficiency of the Spanish economy. Since the
early 1950s, this autarchic philosophy had proved increasingly unworkable.
It relied upon holding down working-class salaries and living conditions
beneath the harshest political repression. The domestic market was narrow
and irrationally regulated, and business behaviour was traditionally
uncompetitive. Not only were there no prospects for economic growth on
this basis, but the policy had led in 1956 to the first serious threats to the
stability of the Franco regime (Ros Hombravella, 1979, page 18). The
consequence was a change of government, in early 1957, from Falangists
whose roots were in landowning, commerce, small business, and local
caçiquismo (rule by party bosses), to members of the Opus Dei movement[1]
with a technocratic big-business orientation and connections with multinational capital. In the words of Professor Paniagua, the change of
government transformed the Spanish state "through the establishment of a
greater harmony between the political and the economic power of the
Spanish ruling class" (Paniagua, 1977, page 26; Moya, 1972, pages 55, 116).
   At once the government set about demolishing the protectionist apparatus
of the autarchy and constructing a new economic order based on measures
for sustained and general growth. In 1959, a Stabilization Plan was
launched, with the support of the World Bank, the International Monetary
Fund, and the Organization for European Economic Cooperation; it
embraced the devaluation of the peseta, credit restrictions, a wage freeze,
public expenditure cuts, tax increases, and the easing of restrictions on
overseas trade and foreign investment, as well as making a tentative start
on the reform of the financial system. These reforms were the turning
point of the Franco era. After a short period of stagnation, they duly
precipitated the 'miracle'.
   The timing was fortunate. Externally Spain's integration in the world
economy was favoured by a buoyant international climate. As well as
directly attracting foreign capital, which rapidly assumed a dominant
position in several key sectors, she enjoyed substantial flows of foreign
currency from the rest of Europe through the remittances of emigrant
workers and the expansion of mass tourism. Over a billion pesetas entered
the country from these sources during the decade[2].

[1] The Opus Dei movement is a Catholic society of lay professionals with a
predominately secular mission.
[2] 30·5% from private foreign capital, 54·4% from tourist receipts, and 15·1% from
emigrant remittances. Source: Banco Exterior de España (1978, page 149).

Internally the country was endowed with a plentiful, cheap, and amenable labour supply, as rural workers abandoned a backward and impoverished agriculture for employment in manufacturing and construction industries and in the menial service sector. This shift of labour took shape in an internal migration of some four million people, amounting to no less than 12·5% of the total national population at the middle of the decade. The majority of the migration was channelled into just four metropolises: Madrid, Barcelona, Bilbao, and Valencia (INE, 1974; Barbancho, 1975). The resulting property-development boom in the expanding urban areas was itself a significant factor in the buoyancy of the period, particularly in the contribution that it made towards the development of a large-scale financial sector within the economy (see Ferreira, 1977).

At least in the short run, the modified authoritarianism of the Opus Dei reforms offered a peculiarly favourable climate for investment. On the one hand, Spain was a dictatorship. It had low wage rates because of the repression of independent working-class organization, and low taxes because of the absence of democratic institutions, central or local, through which demands for public services could be articulated and investment diverted from directly profitable production or property speculation to supportive social infrastructure. Public expenditure comprised a smaller proportion of GNP than in any other European country: the figures for Spain and The Netherlands, respectively, are 16% and 37% in 1961, and 24% and 40% in 1970 (Banco Exterior de España, 1978, page 202). On the other hand, as national publicity emphasized, it was now a 'new' Spain, with a technocratic government which showed a real capacity for reform in the years 1959–1963 with the liberalization of internal and external trade, the partial reordering of the financial system, and the introduction of indicative sectoral planning on French lines, in the First Development Plan of 1964 (Ros Hombravella, 1979, pages 32–37).

The Opus Dei strategy was to achieve economic modernization within authoritarian structures, in such a way that the pursuit of prosperity—*desarrollismo*—would serve as a substitute for the politics of class or regional ideology. The growth rates of the early 1960s seemed to vindicate this classic managerialist strategy. By the mid-1960s, however, certain basic contradictions were becoming apparent between the self-preservation requirements of the authoritarian state, and the exigencies of economic growth[3]. The opening up of the Spanish economy to foreign investment also opened it up to international fluctuations, and this required improved instruments of economic management. Internally, the massive shift of labour to the industry and service sectors created demands for public infrastructure and service development which could only be met by stronger local governments. The extreme geographical imbalance of economic growth created new claims for agrarian and regional development.

[3] See the intelligent comments by L A Rojo in Paniker (1969, pages 159–161).

The tax base needed to be strengthened in order to finance a strengthened public sector, and made more flexible so as to serve as an economic regulator[4]. However, to achieve such reforms, against the resistance of the civil service and dominant financial interests, was beyond the political capacity of the Francoist state, especially as Franco himself was now ageing and unable to maintain a directive role[5]. The external appearance of technocratically-led development was maintained in the Second Plan of 1967 and the Third Plan of 1972; but in practice indicative planning was being abandoned for simple stop–go policies to keep the economy out of inflation and balance-of-payments deficits, and the planners had lost their reformist impetus within government. Indeed, as Harrison (1978, page 56) observes, "the very existence of the 'plan' served as an excuse for the refusal on the part of the regime to undertake even the most elementary structural reform which might have upset vested interests".

The widening gap between the formal objectives of the plans and their actual impotence is especially clear in the case of regional policy, which is reviewed by Richardson (1975), and by Buttler (1975). Regional objectives featured increasingly prominently as the development plans themselves grew weaker. The First Plan contained a simple growth-pole policy. This had a spatial aspect but was not, for two reasons, an instrument of regional planning; it provided for intensive industrial development in a few centres, but not for supportive social infrastructure or labour-market development (Buttler, 1975, pages 188–191; Richardson, 1975, pages 49 and following), whereas from a political perspective the poles were managed by central government on behalf of the national business community to the deliberate exclusion of local interests (Richardson, 1975, page 116). The Second and Third Plans spoke of improving the involvement of provincial and municipal governments in the preparation and implementation of plans, and of giving more priority to social needs and regional geography (Richardson, 1975, pages 95–98). The Third Plan aimed ambitiously for a national settlement strategy based on the containment of Madrid and the promotion of a system of 'equilibrium metropolises'. It also broadened the range of growth-pole incentives to extend over whole regions (*grandes areas de expansión industrial*) (Richardson, 1975, pages 98–105). By the time the planners—now based at an independent Ministry of Development Planning—came to prepare the abortive Fourth Plan in 1973, they intended to include a policy for the whole national settlement system, and to base the plan for the first time on regional, as well as sectoral, targets[6]. But despite these developments in the style and

[4] Neither the tax reform of 1957 or of 1964 solved the basic problem of the highly regressive character of the system arising from its reliance on consumption rather than on taxation of income or capital.
[5] Ros Hombravella (1979, page 52) lists the 'pending reforms' that never occurred after 1964.
[6] See Richardson (1975, pages 185–187). These policies never materialized, however.

objectives of regional planning, in content it remained little more than a narrow instrument for direct or indirect industrial subsidy (see Leira, 1973).

Two aspects of the regional policies of the Development Plans particularly exemplify the institutional limits on reform within the Franco regime. First, the failure of the growth poles was due partly to their strongly centralized management, and to the exclusion of local authorities from designation of the poles and from gauging and meeting urban needs in the wake of industrial expansion. The Franco government mistrusted strong local authorities and preferred to rely on special agencies directly dependent on the central state to provide housing and other urban services; "the result has been", Medhurst (1973, page 178) observes, "to increase the size and ultimately the cost of urban growth". Second, the policies were ad hoc programmes administered by a single ministry, not a horizontal strategy for the concerted action of several departments within a given region. Franco inherited a strongly departmentalized civil service structure; its internal rivalries extended from field service up to cabinet levels (see Medhurst, 1973, chapter 6). It was one of the aspects of Spanish government on which he and the Opus Dei reformers made the least impression (Medhurst, 1973, chapter 4; Arango, 1978, chapter 9). Lack of interdepartmental coordination was particularly evident at the regional level; this was in sharp contrast to the French planning model, which was otherwise scrupulously copied to the last detail by the Spaniards, "... even down to the designation of the smallest bureau", as Harrison (1978, page 155) comments. No supraprovincial territorial units were created in order to provide a coordinative framework for public action and to mobilize private initiative[7], for any such framework would have provided a politically intolerable focus for regional loyalties and demands. Writing in 1973, Medhurst noted the fundamental contradiction which confronted regional planners under Franco: "they cannot create institutions and foster political participation that might facilitate the planning process but which could also imperil the regime's existence" (Medhurst, 1973, chapter 7).

The same contradictions are present in the physical planning system operated under the Land and Urban Planning Act of 1956 by the Ministry of Housing and, subject to its control, by municipal governments (see Bassols Coma, 1973, pages 555–578; Richardson, 1975, chapter 10). The 1956 Act was a remarkable piece of legislation, embodying strong interventionist powers over suburban land development whereby all municipalities, urban and rural, were to prepare comprehensive development plans, coordinated hierarchically at the provincial level in a complete set of provincial plans which, in turn, were to be integrated under a National Urbanization Plan[8]. From an underlying ideology of town–country

[7] Medhurst (1973, pages 174-179). The Hudson Institute Europe (1975, page 271) compared Spain unfavourably with Italy in this respect.
[8] Legal provision had been made for the preparation of a national urban plan since 1949 (Teran, 1978, page 240).

balance and the organic urban community[9], the law provided powerful means for maintaining public over private interests in urban development, and for redistributing the costs and benefits of plans through the physical reordering of land parcels (Garcia de Enterria and Parejo, 1979; Fernandez, 1980). But these progressive characteristics, prized by the democratic local authorities of contemporary Spain, were inoperable in the context of the Francoist political system, as we will show later. The Law of 1956 failed for the same reason as the regional policies of the development plans. Weak and corrupt local authorities, dominated by local business interests, ignored its interventionist potential; in the absence of democratic channels, such planning as was done by municipalities lacked the legitimacy to be effective (Borja, 1977, pages 190–191). In the boom years of suburban expansion in the 1960s and early 1970s, planning provisions favoured the interests of developers, and where they did not do so they were transgressed with impunity (Pereiro, 1981, pages 150–160). As for the provincial and national plans, these presupposed a level of interdepartmental coordination which was quite beyond the capacities of the regime (Romay Beccaria, 1974, pages 797 and following; Teran, 1978, pages 342 and following). In the absence of formal plans at the provincial level[10], physical coordination of public expenditure on an annual basis was attempted through permanent Provincial Commissions of Technical Services (*Comisiones Provinciales de Servicios Tecnicos*); but these were no more effective (Richardson, 1975, chapter 9). They were always, or nearly always, chaired by the civil governor, and "in the gravely inhibiting context of the developmentalist ethos of the period, to point out the problems of some territorial operation whose possible repercussions were insufficiently considered, was little less than antipatriotic. Of course this was hardly beneficial for the political career of any aspirant to power" (Teran, 1978, page 492).

In the words of the economist Ros Hombravella (1979, page 59) the 1960s were for Spain "... one of those periods in which capitalism could justify itself by its 'global' results". The global results were impressive, but they had been achieved at great cost. Spain had ceased to be underdeveloped, but had become, as the philosopher Julian Marías puts it "badly developed" (see Carr and Fusi, 1979, page 59). For many years to come, the country will be paying the bill for the manner in which the economic 'miracle' was achieved, and particularly for the massive rural–urban migrations and the extreme geographical concentrations of prosperity and wealth[11]. Growth rates such as that experienced by the province of

[9] See Teran's description of the key role of Pedro Bidagor in the development of theory and practice after the Civil War (Teran, 1978, pages 161 and following).

[10] Only two such plans had been attempted by 1969, after which the enterprise was postponed indefinitely (Teran, 1978, pages 415–448).

[11] See, in general, the *Anuario del Mercado Español*, published by the Banco Español de Credito, Madrid, for data on the distribution of population and income at provincial and municipal levels.

Madrid, whose population grew by 45·5% between 1961 and 1970 (an increase of 1 200 000), would themselves be sufficient to explain the inadequacy of urban provision, even if local government had not been hamstrung by lack of finance and by centralist control. Although Spain has comparatively little shanty development, a great deal of its modern housing has been built under minimal public supervision at extremely high densities, in such a way that social infrastructure has to be provided belatedly and expensively[12]. A country which has justifiably prided itself on its urban tradition now contains some of the grimmest, most inconvenient, and most foully polluted urban environments in Europe. On the other hand, the rural periphery offers an equally classic spectacle of decline in decaying agricultural villages with ageing populations. The most extreme examples are absolute population losses of the regions of central and western Spain, 18% for La Mancha between 1955 and 1975, and 22% for Extremadura in the same period; whereas the population of Spain as a whole increased by 23%, and that of Madrid by 96%. A process set in motion by underindustrialization and agricultural poverty has been accelerated by the inferiority of rural services and the concentration of new infrastructural investment in the urban areas[13] (see figures 2 and 3)[14].

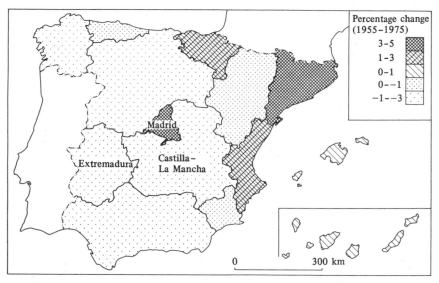

Figure 2. Gains and losses in regional shares of the national population, 1955 – 1975. [Source: Banco de Bilbao (1978, table R-11).]

[12] Barbancho (1975, pages 114 – 115) notes that the provision of schools, social services, and infrastructure often has the effect of *intensifying* congestion.
[13] Barbancho (1979) analyzes this and other 'push' factors.
[14] These maps are based on the Banco de Bilbao's statistical regions, which correspond imperfectly with the autonomous regions depicted in figure 4.

It is instructive to recall the controversies which took place, when Spain
was poised for expansion, between those who argued for a strategy of
regionally balanced growth and those who saw this as an extra to be
achieved once global growth had occurred. In addition to the public
debate between economists of either persuasion (Antolin, 1979, page 203),
there was an internal struggle between the new exponents of economic
development planning and the rather ineffectual department of physical
planning, located in the Ministry of Housing, with its statutory responsibility
for a National Urban Plan under the 1956 Act (Teran, 1978, pages 409
and following). Work on this plan was terminated in 1962, despite the
argument of the economist Lasuén that it should be retained as a counterpart to the Development Plans; this was a decisive victory for the Opus
Dei ministers López Rodó and Alberto Ullastres[15]. In the words of Carr
and Fusi (1979, page 60), both ministers were "... unrepentant believers in
unbalanced growth: to spend public money in poor regions where there was
neither the infrastructure nor the skilled labour for industrial take-off
was to fling good money after bad. Poor regions would benefit more
effectively from the spillover effects of investment in areas where returns
were high". We have shown how clearly these priorities were reflected in
the Development Plans. Indeed, the growth-poles policy in the First Plan
was only included in a late draft as a result of pressure from syndicates

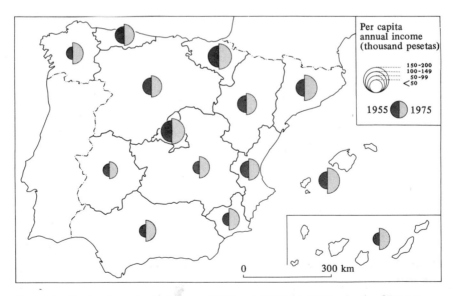

Figure 3. Regional per capita income, 1955 and 1975 (at 1975 values). [Source:
Banco de Bilbao (1978, table R-25).]

[15] Teran (1978, pages 389 and following) notes the personal antipathy and public
hostility between Bidagor, director-general of urban planning in the Ministry of
Housing, and López Rodó.

(the Francoist labour organizations) in the depressed regions[16]. The traditional trade-off between equity and efficiency objectives in regional planning, magnified in Spain's case by the extent of its regional income disparities, was resolved unambiguously in favour of global growth, regional development policy being no more than a by-product of national sectoral indicative planning (Richardson, 1975, pages 33, 45).

The development of Spain under these priorities was the most imbalanced in Europe, significantly more so than that of Italy, with its greater institutional and resource commitment to regional policy (see Hudson Institute Europe, 1975). Instead of a benign diffusion, or 'trickle-down', of national prosperity as predicted by orthodox theory, a malign disequilibrium was established between—in the words of Barbancho (1975)— "great convergence in just a few areas and the desertization of the rest of the country". Any levelling of provincial average per capita income that occurred in the period 1955–1975 arose from changes in the denominator (provincial population) through migration. The partial diffusion of growth in the late 1960s and early 1970s was due to acute bottlenecks of infrastructure in the leading areas, and to the shift of mobile industry, facilitated by regional policy incentives, to second-order centres, particularly those in northeast Spain. It in no way improved the relatively disadvantaged state of the poorer provinces (see Barbancho, 1979). It may be that the economic crisis has provided the first real respite for the declining periphery, a question outside the scope of this paper. But the trends of 'desertization' and metropolitan concentration, so strongly established in the period 1960–1975, will not be easily reversed.

3 Political and economic changes in the 1970s

So far, we have sought to explain the vigorous but unbalanced expansion of the Spanish economy after 1960 in terms of the political characteristics of the Franco regime, just the aspects ignored by the economists of the Hudson Institute Europe (1975) in their optimistic forecasting report *The Spanish Economic Resurgence*[17]. Subsequent events illustrate very well the risks of an analysis which does not take political factors into account. The death of Franco in 1975, the introduction of a new Constitution in 1978, the return to democratic municipal elections in 1979, and the current devolution of regional autonomy, have created a very different framework for economic development, particularly in its regional aspect. The fact that this has coincided with the economic crisis produces a complex picture, with many elements of continuing uncertainty. It is necessary to sketch the main outlines of the post-Franco political system before attempting an assessment of its new urban and regional planning.

[16] The initial draft was just a Plan for Economic Development; it became a Plan for Economic and Social Development (Medhurst, 1973, page 167).

[17] Their neglect of "political aspects of present economic reality and those which will probably characterise it in the future" is defended on pages xxiii and following.

The Spanish economy has suffered severely in the crisis of the 1970s. With a sharp turning point in late 1973, the balance of payments moved from a moderate surplus ($571 million in 1972) to a substantial deficit ($4300 million in 1976). The total number unemployed rose from 192900 in 1970 to 431400 in 1974, and to 831800 in 1977, and has maintained its upward climb to this day (Banco de Bilbao, 1980, page 23); the rate of growth of the GNP fell from 8·4% in 1972 to 5·4% in 1974, and to 1·1% in 1975. The annual increase in the cost of living rose from 8·2% in 1971 to 15·7% in 1974, and peaked at 24·6% in 1977. The deterioration which began in 1973 has been sustained throughout the 1970s (Banco de Bilbao, 1980).

From the first impact of the OPEC oil-price rises, Spain showed itself very sensitive to instabilities in the international capitalist system. This sensitivity was due partly to the successes of the previous decade in opening up the economy to foreign investment and to the position of dependency that had been established by the end of the 1960s (see Banco Exterior de España, 1978, pages 191 and following), and partly to specific factors such as the reduction in the stabilizing inflows of foreign earnings from tourism and remittances from emigrant workers as a result of the recession in Northern Europe. The crisis was worsened by the internal disequilibria inherited from the expansion of the 1960s, most notably those in the agricultural and tourist sectors (Gimenez et al, 1978, chapter 1). The most important internal factor, however, was a political one: the exhaustion of the regime, particularly after the departure of the Opus Dei technocrats from the Cabinet and the assassination of President Carrero Blanco in 1973 (Ros Hombravella, 1979; Tamames, 1978b; Garcia Delgardo and Segura, 1977). The Spanish economy could only drift with the winds until political change occurred.

Throughout his last years, the ageing dictator was preoccupied by the problem of *continuismo*, that is, the continuance of the authoritarian system under his nominated successor King Juan Carlos; this was attempted by the government of Arias Navarro when Franco eventually died in 1975. The effect was to deepen the already serious economic crisis. Instead of the fundamental policies which were needed to meet the crisis, the government merely took limited measures to protect the situation of major financial interests (Garcia Delgardo and Segura, 1977, pages 89–100). Given the country's untenable economic situation, the surrender of economic policy to the representatives of large-scale capital and the blatant use which the latter made of their influence had the effect of reinforcing the pressure of the political opposition and working-class movements (Garcia Delgardo and Segura, 1977, pages 115–116; Tamames, 1978a, volume 2, pages 1188–1189). As Basque separatists stepped up their terrorist campaign, the state showed itself no more capable of maintaining domestic order than it was of responding to the pressures of the adverse economic environment. In the spring of 1976, the king abandoned the

initial strategy of *continuismo* and invited Adolfo Suarez to the premiership
on the understanding that he would lead a government of national unity
with the two priorities of stabilizing the economic situation and preparing
a new democratic constitution. General elections were held in June 1977
(see table 1), confirming this mandate.

The transition involved no break with the previous regime. It left intact
key institutions of the dictatorship within the civil service, the economic
and legal systems, the armed forces, and the mass media. What is more,
after the elections of 1977, the UCD maintained a number of 'converted'
Francoists in key political positions, headed by the prime minister himself.
Nevertheless, this was a period of genuinely consensual government.
Political factions from the communists through the ideological spectrum to
the conservatives around Fraga Iribarne were brought together by the
worsening economic situation and fears of an army coup, as well as by
sheer enthusiasm for democracy. The first product of the consensus was
the Pact of Moncloa, of October 1977, whereby all parliamentary parties
agreed to support certain short-term counterinflationary measures in return
for basic changes in welfare policy and the tax system, amounting—at
least from the viewpoint of the left—to a *ruptura pactada*, or negotiated
break, with the old order (Garcia Delgardo and Segura, 1977, pages 46–50):
the first step in an institutional restructuring which could lead out of the
economic crisis[18]. In the event, the expectations generated by the
Moncloa agreements were to be frustrated by the UCD government, which
retained exclusive control of its implementation (Gimenez et al, 1978,
pages 36–42); but the Pact did serve an important bridging role in
maintaining the political consensus towards its second and permanent

Table 1. Distribution of seats between political parties after the general elections of
1977 and 1979.

Party		Number of seats	
		1977	1979
UCD	Union of the Democratic Centre	165	167
PSOE	Socialist Workers' Party of Spain	124[a]	121
PCE	Communist Party of Spain	20	23
AP	Popular Alliance—a Francoist conservative group, since renamed CD, Democratic Coalition	16	9
PSA } CDC } PNV }	main regional parties of Andalucía, Cataluña and Euskadi	19	21

[a] Includes the five deputies of the PSP (Popular Socialist Party), which subsequently
merged with the PSOE.

[18] See the contributions of the communist economists J Segura and R Tamames in
the communist party journal *Nuestra Bandera* (90), of 1978.

product, the democratic constitution. After months of intense political bargaining which left its mark in the complexity and—as we shall show—ambiguity of the final result, the new constitution came into force on 29 December 1978, and was followed by elections in the spring. The second general election produced broadly the same parliamentary distribution as the first (see table 1), but in the municipal elections (the first since 1931) nearly all the major cities of Spain came under the control of coalitions of the PSOE and PCE. Since then, politics has become more polarized, with significant implications for the operation of the new constitution.

The recovery of democracy has been dominated by two themes, which provide the leitmotifs for the remainder of this paper. The first theme is participation. In every aspect of public life, including planning, the release from authoritarian control has created demands for the direct engagement of groups and of individual citizens in decisionmaking. The strategy of the left is to reinforce these demands wherever possible in the interests of *consolidacion y profundizacion de la democracia* (strengthening and deepening of democracy). The second theme, equally crucial for planning, is regionalism. The history of Spain can be seen in terms of an uneven oscillation between regionalism and centralism, democratic periods being strongly dominated by regional politics[19]. The extreme centralism of the Franco regime, which maintained to the end an entirely uncompromising stance against the Basques and Catalans[20], ensured that after 1975 the regional issue would revive more strongly than ever. There is no necessary correspondence between devolution and democracy or liberty, but they became synonymous in post-Franco Spain (Lazaro Araujo, 1979, page 21; Fernandez, 1977, pages 346 and following).

It was to be expected that some form of devolution would be given to Cataluña, Euskadi (the Basque country), and Galicia, all of which have their own languages and historic institutions and obtained degrees of self-government under the Republic in the 1930s[21]; but the opening of formal negotiations with the Basques and Catalans at once precipitated a centrifugal wave through other parts of the country, including areas such as Andalucía with little previous history of regional consciousness. The sources of the new regionalism are complex, although much of the explanation lies in the experience of uneven development and authoritarian centralism described in the previous section (see also Linde Paniagua, 1977, pages 261 and following). Paradoxically, the government and the parties

[19] Compare the periods 1868–1874 and 1931–1939, analyzed by López Rodó (1980). In the words of Arango (1978, page 9): "from the point of view of the political scientist modern Spanish history is an account of unsuccessful attempts to sustain a viable nation-state".

[20] As in the Burgos trial of Christmas 1970, at which ETA members were sentenced to death by a military court despite national and international appeals for clemency.

[21] López Rodó (1980, page 15) lists the other, abortive, initiatives for autonomy under the Republic.

of the nationalist right fuelled the movement by their insistence on equality of treatment for other regions of Spain in the face of the demands of the Basque and Catalan nationalists. It was stated in the 'decree-law' of September 1977, which provisionally reestablished the Catalan parliament (the *Generalitat*), that no privileged status was implied for Cataluña, so opening the door for the establishment of similar provisional autonomy in other regions, which the government was at once under intense political pressure to grant. Thereafter, preautonomous regional regimes multiplied with astonishing rapidity throughout Spain. Hence the veiled bitterness of the Francoist López Rodó (1980, page 24), when he observes: "if what was sought was to dilute the Basque and Catalan problem so it would lose its virulence, what followed in fact was rather to extend the autonomist fever to the rest of Spain".

The task of the Constitution of 1978 was to establish a new structure for the Spanish state. It is an extremely complex document, by no means a model of juridical clarity, but a considerable achievement of political negotiation in which right-wing protagonists of national unity, centrist supporters of administrative devolution, parties of the left committed both to political autonomy and interregional solidarity, and regionalists out to maximize autonomy all left traces of their influence.

Article 2 states:

"The Constitution is based on the indissoluble unity of the Spanish nation, the common and indivisible country of all Spaniards, and recognises and guarantees the right to self-government of the nationalities and regions of which it is composed and solidarity among them." [22]

The word 'nationalities', which sounds as curious in Spanish as it does in English, was introduced against intense opposition from the right as a recognition of the distinctive status of Cataluña, Euskadi, and Galicia. Just what the 'regions' would be was unclear when the Constitution was drafted, and this is still not entirely resolved today. Given the uneven distribution of regional consciousness within Spain, and the contentious boundary issues between certain regions, no attempt was made to draw a map of them, although boundaries have to be defined in the statute of autonomy of each region. Instead, the Constitution sets out procedures by which existing provinces could jointly or separately seek to obtain devolved powers. To be precise, it set up three principal procedural paths[23]. First, under a transitional provision, the 'nationalities' of Cataluña, Euskadi, and Galicia were enabled to proceed forthwith to full autonomy, to be approved by referendum. Second, under Article 143,

---

[22] Compare the weaker formulation of Article 1 of the Constitution of 1931: "The Republic constitutes an integral state, compatible with the autonomy of the municipalities and the regions". The 1931 Constitution is analyzed by Parejo Alfonso (1977, pages 162 and following).

[23] In his detailed analysis, López Rodó (1980, chapter 4) lists no less than twelve distinct procedures.

regions could initiate a lengthy process of local consultation and central negotiation resulting in a statute of autonomy which passes through parliament as a bill. Third, under Article 151, an alternative procedure is set out whereby a degree of autonomy equivalent to that enjoyed by the 'nationalities' can be obtained by regions through local referendum. This path is swifter, but it is also much more exacting in its requirement of local support—the referendum must give an absolute majority in favour of devolution in each province of the region. It was included to avert future accusations that the Constitution had discriminated in favour of the Basques and Catalans. In February 1980, however, the UCD decided to ban its use. In the words of the party's executive committee, "... without high economic and social costs a strongly centralized state cannot be swiftly transformed into a decentralized one". The critical case was Andalucía, with a militant preautonomous government dominated by nationalists, socialists, and communists. Despite much higher referendum rates in support of autonomy than in Cataluña or Euskadi, the region's progress to autonomy by the path of Article 151 was blocked for many months by the central government, which since this confrontation has tended to act as a reluctant partner in the devolution process, assisted by the procedural complexities of Article 143[24].

Unfortunately, the ambiguities of Articles 143 and 151 extend not only to the procedure for obtaining autonomy, but also to its exact nature. It is stated in Article 151 that communities which attain autonomy by referendum should have a legislative assembly, a council of government with elected president, and a court of justice. These institutions are not prescribed for communities which attain autonomy by the slower route. Does the Constitution then implicitly create first-class and second-class levels of autonomy, with only the former enjoying independent legislative power? Expert opinion has been divided (Munoz Machado, 1979, chapter 3; Lazaro Araujo, 1979, pages 59 and following; Peces-Barba Martinez, 1980; López Rodó, 1980, chapter 5). What is certain is that the Constitution of 1978, although reserving certain powers to the state, retains more flexibility than did the Constitution of 1931 for the negotiation of unique packages of powers by the autonomous regions. Much depends on the balance of political forces within each province and region (Lazaro Araujo, 1979), and can range from the militancy of the Basques to the conservatism of a province such as Segovia (UCD dominated), which attempted for a while to stay out of the devolution process altogether.

Figure 4 shows the geographical division into autonomous communities that had occurred by the end of 1980. In 1980, only Cataluña and

---

[24] The climate of central–regional relations fluctuates markedly. It was cold in the early part of 1980, warmer after the censure motion of 28–29 May (in which the UCD obtained the support of regional parties), but was already chilling again by the time of the attempted army coup in February 1981, which ominously reinforced the spirit of centralism within both the UCD and the PSOE.

Euskadi had obtained statutes of autonomy. The other communities possess provisional governments whose prime purpose is to negotiate full autonomy, but which meanwhile exercise varying degrees of delegated executive power. The provinces of Madrid and Navarra are special cases, as yet unresolved: Madrid because it contains the capital city; Navarra because, being internally divided between Basque and Castillian areas, its affiliation remains to be determined by referendum. The refusal of Segovia to join Castilla–León is a temporary and symbolic gesture of UCD mistrust of the movement towards regional autonomy. Four provinces—Oviedo (now Asturias), Logroño (Rioja), Santander (Cantábria), and Murcia—have opted to stand as autonomous regions on their own. Remarkably, the Constitution places no lower limit on the size of an autonomous region, unlike the one million population required by the Italian constitution of 1947.

The negotiative and voluntaristic nature of the devolution process is producing a regionalization of Spain very different from the neat technical divisions reviewed by Richardson (1975, chapter 4)[25]. The map of regions (figure 4) is irregular, the progress to autonomy is ragged, and no two statutes of autonomy will, it seems, be quite the same. There has been considerable debate among constitutional lawyers over the form of government towards which the country is moving [see Lazaro Araujo (1979) and Cosculluela Montaner (1977) for reviews, and also the

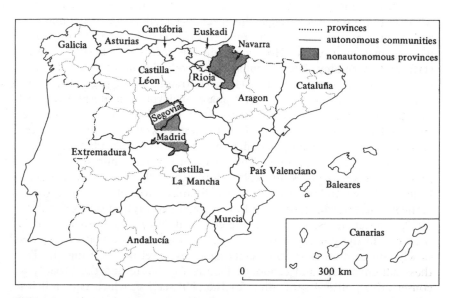

Figure 4. Autonomous communities in 1980.

[25] Linde Paniagua (1977, page 260) notes of this technocratic 'neoregionalism' that "it meant nothing more than a new form of projecting centralist policy and interests".

discussion of the uniqueness of the Constitution by its critic López Rodó (1980)]. It is evidently not a federal system, that is, one in which the subnational units enjoy an equality of legislative independence. It corresponds well with the definition given by Firn and Maclennan of *devolution* as a distinct constitutional category in which economic, legislative, and administrative powers may be unevenly distributed across a set of otherwise similar regions, their respective shares being determined principally by relative bargaining power. As these authors point out, the political origins of devolution involve greater risks of complexity and ambiguity than those of federalism, in that "compromises, contradictions and specific regulations, most of which are produced to meet the demands of an individual region, are likely to condition the rules relating central to regional governments" (Firn and Maclennan, 1979, page 274). The Spanish Constitution attempts to facilitate and regularize an asymmetrical devolution of this sort. Munoz Machado (1979, page 14), analyzing the legislative powers of the new regions, has likened the relevant articles of the Constitution to an *à la carte* menu from which the diners help themselves according to their appetites.

To this metaphor must be added the forbidding role played by the *maître d'hôtel*, that is, central government. The hardest battle for devolution is in the administrative sphere, where the operational transfer of departmental power occurs. In the brief experience of the preautonomous and autonomous governments to date, it has become clear that negotiation with central ministries through the specially created 'mixed commissions' will be protracted, and that the final transfer may be one of formal powers without matching funds. However wide the jurisdiction bestowed in a statute of autonomy, it can remain completely devoid of content for lack of sufficient economic resources (Lazaro Araujo, 1979, page 50). This has evidently been the case in the first phase of devolution, despite the fact that the powers involved have chiefly been regulatory or administrative and involve no capital budget. The problem is well exemplified in the devolution of responsibilities under the Land and Urban Planning Acts, discussed in the next section. The reluctance of state ministries to devolve executive power requires no explanation, especially if we bear in mind the traditionally centralized pattern of the Spanish civil service, with its vertical structures of control and of professional promotion (Medhurst, 1973, chapter 6). Moreover, in the economic crisis the argument for economy in the public sector is frequently invoked as a reason for moving slowly and cautiously towards creating a new level of government. To these administrative and economic factors we should add the broadly conservative political sympathies of the civil service, which is as much a relic of the old institutional order as are the army or the police, and above all the unwillingness of the UCD to countenance a restructuring which would weaken the central and provincial levels of the hierarchy of government—where the traditional influence of the right is most firmly established—to the benefit of the regional and municipal levels where it is weakest. The Constitution is unclear on this matter, but the UCD has increasingly chosen to emphasize that autonomy for regions should not be at the expense of autonomy for provinces. In the spring of 1981, for example, the Catalan *Generalitat* was forced to relinquish certain powers that it had taken over from the provinces.

Although the transition to democracy has produced major changes at the regional and municipal levels, in the form of the autonomous regions and the vigorous revival of party politics in local government, we should not overemphasize the scale of the changes. The greater part of the work of the government proceeds through the same executive machinery as it did before 1975, that is, through strongly centralized ministries running field services in each province under the coordination of a centrally appointed civil governor. Whereas the provinces are going concerns, operating with great uniformity throughout Spain, the regions vary widely in strength and coherence. Yet despite the fact that progress to autonomy in all regions—even Cataluña—is slow and liable to frequent deadlock, political support for regionalism shows no signs of fading away as UCD party leaders perhaps once hoped it would. Similarly, at the municipal level, local political consciousness remains keen notwithstanding the fact that the local authorities voted into power in 1979 have found their room for manoeuvre tightly constrained by central bureaucratic supervision and by monetary controls. The established hierarchy of government is still in the process of adjusting, with great reluctance, to the new centres of democratic legitimacy at the regional and municipal levels, but adjust it ultimately must. The process can be seen particularly clearly in urban and regional planning, to which we now turn.

4 Urban and regional planning since 1975
The institutional and political changes which have occurred since 1975 have transformed the character of regional policy. Before examining the changes, however, it should be noted that the objective character of the regional problem has also been changing during the same period. The key factor here has been the unemployment rate. In 1974, 400000 were unemployed (2·9% of the economically active population). By the first quarter of 1980, the total was 1470900 (11·2%), placing Spain well at the head of the OECD countries, and unemployment was rising by 1500 persons per day (Banca Mas Sarda, 1980, page 16). The trend has not been dampened by the economic policies of the UCD government which, despite declarations of concern[26], has in practice been exclusively occupied in the years 1978–1981 with inflation control (Lazaro Araujo and Panizo, 1978). As for the regional incidence of unemployment, the poor but relatively densely populated south of Spain maintains its place at the top of the table,

[26] For example, the proposals in the medium-term programme by the Ministry of the Economy *Programa a Medio Plazo para la Economia Española*, 1979, pages 55–60

as it did in the 1960s: Andalucía—a region of consistent long-term decline in all economic sectors—has more than double its proportionate share of the national total. But a new and highly significant phenomenon, which has no precedent in the 1960s, is the rise of the regional rates for the most urbanized and economically dynamic regions, Cataluña and Euskadi, up to, or above, the national average level of about 11%. Urban areas as a whole account for a growing share of total unemployment. These trends reflect the sectoral impact of the recession: 28% of the current registered unemployment is in one of the biggest employers of the 1960s, the construction sector (see Angelet and Rafols, 1977; Olive and Valls, 1976), whereas 27% is in manufacturing, much of this in some traditional and geographically concentrated industries such as the Basque iron and steel industry, Catalan textiles, or Galician shipbuilding.

Internal migration rates are always highly sensitive to changes in the job market. Although we shall not have quantitative confirmation of the trend until the Census of 1981, there are clear indications that rural–urban migration fell steeply between 1974 and 1976, and has declined steadily thereafter (Banco de Bilbao, 1980, page 96). Descriptions of the regional problem, hitherto primarily defined in terms of depopulation and underindustrialized areas, are being reorientated towards the industrial composition of the established urban centres; an important political factor here is the superiority in organization and political leverage of industrial workers over those of the dispersed and traditional rural sector. Irrespective of the general recession, the issue of urban unemployment is likely to be aggravated by the long-term restructuring requirements of Spanish industry, particularly in the light of EEC membership[27]. Such trends give some indication of the nature of interregional disparities in the 1980s, and the tensions that will exist between the claims of national economic competitiveness, development of backward areas, and relief of urban unemployment.

There is an obvious risk that the regional differentials opened up under authoritarian rule will widen further under the Constitution of 1978. The first regions to get their statutes of autonomy, Cataluña and Euskadi, which are the wealthiest, most vocal, and most politically articulate, will seek to use autonomy as a stepping stone for economic recovery. The prospects for poorer areas are less favourable. Regionalists argue, reasonably enough, that they could be no worse off than they have been under centralism; yet they may be overestimating the ability of new regional governments to reverse, through the exercise of independent political power, the thirty-year trends of economic decline. In this context, it is instructive to note the cautions of Nevin (1978) against the economic optimism of Scottish and Welsh devolutionists. Firn and

[27] See Cinco Dias (1980, pages 140–160) and Pajaron Collada (1979). In the light of Italy's north–south tensions, the Hudson Institute Europe (1975, page 251) urged that Spain should resolve its regional problem before it joined the EEC.

Maclennan (1979, page 292) also note that: "The industrial expectations raised by the prospects of devolution [of Scotland] have run substantially ahead of the possibilities of implementation". Government at the regional level may be able to promote development marginally more effectively by enlisting local participation, by encouraging indigenous (as opposed to externally induced) growth, by identifying local priorities, and by applying policies for the redistribution of local resources. In the last resort, however, the existing disparities between regions are only capable of governmental correction—if at all—by distributive policies at national level. The most effective economic policy tool available to individual regions may not be the local use of resources under their control, but the political backing, extending to the ultimate potential threat of secession, which they can deploy in bargaining with the central state (see Firn and Maclennan, 1979, page 290).

The basis for such bargaining is set out in Article 2 of the Constitution—cited in the previous section—which at one and the same time guarantees the right to self-government and the principle of 'solidarity'. Solidarity is the other side of the coin to the generalized autonomy which the new Constitution—unlike that of 1931—offers as a political liberty to all regions of Spain. In Article 138,

"the state guarantees the effective implementation of the principle of solidarity consecrated in Article 2 of the Constitution, safeguarding the establishment of a just and adequate economic balance between the different areas of Spanish territory".

This distributive principle has both a general and a specific application. Generally, it constitutes one criterion, among others, by which central government will operate its continuing responsibilities for national finances, economic planning, energy and water, the national transport system, and so on. Some of these responsibilities already involve an interregional transfer of resources from areas of high productivity to those of low productivity. Concealed while government is centralized, the transfer will become more apparent as the autonomous regional governments become established. Specifically, the principle of solidarity is realized through two new means of interregional balancing. First, the general budget made over to the regions includes an allocation intended to guarantee a minimum level of basic public services throughout Spanish territory. Second, an 'interregional clearing fund' has been set up for financing capital investment. Its distribution is at the disposal of parliament, with the objectives, specified in the Constitution, of "correcting interterritorial economic imbalances and implementing the principle of solidarity". Although the nature and scale of the fund remain ill-defined, its distributive impact will presumably be of minor importance beside the resource transfers occurring in general public expenditure.

It is still too early to assess how the new mechanisms for interregional balancing will operate (see Fernandez Rodriguez and Lopez Nieto, 1980). The claims of poorer regions for preferential treatment on grounds of solidarity will now have to compete politically not only against considerations of national economic performance, but also against the goal of regional self-determination. The greater the autonomy enjoyed by regions, the greater the proportion of public revenue they will retain to use as they see fit, and the fewer resources there will be for redistribution. In the new circumstances of urban unemployment, the autonomous governments of Cataluña and Euskadi are doubly unlikely to favour redistributive policies operating to their disadvantage. It might even transpire that for solidarity considerations to carry weight, some form of central assembly based on regional representation would be needed, a 'senate of the regions' unenvisaged in the Constitution of 1978.

It will be apparent that in discussing regional policy in contemporary Spain we are no longer dealing, as Richardson (1975) was, with a discrete policy area under unified executive control, but with a ramifying problem at the heart of the nation's transition to a democratic constitution. Regional planning in the traditional sense continues to exist in name, but in practice it has been overtaken by events. The various area-based tax exemption and subsidy schemes of the earlier instruments have now been pooled under the general heading of *grandes areas de expansión industrial*, which are designated so broadly that they cover most of southern and western Spain. They operate at a very low level and their inappropriateness in a changed institutional and economic environment is widely recognized. Even the Ministry of Industry admits, in its annual report for 1979, that "the low absolute levels of investment, the scanty generation of employment, and the reduced level of fulfilment of targets either for investment [33%] or employment [32%] do not permit much optimism about the efficacy of this instrument of regional action" (Ministerio de Industria y Energia, 1979, page 31). The development of new and more potent instruments must await the consolidation of the system of autonomous regions.

The same is true of the attempts by national planners, since 1973 when long-term macroeconomic planning was abandoned, to develop stronger instruments for what is called *ordenacion del territorio*[28], that is, strategic planning for the physical coordination of public and private investment in a region or subregion. In 1977, when the Ministry of Development Planning was broken up, and responsibility for physical planning was removed from the Ministry of Housing, *ordenacion del territorio* became a major interest of the expanded Ministry of Public Works and Urbanism. The legal framework is provided, under the Land and Planning Act of 1956 in its 1975 revision, in the form of *Planes Directores Territoriales de Coordinacion* (PDTCs). Unlike earlier regional plans, which were merely consultative, these are statutory documents with legal powers. Unlike the earlier provincial plans, whose failure we noted earlier, they can embrace areas wider than the province, making explicit for the first time the possibility of formal planning at the regional level. In other respects the PDTC

[28] The equivalent to the French *aménagement du territoire*. The term was first used in the preparation of the Fourth Economic Plan.

retains important elements of the earlier law—one of these being the concept of a nested hierarchy of spatial plans, with a *Plan National de Ordenacion* at the top and local municipal plans and regulations at the bottom. Another important element retained by the PDTC is its comprehensive character, based upon the coordination of decisionmaking across a wide range of functions[29]. As an executive document, the PDTC must be approved at the highest level by the Council of Ministers, and is binding both on the private sector and on the public sector.

Work on two PDTCs was begun in 1977: one for Andalucía (eight provinces covering 17% of the country) and one for Galicia (four provinces). The timing could not have been more unfortunate, coinciding as it did with the height of the regionalist revival. Both plans were very strongly criticized as centralist and antidemocratic. After the election of 1977, the Andalucía PDTC was officially condemned by the left-wing majority parties in the regional government, and virtually abandoned by the Ministry of Public Works. The political reaction was less evident in Galicia, but its outcome—effective abandonment of the PDTC as a comprehensive decisionmaking instrument—appears to be the same. The future role of PDTCs in providing the framework for regional and subregional planning remains unclear.

Democratization has produced a strong reaction against a type of rational comprehensive planning which promises much but achieves little. The first PDTCs were highly ambitious in physical scale and in policy coverage; they were technocratic, and their hierarchical character, whereby measures of central coordination became binding upon local authorities, was fundamentally at variance with the development of autonomic institutions and the vigorous revival of municipal democracy. Future PDTCs will need to be prepared more from the bottom upward and perhaps be more modest and problem-oriented in content (see Ministerio de Obras Publicas y Urbanismo, 1978). As with interregional policy, however, little progress can be made until the new regional governments have established themselves as planning authorities.

Although Article 148 of the Constitution provides for autonomous areas to assume the functions of *ordenacion del territorio* and urban planning or *urbanismo*, devolution of the two functions is proceeding at very different rates. Regional control of *ordenacion del territorio* is problematic, not only because of the implications that a PDTC has for public expenditure (which must in any case be centrally approved), but also because Madrid retains control of so many key elements of sectoral and infrastructural investment. The negotiations over this aspect of devolution are very protracted, and can only be resolved in the light of the legal and financial provision for autonomy in each region. In 1981, even Cataluña and Euskadi had still to obtain the full powers.

[29] *Ley Sobre Regimen del Suelo y Ordenacion Urbana*, 1976, Article 8.1.

In contrast, urban planning has been one of the first responsibilities to be devolved since 1978. Nominally the state reserves responsibility only for the control of developments affecting more than one region or the national defence. It also retains responsibility for the public housing programme pending the completion of substantial new legislation in this field and, more importantly, control of what is potentially a most effective instrument of positive intervention (as opposed to mere regulation)—the Instituto Nacional de Urbanización (INUR)—a public development corporation which buys land and resells it for industrial and residential building[30]. The potential concentration of powers in the hands of the new regions is nevertheless a significant one, particularly as it includes the powerful controls exercised previously by the central state over provincial planning activities[31]. Hitherto, provinces have referred the plans for large towns and proposals for major projects to Madrid; these are now approved at regional level. What is more, whereas the provinces retain their powers of final approval over the plans for smaller towns and villages, regional governments will be able to exercise direct control by virtue of their right to chair the provincial planning commissions, determine their structures, and nominate members to them. Thus the direct powers exercised by central government under the Land and Planning Act, and the powers delegated to the provinces, have both come into the hands of regional governments. Of course, the regional government may choose not to use these powers. In Aragon, the UCD has decided to devolve them to the provincial assemblies, thus giving them virtual independence in planning matters.

What has proved difficult, of course, is developing the executive arms of autonomous regions to match their formal responsibilities. Up to the present, regional governments have been entrusted with wide powers but narrow resources—merely a transfer of local officers of the Ministry of Public Works, with minimal provision for the overheads and manpower costs of functions which are supposedly being taken over from the centre. The Andalucian region, which assumed planning powers in June 1979, has found itself barely able to sustain its basic administrative responsibilities, and has been involved in a continuous wrangle with the Ministry over funds. Even Cataluña, financially and politically the strongest of the autonomous areas, was unsuccessful for two years in getting an adequate allocation for urban planning, which it had controlled since 1978. The Catalan Ministry of Territorial Policy and Urbanism was able to operate only by co-opting the well-established planning department of the province

[30] In the summer of 1980, the activities of the INUR in Cataluña were transferred to the autonomous government, a symptom of the cordiality of relations then existing between right-wing Catalan nationalists and the UCD. See footnote (24).

[31] One aspect of the central–regional conflict in Andalucía has been the government's attempt to continue dealing directly with the provincial assemblies (generally UCD-controlled) in planning matters, over the heads of the regional government.

of Barcelona and by the expensive expedient of temporarily supplementing its budget with private credits. What broke the deadlock was the victory of the right-wing nationalist party in the Catalan general elections of May 1980, after which a real devolution of planning powers began to occur. It remains to be seen whether other regions will be able to follow this breakthrough, or if it was a unique product of political trading between central and regional governments.

One factor which may sustain the impetus is that the devolution of planning powers has occurred at a period when the question of *urbanismo* is attracting intense political interest. Under Franco, one of the focal points of the clandestine organizations of the left, and an important means to its objective of developing democratic consciousness, was the *movimientos de barrios*, or neighbourhood movement, which was initiated primarily by the PCE and some fringe parties of the extreme left, and mobilized around the social and community issues of the urban development boom (see Castells, 1978; Borja, 1977). When, after a year of pressure from the parliamentary left, Prime Minister Suarez declared local elections in 1979, it was inevitable that the two themes of citizen participation and the improvement of urban life would be at the centre of the campaign, and that as soon as PSOE–PCE coalitions had obtained control of all the major urban areas, *urbanismo* would be a first priority. The two main tasks are clearing up the backlog of illegal development which contravened planning regulations under the lax regime of the Francoist municipalities, and revising the plans themselves so as to use more effectively the potentially strong powers available—at least over suburban development, although less over the current private sector redevelopment boom—under the Land and Planning Act. An extensive legal literature and system of support services has sprung up to assist the municipalities[32], and the new regional governments can—if so inclined politically—play an active role in this regard. For instance, most of the work of the Catalan Ministry of Territorial Policy and Urbanism has so far been aimed at facilitating municipal planning initiatives. In part, this acknowledges the legal reality that regional governments at present possess powers only for urban and not regional planning. But it also reflects a more generalized disillusion with the strategic and comprehensive approach, balanced by a new enthusiasm for participatory democracy.

5 Conclusion
Regional planning in Spain used to be rather easy to describe. It was a self-contained policy area with good official documentation, lending itself well to the kind of monitoring and evaluation exercise carried out by

[32] See especially the publications of CEUMT, the Centro de Estudis Urbanistics Municipales y Territorials, which is based in Barcelona, but has nationwide connections with groups of the left.

Buttler in his study *Growth Pole Theory and Economic Development* (1975). Events after 1975 have muddied the waters. Not only is the new framework very complicated, but at the time of writing (1980) it is still in an early stage of evolution—evolution that often occurs by unexpected turns of events such as the postelection breakthrough in Cataluña. Although the developments of the past few years have shed light on the shortcomings of Francoist regional planning, it is still much too early to judge the consequences of the new Constitution for the geographical distribution of prosperity. What is already clear is that the disillusion with the ambitious rational–technocratic exercises so prominent before 1975 does not imply, as it does elsewhere in Europe, a negative retreat to a more limited, bureaucratic, and apolitical mode; on the contrary, it has resulted in a deliberate attempt to transfer the issues of urbanization and imbalanced development from the technical to the political sphere. We end with this emphasis. Contemporary Spain stands out from its European neighbours as a country where, despite the economic crisis, there still exists a political will to strengthen democratic institutions, particularly at the regional and municipal levels, and to demonstrate that they can improve upon the authoritarian state in matters of urban and regional development.

Acknowledgements. We owe especial thanks to Mario Rui Martins, Vicente Granados, Manuel Escudero, and Augustin Rodriguez-Bachiller, who contributed detailed and helpful comments on an earlier draft; responsibility for the final product, however, rests with us alone.

References
Angelet J, Rafols J, 1977 "La crisis del sector y la crisis del modelo de proteccion oficial" *Cuardernos Architectura y Urbanismo* (March–April) **42** 38–44
Antolin R P, 1979 *Emigracion y Desigualdades Regionales en España* (Editorial Magisterio Español SA, Madrid)
Arango E R, 1978 *The Spanish Political System—Franco's Legacy* (Westview Press, Boulder, Col.)
Banca Mas Sarda, 1980 *La Coyuntura Economica, en Breve* (Banca Mas Sarda, Barcelona)
Banco de Bilbao, 1978 *Renta Nacional de España y su Distribucion Provincial (Serie Homogenea 1955-1975)* (Banco de Bilbao, Bilbao)
Banco de Bilbao, 1980 *Informe Economico 1979* (Banco de Bilbao, Bilbao)
Banco Exterior de España, 1978 *La Crisis de los 70* (Servicio Estudios Economicos, Banco Exterior de España, Madrid)
Barbancho A G, 1975 *Las Migraciones Interiores Españolas en 1961-1970* (Instituto de Estudios Economicos, Madrid)
Barbancho A G, 1979 *Disparidades Regionales y Ordenacion del Territorio* (Editorial Ariel, Barcelona)
Bassols Coma M, 1973 *Genesis y Evolucion del Derecho Urbanistico Español 1812-1956* (Montecorbo, Madrid)
Borja J, 1977 "Urban social movements in Spain" in *Captive Cities* Ed. M Harloe (John Wiley, Chichester, Sussex) pp 187-211
Buttler F, 1975 *Growth Pole Theory and Economic Development* (Saxon House, Farnborough, Hants)
Carr R, Fusi J P, 1979 *Spain: Dictatorship to Democracy* (Allen and Unwin, London)

Castells M, 1978 "Urban social movements and the struggle for democracy" *International Journal of Urban and Regional Research* **2** (1) 138-146

Cinco Dias, 1980 *España ante la CEE* (Diesa, Madrid)

Cosculluela Montaner L, 1977 "Las vertientes del regionalismo" in Fernandez (1977) pp 191-246

Fernandez T R (Ed.), 1977 *Las Autonomias Regionales: Aspectos Politicos y Juridicos* (Instituto Nacional de Prospectiva, Madrid)

Fernandez T R, 1980 *Manual de Derecho Urbanistico* (El Consultor, Madrid)

Fernandez Rodriguez F, Lopez Nieto A, 1980 "El fondo de compensacion interterritorial" *Revista de Estudios Regionales* Extraordinary Volume 2 (Las Autonomias) 549-582

Ferreira F (Ed.), 1977 *Politica de Vivienda* (Ayuso, Madrid)

Firn J, Maclennan D, 1979 "Devolution: the changing political economy of regional policy" in *Regional Policy* Eds D Maclennan, J B Parr (Martin Robertson, Oxford) pp 273-296

Garcia de Enterria E, Parejo L, 1979 *Lecciones de Derecho Urbanistico* (Civitas, Madrid)

Garcia Delgardo J L, Segura J, 1977 *Reformismo y Crisis Economica: La Herencia de la Dictadura* (Saltes, Madrid)

Gimenez A, Lopez Hernando J, Pons L, 1978 *La Descentralizacion Fiscal Frente a la Crisis Economica—Aspectos Economicos de las Elecciones Municipales y de las Autonomias Regionales* (Blume Ediciones, Madrid)

Harrison R J, 1978 *An Economic History of Modern Spain* (Manchester University Press, Manchester)

Hudson Institute Europe, 1975 *El Resurgir Economico de España: Informe del Hudson Institute Europe* (Instituto de Planificacion, Madrid)

INE, 1974 *Las Migraciones Interiores en España* Decnio 1961-1970 (Instituto Nacional de Estadistica, Madrid)

Lazaro Araujo L, 1979 "Sector publico, descentralizacion y autonomias en la Constitucion Española de 1978" *Revista de Estudios Regionales* (4) 17-66

Lazaro Araujo L, Panizo F, 1978 "Desempleo y politica regional en España" in *Seminario Franco-Español sobre Problemas Actuales de la Economia del Empleo* (Ministerio de Economia, Madrid) pp 403-428

Leira E, 1973 "Growth poles in Spain: a legitimising instrument for efficiency-oriented policy" mimeograph, University of California, Berkeley, Calif.

Linde Paniagua E, 1977 "La ideologia regionalista" in Fernandez (1977) pp 247-298

López Rodó L, 1980 *Las Autonomias: Encrucijada de España* (Aguilar, Madrid)

Medhurst K N, 1973 *Government in Spain: The Executive at Work* (Pergamon Press, Oxford)

Ministerio de Industria y Energia, 1979 *La Industria Española en 1978* (Ministerio de Industria y Energia, Madrid)

Ministerio de Obras Publicas y Urbanismo, 1978 *Planeamiento Local y Planificacion Regional: Contenido Urbanistico de los Planes Directores Territoriales* Estudio Monografico 3, Direccion General de Urbanismo, Madrid

Moya C, 1972 *Burocracia y Sociedad Industrial* (Edicusa, Madrid)

Munoz Machado S, 1979 *Las Potestades Legislativas de las Comunidades Autonomas* (Editorial Civitas, Madrid)

Nevin E (Ed.), 1978 *The Economics of Devolution, Proceedings of Section F of the British Association for the Advancement of Science, Aston University, Birmingham, 1977* (University of Wales Press, Cardiff)

Olive M J, Valls X, 1976 "El sector de la construccion en el modelo de desarrollo Español" *Cuadernos Architectura y Urbanismo* (July-August) 38-46

Pajaron Collada V, 1979 "La industria Española ante las comunidades Europea" *Informacion Comercial Española* **551** (June-July) 61-73

Paniagua F J, 1977 *La Ordenacion del Capitalismo Avanzado en España 1957-1963*
  (Anagrama, Barcelona)
Paniker S, 1969 *Conversaciones en Madrid* (Kairos, Barcelona)
Parejo Alfonso L, 1977 "La region y la legislacion historica de regimen local" in
  Fernandez (1977) pp 13-187
Peces-Barba Martinez G, 1980 "El acceso a la autonomia: la via del Articulo 143"
  El Pais 17 January 1980, p 13
Pereiro A J L, 1981 *Desarrollo y Deterioro Urbano de la Ciudad de Vigo* (Colegio
  Oficial de Arquitectos de Galicia)
Richardson H W, 1975 *Regional Development Policy and Planning in Spain* (Saxon
  House, Farnborough, Hants)
Romay Beccaria, J M, 1974 "La politica urbanistica" in *La España de los Años 70*
  volume 3, Ed. M Fraga Iribarne (Editorial Moneda y Credito, Madrid)
Ros Hombravella J, 1979 *Politica Economica Española 1959-1973* (Editorial Blume,
  Barcelona)
Tamames R, 1978a *Estructura Economica de España* (Alianza Universidad Textos,
  Madrid)
Tamames R, 1978b *Introduccion a la Economia Española* (Alianza Universidad Textos,
  Madrid)
Teran F de, 1978 *Planeamiento Urbano en la España Contemporanea: Historia de un
  Proceso Imposible* (Gustavo Gili, Barcelona)

Postscript—spring 1982
In the twenty months since our paper was completed there has been some stagnation, but also some significant movement in the 'autonomic process', as it is now generally called. We can briefly bring the story up to date.

(1) The Basque country and Cataluña remain far and away the most important autonomous communities, operating genuinely decentralized powers on substantial budgets across a wide range of functions. The political leadership of both regions has remained with centre-right nationalists who have built up strong policies of industrial regeneration on a foundation of business confidence among their respective regional bourgeoisie. Both governments have made much use of direct political negotiations with the UCD in Madrid, with whom their relation is best described as tough but constructive. There have been some setbacks in the transfer of powers and also some unfavourable rulings by the constitutional tribunal, of which perhaps the most serious was a veto on Cataluña's attempt to dissolve the provinces and restore the historical structure of local government by *comarcas*. But for the most part the picture is one of steady consolidation.

(2) The picture is very different in the long, straggling tail of the remaining thirteen autonomous communities. Since our paper was completed, Galicia and Andalucía have obtained their statutes of autonomy; the remaining statutes are at various stages of drafting and consultation. Opinion poll data and the generally low turnout rates for regional referenda continue to indicate a lack of public interest in, or knowledge of, the autonomic process. The transfer of powers continues slowly against resistance from central ministries, and in the absence of effective powers the regions are chiefly engaged in a somewhat unsatisfactory kind of 'planning' with a high ratio of data collection and general policy formulation to operational content.

(3) The gap between field leaders and stragglers, exacerbated by the UCD government's policy of passive neglect, caused growing political tension and administrative confusion during 1980. After the unsuccessful military coup of 23 February 1981, national political leaders were jolted into corrective action, and the UCD entered a series of agreements with PSOE about the future management of the autonomic process. They agreed on a firm timetable for the completion of the process by spring 1983, and on a number of reforms to tidy up and introduce a greater consistency in the powers being decentralized. Sectoral commissions, one for each major department of state, are replacing the bilateral mixed commissions which negotiated the Basque and Catalan autonomies. This may reduce the scope for political bargaining by individual regions, but it should enhance the prospects for a reform of the central machinery, which logically must accompany any effective devolution. The agreements also led to the

setting up of the 'organic' (that is, framework) law on the financing of the autonomous communities—LOFCA—and the incorporation of the solidarity fund for the first time into the national budget for 1982. Another framework law—LOAPA—relates to the 'harmonization' of the autonomic process, and contains certain legal clarifications of the distributions of powers between centre and region where these had been left open or ambiguous in 1978. Where the Constitution tended to favour a decentralist interpretation, LOAPA's emphasis is clearly centralist. This may have something to do with the fact that it was drafted under the shadow of a military coup (it contains some gratuitously offensive provisions banning the use of the word 'nation' by regionalists), but it is worth remembering that in formal constitutional terms the new system remains one of the most decentralized in Europe.

(4) The implementation of the UCD–PSOE agreements since summer 1981 has been variously criticized. The Basques and Catalans have condemned LOAPA as an indirect attack by the centralist parties on their statutes of autonomy: 'harmonization', they argue, is a euphemism for homogenization to the lowest common denominator of the weakest region. But PSOE for its part has attacked UCD for failing to honour the agreements and continuing to negotiate with Cataluña and the Basque country on a special basis, at the expense of the 'harmonization' and 'solidarity' principles.

The balance of forces remains unstable and it is still too early to predict how the 1978 regionalization will settle down. Since we wrote our paper, the consolidation of autonomy in the leading regions has increased uncertainty about the devolution process as a whole. Even under the most favourable conditions it would be a delicate political puzzle to achieve simultaneously the three constitutional objectives of recognizing the historical nationhood of the Basques, Catalans, and Galicians, and creating effective regional governments elsewhere in Spain, while maintaining the capacity of the centre to redistribute resources in the interests of solidarity. But the principles agreed by UCD–PSOE do go some way towards defining the path for future compromise between centre and periphery, and between rich and poor regions.

The Demise of Growth-centre Policy: The Case of the Republic of Ireland

P BREATHNACH
St Patrick's College, Maynooth, Republic of Ireland

1 Introduction

This paper examines the implications for conventional industrial location and regional planning theory of the locational behaviour of new industry that has been established in the Republic of Ireland (henceforth 'Ireland') in the last twenty years. The widely dispersed spatial pattern exhibited in this recent phase of industrialisation calls into question the extent to which agglomerative tendencies influence modern manufacturing industry, and consequently the efficacy of growth centres as a means for promoting regional industrial expansion. The paper is divided into four main parts. Section 2 reviews briefly the evolution of growth-centre theory and its influence on regional development thinking in Ireland in the 1950s and 1960s. This part concludes with an examination of the Irish government's rejection of a growth-centre policy and an outline of the alternative industrial location policy actually put into effect, which involved a strong dispersionist orientation.

Section 3 then analyses the actual pattern of industrial location in Ireland between 1960 and 1980, highlighting the wide dispersal of plants achieved in this period. This locational pattern is related in section 4 to the postwar reorganisation of industrial capital, with particular significance being ascribed to the growth of multinational investment, which has played the leading role in recent Irish industrialisation. Finally, in section 5, the role of regional policy in influencing industrial location is assessed, and some questions are raised concerning the role of the state in the capitalist system.

2 Growth-centre theory and Irish regional planning

The theoretical basis for concentrating new industrial investment in lagging regions into a limited number of 'growth centres' began to crystallise in the late 1950s, after the pioneering work of Perroux and Hirschman, among others[1]. In the two subsequent decades, such has been the degree of academic interest generated by growth-centre theory that Kuklinski (1978, page 21) has recently observed that: "Sometimes the judgement is expressed that growth-pole theory is the closest approximation to the general theory of regional development". Indeed, the growth-centre concept would appear to have captivated the imagination of regional

[1] The evolution of growth-centre theory is discussed in Brookfield (1975, chapter 4), and in Friedmann and Weaver (1979, pages 125–129).

planning practitioners as much as academic theorists, according to the suggestion of Higgins (1978, page 229): "There is probably not a major retarded region anywhere in the world where some planners or politicians have not proposed the creation or strengthening of one or more *pôles de croissance* as a solution to its economic and social problems".

Essentially, growth-centre thinking is based on the readily observed fact that in the past, manufacturing industry has tended to agglomerate at particular locations because of the economies to be gained by so doing. These agglomeration economies have been divided by Richardson (1969, pages 70–87) into *localisation* economies, shared by firms in the same industry, and *urbanisation* economies, shared by all firms located in large urban centres regardless of industrial sector. In practice, regional planners have tended to emphasise the creation of the latter category of external economies at selected growth centres through the operation of general incentive schemes applicable to all types of industry, as the establishment of complexes of interrelated industries necessary for the generation of localisation economies requires financial and planning powers usually beyond the capabilities of government in a free-enterprise society. A key element in growth-centre policy has been the idea that once the industrial base of the selected centres has passed a certain threshold level, sufficient urbanisation economies will have been generated to ensure 'self-sustaining' growth through the automatic attraction of further industries without the need of special inducements, and indeed, much attention has been devoted to establishing what this minimum threshold might be (Moseley, 1974, chapter 5).

A variety of supplementary advantages have been attributed to growth centres as a regional planning device, including the more efficient use of public funds for infrastructure investment; the creation of a diversified social interaction milieu amenable to innovation; the interception of migratory flows from surrounding areas; the more efficient utilisation of those public services which are subject to scale economies; and the ability of growth centres to generate spread effects in their hinterlands (Moseley, 1974).

Most of these arguments were advanced at one stage or another, as a campaign to have a growth-centre policy implemented in Ireland gathered momentum during the 1960s. Formal regional policy in Ireland dates from 1952, when the western half of the country, characterised by a profusion of small farms, an inhospitable environment, and heavy out-migration, was scheduled as a block of 'Undeveloped' (now 'Designated') Areas (figure 1) within which special grants were made available for the establishment of new industry. Although industrial grants were introduced to the rest of the country in 1956, the western areas have always maintained a marked superiority in the level of grants available[2]. These grants apply

[2] Currently, the effective maximum grant is 50% of fixed assets in the Designated Areas, and 35% elsewhere.

ubiquitously within their respective areas, and from the beginning the Irish government has favoured a policy of maximum dispersal of industrial investment, with the ideal objective of allowing each community to provide adequate industrial employment locally.

The development of a growth-centre school of thought in opposition to this locational policy generally reflects the evolution of the concept internationally[3]. Thus the first suggestion of a spatially selective industrial policy appeared as early as 1958 in an influential government discussion document (*Economic Development*, 1958). Subsequently, after a series of official reports, all favourable to a growth-centre policy, the campaign to have such a policy implemented in Ireland reached its peak in 1969 with the publication of a comprehensive growth-centre strategy embracing the entire country (Buchanan and Partners, 1969). It was around this time that Smith, in his definitive review of the field of industrial location,

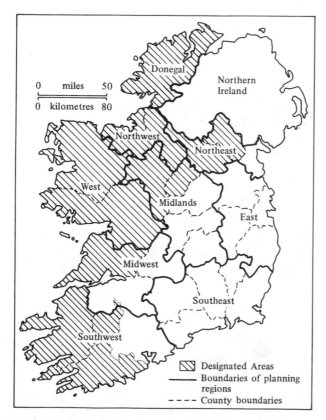

Figure 1. Ireland: planning regions and Designated Areas.

[3] A detailed account of the evolution of growth-centre thinking in Ireland may be found in Walsh (1976).

wrote regarding the question of "the spatial allocation of investment in industrial development" that "the concentration at selected points as an alternative to even distribution has gained widespread acceptance in recent years", and further that "The growth-point concept has become a central and almost essential feature of the spatial strategy of industrial development planning" (Smith, 1971, page 157).

The so-called Buchanan Report certainly reflected this line of thinking, proposing that 75% of new industrial employment over a twenty-year period should be concentrated in nine urban centres (figure 2). The main element in the plan was the development of two 'national' growth centres at Cork and Limerick which would be enabled to attain a sufficient size to compete effectively for new investment with the national capital, Dublin, which alone accounted for 40% of national industrial employment.

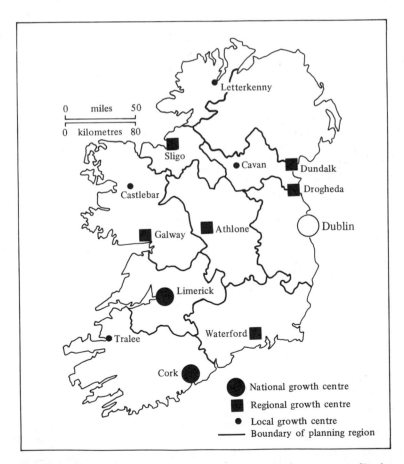

Figure 2. Growth-centre strategy proposed in the Buchanan report (Buchanan and Partners, 1969).

In addition, six 'regional' centres were to receive preferential treatment as regards industrial investments within their respective regions, and four 'local' centres in isolated districts were essentially to become foci of service provision for these districts.

A major problem with this plan was that, by building on the existing industrial centres which were located mostly in the East and South, it offered little to the most underdeveloped areas in the Midlands, Northwest, and Southwest, where the ruling party (Fianna Fáil) derived a major proportion of its electoral support. In addition, the proposals brought forth a predictable clamour of protest from those urban centres elsewhere which had not been favoured by the report. Accordingly, it was hardly surprising that the government shied away from the Buchanan proposals, opting instead for a continuation of the dispersal policy. This was given formal expression in 1972 when the Industrial Development Authority (IDA), the state agency responsible for promoting industrial development at both the national level and the regional level, published its first five-year plan (IDA, 1972a; 1972b), which effectively tolled the death knell for growth-centre policy in Ireland.

In justifying a continuation of the dispersionist policy, the IDA criticised the Buchanan Report for being too pessimistic about the prospects of attracting industry to remote locations, using as evidence the excellent industrial growth rate of the weaker regions in the late 1960s. Developments in transport and communications, argued the IDA, had conferred on industry much greater locational flexibility. Thus, during the 1960s, industrial plants had been established in 271 separate locations, and one-half of the plants established in this period had been located in towns of less than 3000 population. Nor had this degree of dispersal had any apparent negative effect on the enthusiasm of industrialists (a major argument of the growth-centre proponents): the rate of new industrial employment promoted in the period 1968–1971 ran at twice that of the previous four-year period (IDA, 1972a, pages 44–49).

The main thrust of the IDA's plan, therefore, was to systematise the dispersal policy by dividing the country into forty-eight clusters of spatially proximate towns and their hinterlands, each cluster forming a common labour-catchment area and being assigned a target for industrial job creation during the period of the five-year plan. Such a degree of spatial disaggregation of the overall national job-creation target implied an impressive capacity to control the location of new industry on the part of the IDA. The principal means of achieving this were to be a comprehensive programme of acquiring and preparing fully serviced industrial sites throughout the country, in most cases with ready-built advance factories immediately available to prospective industrialists (figure 3), and a much greater degree of discretion than that applied previously in the allocation of grants, with the percentage grant offered being varied in accordance with the IDA's locational priorities.

At the same time, the IDA did allow that large centres possessed certain advantages, particularly for 'high-technology, large-scale' industries, and proposed that such industries should be located in the larger centres, with smaller-scale industries being located in smaller communities. All in all, then, the IDA expected that during the period of the plan, some 50% of new industrial employment would locate in Dublin and in the eight national and regional centres identified by Buchanan (compared with 75% over a twenty-year period, as proposed by Buchanan). Although marking a substantial dilution of the degree of concentration envisaged by Buchanan, the IDA plans did, nevertheless, entail a significant element of centralisation. However, it may be that the IDA was merely making a formal gesture to the weighty body of pro-growth-centre opinion in this respect, as the indications are that in practice, the IDA has been implementing an even greater degree of dispersion than that anticipated in its plan. It is to an analysis of the IDA's locational performance that the paper now turns.

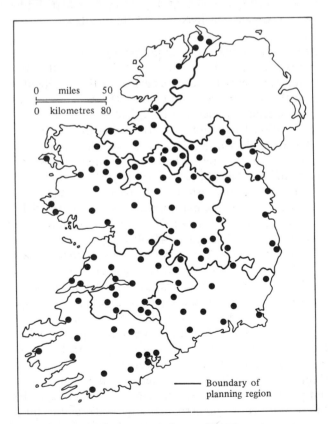

Figure 3. Locations of IDA advance factories.

3 Industrial location in Ireland 1960-1980

To enable it to monitor the performance of its industrial plans (the plan for 1978-1982 has maintained the approach adopted for 1973-1977), the IDA has, since 1973, carried out a comprehensive survey of employment trends in all Irish manufacturing firms, and has published the results at the regional level. Table 1 compares the regional job targets with actual gains for the period of the first five-year plan, and includes job losses over the period to give the overall net change in manufacturing employment. In this table, the first four regions listed may be characterised as the 'weak' regions, displaying a low level of urbanisation and manufacturing employment; the remaining five regions can generally be placed in the 'strong' category, although some—especially Southwest and Northeast— possess significant internal variations. Thus it can be seen that whereas three of the four weak regions surpassed their targets, only one of the five strong regions did likewise. Indeed, the three regions containing the largest urban centres in the State—East (Dublin), Southwest (Cork), and Midwest (Limerick)—all fell short of their targets. This indicates an even greater degree of dispersal away from urban areas than even the IDA itself envisaged.

Table 1 also shows that whereas all four weak regions experienced net gains in manufacturing employment over the period, only two of the strong regions did so. The most significant development in this respect was the spectacular level of job losses in the metropolitan East region. The bulk of industry in this region had been established under conditions of heavy protection between 1932 and 1959, and consisted for the most part of small, inefficient firms serving the limited home market (Walsh, 1980a). These firms were hit particularly hard by the coincidence of Ireland's accession to the EEC in 1973 (and the consequent exposure to international competition) and the international recession which followed the rapid escalation in oil prices in the same year.

Table 1. Regional pattern of job gains and losses in manufacturing industry, 1973-1977. Source: IDA (1979a, page 44).

Region	Gross job target	Actual job gains	Job losses	Net change
Donegal	2800	2300	1500	+800
Northwest	1700	1800	700	+1100
West	5300	7350	2200	+5150
Midlands	3400	5350	2200	+3150
East	17000	14600	25650	−11050
Southeast	4700	7200	4450	+2750
Northeast	5300	4500	5500	−1000
Midwest	5400	5300	5300	−
Southwest	9400	9100	8100	+1000

The different regional patterns in the distribution of gains and losses indicated in table 1 has accelerated the regional redistribution of manufacturing employment in Ireland which had already become apparent in the 1960s. The IDA's ultimate objective would appear to be to allocate to each region a proportion of national industrial employment similar to that region's share of the national population, and the remarkable progress that has been made in this direction is indicated in table 2, in which the ratio between these two proportions for each region is given for three different years, 1961, 1973, and 1979. The degree to which there has been movement towards the optimum universal ratio of 1·0 is evident: for example, in the period 1961–1979, the East region's ratio has been cut back from 1·62 to 1·11, and those of the weakest regions, West and Northwest, have increased from 0·34 and 0·39 to 0·76 and 0·83, respectively. To a certain extent, the relative regional redistribution indicated in table 2 is due to industrial decline in established industrial regions, and to a degree of population redistribution; nevertheless, there is no doubt that the major cause has been the ability of the traditionally weak regions to attract a relatively large proportion of new industrial investment during the period under consideration.

This, in turn, is reflected in corresponding trends in other economic indicators. Thus the number of counties experiencing population decline fell from twenty-five (out of twenty-six, the exception being Dublin) in 1951–1961, to fourteen in 1961–1971, and to only one in 1971–1979 (*Census of Population of Ireland 1979*, 1980, table 1), indicating that population stabilisation has spread throughout the country in response to the IDA's efforts at industrial redistribution. This trend is further corroborated by the data on regional per capita incomes for the period

Table 2. Regional distribution of manufacturing employment and population.

Region	1961			1973			1979		
	ME[a]	NP[b]	ME/NP	ME[c]	NP[d]	ME/NP	ME[e]	NP[b]	ME/NP
Donegal	2·4	4·0	0·60	2·3	3·6	0·64	2·7	3·6	0·75
Northwest	1·2	3·1	0·39	1·4	2·6	0·54	2·0	2·4	0·83
West	3·3	9·7	0·34	3·8	8·6	0·44	6·4	8·4	0·76
Midlands	4·2	8·5	0·49	3·9	7·7	0·51	5·9	7·5	0·79
East	52·2	32·2	1·62	48·2	36·0	1·34	41·5	37·3	1·11
Southeast	8·9	11·4	0·78	10·0	11·0	0·91	11·6	10·9	1·06
Northeast	6·7	6·1	1·10	7·3	5·8	1·26	6·9	5·7	1·21
Midwest	6·0	9·3	0·65	8·6	9·1	0·95	8·8	8·9	0·99
Southwest	15·1	15·9	0·95	14·5	15·6	0·93	14·5	15·3	0·93

ME ≡ percentage of national manufacturing employment
NP ≡ percentage of national population

Sources: [a] O'Farrell (1975, page 15); [b] *Census of Population of Ireland 1979* (1980, table 2); [c] computed from data in IDA (1979a, page 43); [d] IDA (1972b, page 8); [e] IDA (1980).

under review (table 3), which show a steady decline in the relative position of the East region, a slight improvement in the combined Northwest and Donegal regions, and a significant improvement in the West region, although there has been a deterioration in the relative position of the Midlands region. In the four weak regions, the proportion of total personal income attributable to employee remuneration in manufacturing and mining rose from 8·9% to 11·4% in 1973–1977 alone, and this clearly had a major role in counteracting the regionally uneven distribution of payments under the EEC Common Agricultural Policy, the bulk of whose benefits have accrued to the prosperous agricultural regions in the East and South (Ross, 1980).

Within the individual regions, it has not been possible to monitor the extent to which the IDA has met its target at the town-group level. However, it is instructive that, in November 1980, 87% of all the advance factories which had been constructed were occupied, while over one-half of those under construction were already reserved for clients (Killeen, 1980a). This indicates a high level of attainment of locational targets. Indeed, according to the managing director of the IDA, by 1980 it had become difficult to recruit even unskilled workers in several parts of the country (Killeen, 1980b).

The most recent comprehensive survey of the locational patterns of IDA-sponsored industry was that carried out by O'Farrell in 1973 (O'Farrell, 1975; 1978; 1980). This survey found that of the 418 grant-aided plants which had been established in the period 1960–1973, over half (237) were located in towns of less than 5000 population (O'Farrell, 1975, table 12, page 27). This corroborates the earlier findings of the IDA, referred to above. By contrast, Dublin, with a population twice that of the combined population of all towns of less than 5000 population, attracted only thirty-six plants in the same period.

For the period since 1973, it has been possible to analyse the locations of foreign firms establishing in Ireland, complete lists of which are published periodically by the IDA (IDA, 1979b). Such firms comprise the

Table 3. Regional per capita income as a percentage of the national average, for the years 1960–1977. Source: Ross (1980, page 20).

Region	1960	1973	1977
Donegal–Northwest	75·6	76·4	76·6
West	78·2	81·4	86·1
Midlands	82·9	80·3	78·7
East	124·2	117·2	115·4
Southeast	93·5	94·5	95·3
Northeast	87·7	91·3	91·0
Midwest	94·2	95·9	94·8
Southwest	98·8	98·9	100·2

majority of new manufacturing plants establishing in Ireland since 1960 (see below). It was found that in the period 1973–1978, 41% of the 358 firms in question located in Dublin and the eight national and regional centres designated in the Buchanan Report, with the other 59% locating elsewhere. This indicates a greater degree of concentration than in the earlier period studied by O'Farrell, when over 70% of plants located outside the nine main centres. However, numbers of plants in themselves do not necessarily provide an accurate reflection of the distribution of industrial employment, owing to variations in plant size. Accordingly, an analysis was carried out on plants with a projected employment target of over 500, which had begun production, were under construction, or had been approved for grants by the IDA during the period 1974–1978, according to the IDA's periodical, *IDA News*. Of twenty-four plants in this category, only eleven were located in the nine main centres (of which only four were located in the three major centres: Dublin, Cork, and Limerick). Thus, the IDA has not been adhering to its own proposals for locating large plants in the larger urban centres, nor have these plants themselves shown any systematic preference for such centres.

All in all, then, it is clear from the evidence presented above that, despite the assertion of Smith (1971, page 503) that: "External economies of agglomeration and interindustry linkages are becoming increasingly important determinants of plant location in advanced industrial nations", in the Irish case the experience of the last twenty years suggests that, if anything, industrial firms have displayed a preference for small communities rather than large urban centres. O'Farrell attaches particular importance to the IDA's financial incentives and organisation of itineraries to prospective sites for potential investors as an explanation for this phenomenon (O'Farrell, 1980, page 149). Although these factors are certainly relevant, they nevertheless fall a long way short of providing an adequate explanation for the pattern of industrial dispersal apparent in Ireland. Rather, it is argued that this locational pattern is reflective of fundamental changes which have been taking place in the nature of modern manufacturing industry at a global level, and which are discussed in section 4.

4 Industrial reorganisation and locational choice

In the first instance, it is clear that industrial dispersal in Ireland has coincided with the introduction in 1959 of an 'open door' policy with respect to foreign investment, thereby ending a twenty-seven-year experiment in protectionism during which foreign investment was officially discouraged. The principal financial incentive for foreign firms, apart from the industrial grants scheme, was a fifteen-year period of exemption from tax on profits derived from export sales, reflecting a new policy of basing economic growth on the expansion of exports. Since 1959, the proportion of new industrial investment emanating from foreign sources has consistently hovered around the 60% mark, and with indigenous investment doing little more than replacing native firms going out of business, the relative significance of the foreign sector has grown rapidly until a situation has been reached where foreign firms now account for over one-third of manufacturing employment, one-half of manufacturing output, and the great bulk of industrial exports, apart from food (Desmond, 1980). The principal sources of these firms have been the USA, the UK, and West Germany, although in all, over twenty nationalities are represented; the main areas of investment are electronic and other electrical equipment, mechanical engineering, chemicals and pharmaceuticals, synthetic textiles, foodstuffs, healthcare products, and leisure goods (IDA, 1979b).

Whereas the growth-centre proponents of the 1960s argued that the government's dispersal policy would deter foreign firms from locating in Ireland, in fact foreign firms have led the way in terms of complying with the IDA's locational requirements. O'Farrell's analysis of the locational behaviour of industrial firms in the period 1960–1973 identified a greater tendency for foreign firms compared with indigenous firms to locate in peripheral areas (O'Farrell, 1978; 1980), and this tendency has continued as indicated by this recent observation by the IDA's managing director: "... domestic industry isn't very mobile; people tend to expand where they have already located, so for regional development we will want some mobile foreign capital" (Killeen, 1980c).

This points to a fundamental difference between indigenous and foreign enterprise in Ireland, namely the respective scales of corporate organisation. The rapid postwar growth of multinational investment is strongly associated with a corresponding increase in the concentration of industrial ownership within the world's economically advanced countries. Thus, in the USA, the top 100 manufacturing corporations increased their share of net output from 23% to 38% of the total between 1947 and 1970, and their share of manufacturing assets increased from nearly 40% to nearly 50% from 1948 to 1971; in the UK, the share of net manufacturing output controlled by the top 100 companies rose from 20% in 1950 to 50% in 1970 (Holland, 1976a, pages 30–31). Similar trends may be observed in Italy, France, and West Germany (Holland, 1976b, page 44).

The implications for locational behaviour of the concentration of industrial ownership are manifold. For a start, the operation of multiplant, multilocational organisations gives corporate management a broader spatial perspective, making it more aware of spatial variations in various cost factors, and more amenable to considering a range of possible locations for new plant (Hamilton, 1978b, page 37). In addition, the greater resources available to a large corporation enable it to carry out a more intensive and sophisticated search for the 'best' location for a new plant. This greater locational flexibility on the part of large firms is further enhanced by postwar developments in the realm of transport and communications, themselves mainly facilitated by the major research and development efforts brought to bear by these firms. General improvements in transport facilities and technology, and the increasing sophistication (and therefore value per unit weight) of modern industrial products would appear to have reduced transport costs to virtual insignificance over a wide range of industrial production, particularly when these are compared with the various cost advantages (to be discussed below) which may be derived from locational diversity. This, of course, wreaks havoc with traditional Weberian industrial location theory, in which transport costs play such a central role. Rapid improvements in communications systems have further enabled complex and widely dispersed organisations to be efficiently controlled from centralised headquarters, and the standardisation of production technology (to be considered in more detail below) and the routinisation of decisionmaking procedures, by reducing the need for intimate contact between its constituent parts, also contribute to the effective functioning of the multilocational organisation.

The merging of functionally linked activities under unified corporate ownership, which has been a key feature of industrial concentration, also contributes to locational flexibility by reducing the uncertainty concerning supplies and outlets which in the past was a major reason for the agglomeration of small, independent firms at particular locations. In addition, the large scale of operation of many modern firms has allowed them to achieve internally the threshold levels needed to support various specialist services (eg legal, financial, marketing, technical) thereby obviating one of the key considerations favouring agglomeration at urban centres where such services are provided by independent firms. Access to information concerning new techniques and products, which is maximised in the information-rich milieu of major cities, has also declined as a locational criterion for large firms, which rely increasingly on internally produced research and development (Holland, 1976c, pages 211–212). In any case, the information generating, gathering, and processing functions of large corporations have, as is well known, little need for spatial association with production activities. Accordingly, one observes a marked tendency for the former to gravitate in particular towards metropolitan areas, whereas the latter display a contrary tendency towards increasing dispersal. This centralisation of ownership and control of production activities and the simultaneous decentralisation of the latter activities has become an outstanding feature of the spatial organisation of modern capitalism.

A final factor which has played an important role in facilitating the decentralisation of production to peripheral areas has been the development of infrastructural facilities (eg transport, communications, power, education) in these areas by national governments, thereby removing basic obstacles to the successful operation of externally orientated and controlled activities.

The various factors discussed thus far have combined to confer on large industrial enterprises an unprecedented degree of locational flexibility. It remains to explain the particular locational choices which have been made by these enterprises, and in particular the preference for peripheral, largely rural areas, as indicated by the Irish evidence, and the avoidance or abandonment of established industrial centres. With the dilution of the attractive force of such centres owing to the various developments outlined above, it is to be expected that the deterrent aspects of such centres should assume a magnified relative importance. Thus Keeble (1976a, pages 26-27) has cited factors such as managerial residential preferences and high land costs in accounting for industrial dispersal in Britain. One clearly significant factor in this context not mentioned by Keeble is the high cost of labour in established industrial centres. This factor has been particularly highlighted by Massey in her study (in association with Meegan) of the UK electrical engineering and electronics industries (Massey, 1978; see also Massey and Meegan, 1978; 1979). In this context, it should be borne in mind that labour costs are a function not only of wage rates (which in many cases may be standardised nationally), but also of the propensity to industrial action, absenteeism, and low productivity on the factory floor, all of which tend to be higher in established industrial areas. Thus, Massey (1978, page 50) found that:

"... the reserve of labour in cities was seen as being more expensive, more highly unionised and more militant .... So, instead of using this labour, capital is beginning to spread out. Small towns are now favoured locations".

Holland (1976c, pages 217-218), cites evidence to the same effect from the USA.

In the past, a major constraint on the desire by firms to avoid high labour costs in urban areas was the need to have access to the skilled labour available in such areas. More recently, however, many firms have been enabled to free themselves from this constraint by introducing technological innovations which have facilitated the 'deskilling' of industrial work through means such as automation, standardisation of components, and the introduction of conveyor production-line systems and numerically controlled machine tools (Massey, 1978, page 43). As a consequence, virtually no initial skills are required for large portions of modern industrial work; in this situation, any area possessing the requisite supply of general labour is a potential location for such industry, while clearly the preferred areas will be those where such labour is cheapest and/or most productive. Again, in this context, it is necessary to note that the increased scale of corporate organisation has been a key factor in the introduction of deskilling technology, in that only the largest firms possess the scales of output which make such innovation worthwhile, and the research and development capacity to make them possible.

A further noteworthy aspect of Massey's work is that it demonstrates that industrial decentralisation is not simply confined to declining industrial sectors such as textiles (Keeble, 1976b, pages 173-181), whose usefulness as a basis for regional development is questionable, but is occurring also in expanding, technologically advanced industries. In the USA also, Rees

(1979, pages 49–50) has noted a reversal in the 1960s and 1970s of the previous tendency for rapid-growth industries to concentrate in the industrial heartland of the Northeast.

The attractions of peripheral areas for industrial investment complement deterrents operating in central regions. Thus the cost of land, and of infrastructure and labour reproduction (Lipietz, 1980, pages 68–70) are minimised, as is pressure on the physical environment. But perhaps the key factor in this respect is the lower cost of labour in such areas. This may arise simply from lower wage rates due, in part, to lower rates of unionisation, although trade union members in peripheral regions tend anyway to be less militant than those in the main industrial centres. This lack of militancy may be due, to a certain extent, to the lack of alternative employment opportunities locally, and indeed firms moving to peripheral regions may deliberately choose isolated locations in order to monopolise local labour pools and thereby encourage labour docility. In any case, new entrants to the industrial work force emanating from a rural background do not appear to possess (at least initially) the cynical attitude to industrial work which is a common feature of long-established centres, and hence display favourable productivity records.

Although the tendency towards peripheralisation is well documented for firms operating at the national level (Keeble, 1976a; Rees, 1979), the role of multinational firms in this respect is particularly worth noting. There would appear to be some disagreement concerning the locational behaviour of multinational firms within national territories (Yannopoulos and Dunning, 1976, pages 389–390). Referring to Western Europe, Hamilton (1978b, page 27) notes that: "Most [multinational units] tend to be located in or near major cities and ports". Similarly, Holland (1976b, page 51) refers (with respect to the UK, France, and Italy) to "the extent to which multinationals concentrate their activities in more developed regions"[4]. Indeed, Holland has been preoccupied with the ability of multinational companies to frustrate national regional development policies by threatening to move abroad if their desire to locate in the allegedly preferred central regions is not facilitated (Holland, 1976a; 1976b, pages 33–41; 1980, pages 78–79). At the same time, Hamilton (1978b, page 37) does suggest a greater preparedness on the part of multinational firms to locate in problem regions, and Keeble's evidence for the UK certainly seems to bear this out: in the period 1966–1971, 80% of the employment created by foreign firms was located in the assisted peripheral areas, with only 8% going to the central regions around London and Birmingham (Keeble, 1976a, page 30). Nor, indeed, is it the case that firms relocating from, or avoiding, the existing major industrial regions are simply choosing the leading urban centres in peripheral regions, as Holland alleges (1976b, page 52). Keeble (1978, pages 47–48) produces evidence in the UK case

[4] See also Blackbourn (1978) in this context.

to show that *within* regions, greater equalisation of industrial location is taking place, and in the case of the Atlantic provinces of Canada, Hayter and Storey (1978, page 22) have noted a tendency for incoming footloose plants to avoid large urban centres and locate instead in small communities. The Irish experience, therefore, is clearly not unique.

It would appear, then, that Holland's trepidations are based on an outdated view of the locational behaviour of multinational firms. Such firms initially tended to locate in developed countries in order to gain access to local national markets, and accordingly tended to favour locations in central regions where such markets were concentrated. However, during the 1960s, many of these firms began to develop truly multinational production systems, involving international linkages between plants, frequently with global markets being supplied from centralised production units. There is not space at the present time to investigate the reasons for this development in any depth, but the following are worth mentioning: the achievement of economies of scale through the centralisation of component production; the ability to minimise exposure to taxation and to optimise the effects of currency fluctuations through the manipulation of intrafirm transfer pricing, where organically linked production processes are separated internationally; the minimisation of overt corporate presence in any one country (given governmental anxiety over the attenuation of its sovereign powers by the activities of multinational enterprise); and the general freedom of manoeuvre facilitated by not placing too many eggs in any one basket.

Given this tendency towards global integration of production activities, the emphasis on supplying individual national markets has declined, as has the role of transport costs—particularly at the intranational level—in determining locational choice. Combined with the other factors promoting locational change, discussed previously, these considerations can be expected to have produced substantial changes in the locational behaviour of multinational firms in recent years. This is certainly indicated by the evidence from the Irish case, to which we now return.

The large and growing inflow of foreign firms into Ireland since 1960 has been associated with a particularly attractive combination of incentives. Apart from the generous grants available, the fifteen-year 'tax holiday' on export-based profits has been a particularly attractive incentive, not only per se, but because of the opportunity it presents for manipulating transfer prices so that corporate profits are concentrated in the Irish operation. This is indicated by the high profitability of foreign investment in Ireland, which, in the case of US investment, was running at over twice the average level for all US foreign investment in the mid-1970s (Ambrose, 1978, page 3). American firms in Ireland tend to be strongly interlinked with affiliates elsewhere: in 1974 such firms sold over three-quarters of their exports to, and purchased almost one-half of their imports from, these affiliates (McAleese, 1977, page 36–37). In the same year, all foreign firms (excluding those in the food industry) in Ireland imported almost 90%

of raw materials and components and exported almost 90% of output (McAleese, 1977, pages 30, 47). These statistics emphasise Ireland's 'export platform' status.

However, Ireland's attractiveness to foreign investment goes well beyond these considerations. In the EEC context in particular, Ireland constitutes a major labour reserve, with registered unemployment habitually of the order of 10%, a very low proportion of women in the work force, the highest birth rate in the Community, and considerable underemployment in agriculture, particularly in the Designated Areas. Furthermore, this labour is relatively cheap: in 1980, average earnings in Ireland were the lowest in the EEC, and were less than half those in West Germany, The Netherlands, and Belgium (Inbucon Management Consultants, 1980).

Within Ireland, on the other hand, there is a high degree of unionisation in incoming industry, and therefore a high degree of standardisation of wages for most types of industrial work. Wage-rate variations, therefore, cannot be adduced to explain the locational behaviour of foreign firms in Ireland. It is here that the other elements determining labour costs, referred to earlier (namely, militancy and productivity), assume a particularly significant role. Thus, the much longer tradition of union organisation in the older industrial centres, especially Dublin, has engendered in these centres a much greater degree of worker militancy. Most of the major strikes in recent years have occurred in national level organisations (such as the state sector and the banks) which are strongly orientated towards the capital city, and in many of these disputes (eg post office technicians, petrol-tanker drivers) voting patterns have shown a clear-cut division between workers based in Dublin and those elsewhere. A potentially significant factor in restraining trade union militancy in rural areas in particular, apart from the recency of proletarianisation, is the participation of part-time farmers in the industrial work force (Lipietz, 1980, page 70; Carney et al, 1980, pages 22–23). Part-time farming is widespread in Ireland: in 1975, less than one-half of Irish farms were operated on a full-time basis, and in the three counties of the province of Ulster which are in the Republic (all in the Designated Areas) the proportion drops to as low as one-quarter (*Farm Management Survey*, 1979).

It is not surprising, therefore, to find that foreign firms in Ireland have experienced a low incidence of labour disputes. Thus, in the period 1972–1977, 79% of overseas firms in Ireland had no strikes at all, and of the remainder, 92% lost less than one day per worker per year in industrial disputes (McEldowney, 1980). This is borne out in a survey of 114 foreign companies in Ireland, carried out by a British business magazine (*Business Location File*, 1978) which concluded: "The picture of an Ireland brought to a standstill by work stoppages is a fake, because the companies that actually produce in the country are, overall, satisfied with this aspect of the business environment".

Finally, as regards labour productivity, again the evidence indicates a high degree of satisfaction among foreign firms. A survey of such firms Ó hUiginn, 1970), demonstrated that the most satisfactory aspect of their operating experience in Ireland was the performance of the labour force, with respect not only to industrial relations, but also to productivity, availability, cost, and stability. This corroborates the general findings of the earlier *Survey of Grant-aided Industry* (1967).

5 Regional policy and the role of the state

The main conclusion to be drawn from the foregoing discussion is that the basic foundation upon which growth-centre theory is built, namely the 'natural' tendency for industry to agglomerate, is rapidly losing its validity. Admittedly, the traditional considerations promoting agglomeration still apply in many cases to small, independent firms; this is indicated by the lower propensity to dispersal of the indigenous Irish firms, which tend to possess these characteristics. However, the fact remains that the proportion of total output and employment accounted for by such firms is diminishing rapidly. On the other hand, large firms—particularly those with a multi-national organisational scope—either are increasingly indifferent as regards choice of location, or in many cases may be quite desirous of avoiding concentrated locations.

These findings raise serious questions concerning the role of government incentives in influencing industrial location patterns. Such incentives are usually justified as compensating for the extra costs incurred through not locating at preferred sites, which are assumed to be in central regions (Yannopoulos and Dunning, 1976, page 391). Even where firms are locationally indifferent, clearly financial incentives will have a decisive influence in determining the actual locations chosen, although one would expect that the level of incentives required would be less in the latter than in the former case. O'Farrell (1980, page 149), Keeble (1976b, page 36), and Hamilton (1978b, page 37) have all emphasised the role of financial incentives in promoting industrial dispersal. However, Hayter and Storey's (1978, page 22) study of Atlantic Canada shows that even in the absence of an active locational policy on the part of government, incoming firms have tended towards dispersal. This supports the contention of this paper that for a considerable number of firms establishing in isolated peripheral locations, such locations are in fact the preferred locations in the first place, so that for these firms, regional incentives are simply reinforcing trends which would have operated in any case.

Such an argument assumes further significance in the light of the recent growth of interest among geographers in the role of the state in capitalist society (Dear and Clark, 1978; Johnston, 1980). There is a substantial school of thought which sees this role as that of creating the necessary conditions for maximising the process of capital accumulation (Lipietz, 1980, page 73). In the realm of regional policy, for example, Parson

(1980) has argued (in the context of Northern Ireland) that the function of growth-centre policy in peripheral areas is to assemble adequate labour reserves at selected centres in order to facilitate incoming industry. Damette (1980), on the other hand, sees such factors as industrial grants, investment in peripheral infrastructure, and accelerated depreciation of existing plant as facilitating rapid spatial adaptation to the changing conditions within which accumulation takes place. The resulting 'hyper-mobility' of capital, then, is seen at present as one component of the process of capital restructuring (Massey, 1978; 1979). Thus, Massey (1978, page 49) argues "against a-historical assumptions that regional policies of employment dispersal are necessarily contradictory to the process of accumulation at the national level".

It is necessary in this context to avoid perceiving capital as a homogeneous entity; rather, it comprises an amalgam of frequently competing fractions (Holland, 1980, chapter 6). This can have important regional policy implications. Thus Damette (1980, pages 80–81) sees the penetration of peripheral regions by centrally based monopoly capital as potentially undermining the position of regional elites, although elements of the latter may benefit from this penetration by adapting to it (eg via construction activities or the supply of services to incoming firms). The role of the state in this situation involves mediation with these local elites (Lipietz, 1980, page 74), although it may also resort to coercion if necessary (Damette, 1980, page 80).

In the Irish case, there are very few indigenous large-scale capitals. Instead, as is typical of ex-colonies, the Irish economy has been dominated since independence by petty capitalism and petty commodity production. The author has argued elsewhere (Walsh, 1980b) that the Irish political system reflects these circumstances, with the main political parties representing amalgams of the leading business interests. Thus, Fianna Fáil (the usual governing party) has represented the interests of the domestic-orientated 'national' bourgeoisie, which was presented with a guaranteed and insulated, if limited, home market during the protectionist period, and local elites in the western small farming areas, whereas Fine Gael, the main opposition party, has traditionally represented the export-orientated commercial farmers and associated business and mercantile interests—the classic 'comprador' bourgeoisie.

The decision to abandon protectionism and embark on a policy of attracting foreign investment was taken in the light of the accumulation crisis faced by the national bourgeoisie after the recession of the late 1950s. The new policy, and the free-trade conditions which it implied, necessitated a major restructuring of indigenous Irish industry if it was to survive, and although generous schemes to facilitate this were introduced, as we have seen, there has nevertheless been a considerable shakeout of Irish firms in the face of growing external competition. However, whereas most of these firms were suppliers of consumer goods to the home market, a considerable replacement market has been provided in the form of the needs of foreign firms locating in Ireland. This is quite clearly acknowledged in the following statement by the managing director of the IDA:

"Much of our small industries development, which we are concentrating very heavily on now, domestic or Irish industry if you like, is the result of the demand created by large and medium industry, a lot of which is foreign owned. So much of the opportunity for small industries growth would disappear if we were to back off foreign investment" (Killeen, 1980c).

Apart from manufacturing industry, foreign investment has, of course, generated spin-offs both in construction and in services, not only directly, but indirectly in the form of the increasing consumer demands generated by workers in foreign firms. Accordingly, although some Irish businesses have adapted to the new conditions sufficiently well to emerge as large-scale operators in their own right, nevertheless Irish capital in general has allowed itself to be channeled into such small scale 'secondary activities', so characteristic of the process of dependent development (Furtado, 1968)[5].

Finally, the spatially dispersed pattern of foreign investment in Ireland is clearly associated with the correspondingly decentralised petty business interests which control the Irish state (despite the high degree of bureaucratic centralisation of the latter). Indeed, it may be that the attempt to have a growth-centre policy implemented in the 1960s reflected an attempt on the part of city-based industrial interests to replace business lost under the new economic policy (with city-based theorists providing the required 'ideological' input); certainly, opposition to dispersal appears to have declined along with the influence of these interests.

6 Conclusion

The main thrust of the argument of this paper is that manufacturing industry has become increasingly mobile in terms of locational behaviour; that this development is intimately associated with the concentration of industrial ownership; that the function of governmental regional policy has been to facilitate "the rapid development of sites corresponding to the optimal locations in terms of profit maximisation" (Damette, 1980, page 85); and that for a considerable number of firms, these locations are to be found in peripheral areas with suitable labour reserves. As a consequence, established industrial location theory and its derivative, growth-centre theory, are in need of fundamental revision. The industrial areas of urban regions are now emerging as the principal problem regions in advanced capitalist economies, with profound political implications, given the concentrations of militant workers in these areas (Carney, 1980).

---

[5] A major exception to this generalisation is the food-processing sector, which remains largely under indigenous ownership, and has made substantial technological progress, mostly under the aegis of large-scale agricultural cooperatives.

On the other hand, the industrialisation of peripheral regions will inevitably lead to the destruction of those very qualities which currently make these regions so attractive to industry (Carney et al, 1980, pages 22–23; Carney, 1980, pages 33–34). Thus do the imperatives of capital accumulation lead to a never-ending process of spatial reorganisation.

References
Ambrose B, 1978 "Ireland's exports" *Ireland Today* (940) 2–3
Blackbourn A, 1978 "Multinational enterprises and regional development: a comment" *Regional Studies* **12** 125–127
Brookfield H, 1975 *Interdependent Development* (Methuen, Andover, Hants)
Buchanan C, and Partners, 1969 *Regional Studies in Ireland* (An Foras Forbartha, Dublin)
Business Location File 1978, quoted in *The Irish Times* 27 October 1978, p 10
Carney J, 1980 "Regions in crisis: accumulation, regional problems and crisis formation" in Carney et al (1980) pp 28–59
Carney J, Hudson R, Lewis J (Eds), 1980 *Regions in Crisis* (Croom Helm, London)
Census of Population of Ireland 1979 1980 (The Stationery Office, Dublin)
Damette F, 1980 "The regional framework of monopoly exploitation: new problems and trends" in Carney et al (1980) pp 76–92
Dear M, Clark G, 1978 "The state and geographic process: a critical review" *Environment and Planning A* **10** 173–183
Desmond B, 1980, quoted in *The Irish Times* 14 April 1980, p 9
Economic Development 1958 (The Stationery Office, Dublin)
Farm Management Survey 1979 (An Foras Taluntais, Dublin)
Friedmann J, Weaver C, 1979 *Territory and Function: The Evolution of Regional Planning* (Edward Arnold, London)
Furtado C, 1968 "La concentración del poder económico en los Estados Unidos y sus proyecciones en América Latina" *Estudios Internacionales* **1** [quoted in Sunkel, 1973]
Hamilton F E I (Ed.), 1978a *Contemporary Industrialisation* (Longman Group, Harlow, Essex)
Hamilton F E I (Ed.), 1978b *Industrial Change* (Longman Group, Harlow, Essex)
Hayter R, Storey K, 1978 "The distribution of DREE sponsored manufacturing investments in Atlantic Canada 1972–1975", DP-2, Department of Geography, Simon Fraser University, Burnaby, BC, Canada
Higgins B, 1978 "Development poles: do they exist?" in Lo and Salih (1978) pp 229–242
Holland S, 1976a *The Regional Problem* (Macmillan, London)
Holland S, 1976b "Meso-economics, multinational capital, and regional inequality" in *Economy and Society in the EEC* Eds R Lee, P E Ogden (Saxon House, Teakfield, Farnborough, Hants) pp 38–62
Holland S, 1976c *Capital Versus the Regions* (Macmillan, London)
Holland S, 1980 *Uncommon Market* (Macmillan, London)
IDA, 1972a *Regional Industrial Plans 1973–1977: Part I* (Industrial Development Authority, Dublin)
IDA, 1972b *Regional Industrial Plans 1973–1977: Part I. Appendices* (Industrial Development Authority, Dublin)
IDA, 1979a *Industrial Development Plan 1978–82* (Industrial Development Authority, Dublin)
IDA, 1979b *Overseas Sponsored Companies in Ireland* (Industrial Development Authority, Dublin)

IDA, 1980 "Employment survey 1980" mimeograph, Industrial Development Authority, Dublin

Inbucon Management Consultants, 1980, quoted in *The Irish Times* 2 November 1980, p 13

Johnston R J, 1980 "Political geography without politics" *Progress in Human Geography* **4** 439–446

Keeble D, 1976a "Regional development and the attraction of industry" in *Regional and Rural Development* Ed. P J Drudy (Alpha Academic, Chalfont St Giles, Bucks) pp 23–50

Keeble D, 1976b *Industrial Location and Planning in the United Kingdom* (Methuen, Andover, Hants)

Keeble D, 1978 "Industrial migration in the United Kingdom in the 1960's" in Hamilton (1978b) pp 52–55

Killeen M J, 1980a, quoted in *The Irish Times* 3 November 1980, p 12

Killeen M J, 1980b, quoted in *The Irish Times* 21 January 1980, p 15

Killeen M J, 1980c, quoted in *The Irish Times* 26 February 1980, p 15

Kuklinski A, 1978 "Industrialisation, location, and regional development" in Hamilton (1978a) pp 20–24

Lipietz A, 1980 "The restructuration of space, the problem of land, and spatial policy" in Carney et al (1980) pp 60–75

Lo F, Salih K (Eds), 1978 *Growth Pole Strategy and Regional Development Policy* (Pergamon Press, Oxford)

Massey D, 1978 "Capital and locational change: the UK electrical engineering and electronics industries" *Review of Radical Political Economics* **10** (3) 39–54

Massey D, 1979 "In what sense a regional problem?" *Regional Studies* **13** 233–243

Massey D, Meegan R, 1978 "Industrial restructuring versus the cities" *Urban Studies* **15** 273–288

Massey D, Meegan R, 1979 "The geography of industrial reorganisation" *Progress in Planning* **10** 155–237

McAleese D, 1977 *A Profile of Grant-aided Industry in Ireland* (Industrial Development Authority, Dublin)

McEldowney E, 1980, quoted in *The Irish Times* 29 December 1980, p 10

Moseley M J, 1974 *Growth Centres in Spatial Planning* (Pergamon Press, Oxford)

O'Farrell P N, 1975 *Regional Industrial Development Trends in Ireland 1960–1973* (Industrial Development Authority, Dublin)

O'Farrell P N, 1978 "An analysis of new industry locations: the Irish case" *Progress in Planning* **9** 129–229

O'Farrell P N, 1980 "Multinational enterprises and regional development: Irish evidence" *Regional Studies* **14** 141–150

Ó hUiginn P, 1970 "Industrial location and foreign manufacturing companies in the Republic of Ireland" unpublished MSc thesis, University of Edinburgh, Edinburgh, Scotland

Parson D, 1980 "Spatial underdevelopment: the strategy of accumulation in Northern Ireland" *Antipode* **11** (2) 73–87

Rees J, 1979 "Technological change and regional shifts in American manufacturing" *Professional Geographer* **31** 45–54

Richardson H, 1969 *Elements of Regional Economics* (Penguin Books, Harmondsworth, Middx)

Ross M, 1980 *Personal Incomes by Region in 1977* National Economic and Social Council Report number 41 (The Stationery Office, Dublin)

Smith D M, 1971 *Industrial Location* (John Wiley, New York)

Sunkel O, 1973 "Transnational capitalism and national disintegration in Latin America" *Social and Economic Studies* **22** 132–176

Survey of Grant-aided Industry 1967 (The Stationery Office, Dublin)

Walsh F, 1976 "The growth centre concept in Irish regional policy" *Maynooth Review* **2** (1) 22-41

Walsh F, 1980a "The structure of neo-colonialism: the case of the Irish Republic" *Antipode* **11** (2) 66-72

Walsh F, 1980b "Irish economic development 1905-1959" mimeograph, Department of Geography, St Patrick's College, Maynooth, County Kildare, Republic of Ireland

Yannopoulos G N, Dunning J H, 1976 "Multinational enterprises and regional development: an exploratory paper" *Regional Studies* **10** 389-399

Regional and Subregional Planning in Italy: An Evaluation of Current Practice and some Proposals for the Future[†]

F ARCANGELI
Istituto Universitario di Architettura di Venezia

1 Introduction

The aim of this paper is to present an up-to-date survey and a critical evaluation of regional and subregional planning practice in Italy. Section 2 describes the institutional setting after major devolutions of powers to regional councils and governments during the 1970s, and some preliminary consideration is given to the impact of regional devolution upon the institutional framework of physical and economic planning. In section 3 the following three general hypotheses are advanced:

(1) the only possible solution to the crisis of planning in Italy is a radical move towards an active role for regions in national planning. Italy is divided into twenty regions (see figure 1). Special, stronger powers have been devolved to five of them, and all received ordinary powers after the first regional elections, held in 1970. In this paper, only the more general case of the ordinary regions is considered, without dealing with the particular cases of the 'Special Statute' regions of Val d'Aosta, Trentino–Alto Adige, Friuli–Venezia-Giulia, Sicilia, and Sardegna.

(2) Many of the limitations of regional planning in the 1970s can be overcome if the new regional institutions develop close links with the system of local authorities (LAs) and if participation in regional planning becomes more meaningful. The system of LAs comprises two levels of local government: provinces (95 in number) and communes (8053). Analyses of the problems and relationships between different levels of local and regional government before the recent changes, introduced by Law 382/1975[1] and Decree 616/1977, are given by Cassese (1973) and Dente (1977), and since these changes by Barbera and Bassanini (1979) and in the annual handbook published by the 'League for Local Autonomies' (Cassese, 1981; *Guida per le Autonomie Locali*, 1978–1980).

(3) Both efficiency and democracy in planning could be increased through a radical reform in the system of LAs with the setting up of a new

---

[†] This paper is an extended and largely revised version of a preliminary paper "A survey of wide area planning in Italy" that the author submitted, together with Marina Tazzer, to the Annual Meeting of the British Section of the Regional Science Association, held in London in September 1980.

[1] The Italian system of reference to laws and presidential decrees is used throughout this paper: number of the act (or decree)/year of promulgation; in references to regional laws, the relevant region is stated first. Statutes are catalogued according to this system in the *Gazetta Ufficiale* published by the central government.

'intermediate institution' (*ente intermedio*) between the region and the communes.

In section 4 of the paper we examine the new regional problems and the limits of regional policies in Italy in the 1970s in order to justify our proposals for a much larger role for regional councils in the control of their economies and their effective participation in national economic planning. In section 5 we consider three case studies of subregional planning in major urban areas (Milan, Turin, and Venice) where some of the most advanced practice in Italy is to be found, guided by a new attitude to physical planning (somewhat similar to 'structure planning'). The evaluation of these case studies leads to our conclusions (section 6), taken from the

Figure 1. Regional map of Italy.

forthcoming text of the structure plan for Venice, where a precise proposal for the *ente intermedio* is put forward, and the implications of this solution for the working of regional and physical planning are considered.

2 The statutory framework of planning in Italy
2.1 Regional planning
It was more than twenty years after the approval of the new democratic Constitution of the post-fascist era that one of its fundamental reforms was implemented with the election of regional councils in 1970. The timing is not so surprising, as specific social and political conditions of the period gave strength to the 'regionalist' movement demanding the implementation of the Constitution. The social context was dominated by students', workers', and urban movements; behind them, the growing territorial imbalances of growth, the conflicts created by high reproduction costs of the labour force in the metropolitan areas, and the difficulty of tackling simultaneously the differentiation of regional problems and growth paths ("the three [or more] Italies"; see Bagnasco, 1977). The political situation since the beginning of the 1970s has been dominated by the crisis of the 'centre-left' coalition[2] and the search for new equilibria; this crisis is the basis of a more flexible attitude by sections of the ruling classes (mainly the most dynamic industrialists of northern Italy and the emerging 'peripheral' areas of Emilia–Romagna and central Italy) toward the role of the Italian Communist Party (PCI). Hence the argument that devolution to regions would produce the 'taking over' of many regions by the Communists and the 'breakup' of Italy lost its hold.

Regional councils and governments have been set up with considerable powers of intervention in productive sectors as well as in social services and spatial planning, especially after recent (1975–1977) major improvements in the devolution of powers from central government to the regions: many limitations and restrictive interpretations of the Constitutional Law in the first devolution of 1972 have been overcome, mainly in the field of territorial policies though not in that of economic issues[3].

[2] It is impossible to summarize here the evolution of the main trend in postwar Italian politics, associated with the origins, rise, and decline of the centre-left coalition (see Pallante and Pallante, 1975). The 1968 workers' struggles marked the end of this as a stable solution to the problem of government (see Tamburrano, 1971) and, as far as economic and planning policies are concerned, the roots of this decline can be traced to the failure of incomes policies (a much wider issue, on which see Cacciari, 1971; D'Antonio, 1973, pages 198–201; Tarantelli, 1978).

[3] Regional powers are listed in Article 117 of the Constitutional Law and can be classified as dealing with physical planning, agriculture, social services, cultural promotion, and location of other activities. Law 281/1970 and Decrees 1/1972–11/1972 gave a restrictive interpretation to this Law. A much greater devolution to regions was granted in Law 382/1975 and Decree 616/1977. To date, agriculture, craft industries, and tourism are the activities most tightly controlled by regions, but demands are being made for more control over labour-market regulations and small firms in the private industrial sector.

An evaluation of the outcome of the first generation of regional councils between the 1970 and 1975 elections can be summarized as follows: there is a "crisis of regional planning" because of a "lack of a national planning policy, problems of regional finances, a lack of binding force and implementation of the regional development plans, inappropriate attitudes of regions in dealing with sectoral planning and in the delegation of their own functions to technical agencies (regional financial companies), without adequate control and without any global and systematic planning frame of reference" (Merloni and Urbani, 1977, page 150).

No price solution has been found in recent years to the problems of the indefinite character of Italian regional planning, of the power conflicts between regions and the central state (including those over regional policy), and of the active role that regions should play as a source of innovation and democracy in the working of the state. These contradictions will be further analyzed in sections 3 and 4. This section only considers, briefly, interaction between the new regional bodies and the working of economic and physical planning.

2.2 Economic planning

The roots of state economic planning in Italy can be traced to the early proposals from the trade unions (see *Il Piano del Lavoro delle CGIL 1949–1950*, 1978), and from the government in the *Schema Vanoni* of 1954 (reprinted in Ministero del Bilancio, 1967, volume 1). Although there were many differences in their contents, a common element in these early proposals was the stress on the role of 'autonomous investment' to attain employment and growth-rate targets, with particular reference to housing investment, public works, and agriculture. The process of accumulation in itself was not analyzed with a view to keeping it under control.

A consciousness of the impending limits to and the 'dualistic' character of growth [with special reference both to agriculture and underdevelopment in the South (or Mezzogiorno) and to the private consumption boom and lack of social capital accumulation] only emerged at the beginning of the 1960s at the peak of the 'economic miracle'. However, the very large 'reformist alliance' in parliamentary power during that period was not fully conscious of power relations or of the strength of conservative attitudes opposing any change; moreover, sectoral and regional disequilibria were only interpreted as 'limits to growth' and not also as functional elements in a specific model of growth (see Andriani et al, 1981, page 14). In addition, the economic and political culture of the 1960s lacked the necessary technique and operational attitudes necessary for successful reformist planning (see many contributions in Lunghini, 1981).

The movement toward the first (and last) Five-year National Plan, 1965–1969, started from a government paper in 1962 written by Minister Ugo La Malfa (reprinted in Ministero del Bilancio, 1967, volume 2, pages 87–134), and came to an end in 1967 when Parliament passed two bills, the first constituting the special Committee of Ministers for planning (CIPE), and the other formally approving the Five-year Plan. The outstanding features of this period, as far as the regional impact of national planning is concerned, can be summarized as follows.

(a) Major institutional reforms were initially proposed but then abandoned (in the context of the evolution from more radical to more moderate equilibria of the new government coalition, including the Socialist Party). Foremost amongst these reforms were the election of regional councils and a new bill on physical planning to replace the inadequate 1942 Act (Law 1150/1942). A radical proposal of Minister Sullo, based upon a general mechanism of expropriation of development land, was strongly opposed and never considered by the government; for discussions of land reform in the 1960s, see Carabba (1977, pages 62–64), Tamburrano (1971, pages 167–169), and also Secchi (1974; 1977).

(b) No real integration of the special policies for the Mezzogiorno (for accounts of these, see Amato, 1972; Secchi, 1974; Graziani and Pugliese, 1979; Del Monte and Giannola, 1979; Saraceno, 1981) and national planning policies was achieved: the National Plan did not emphasize this central problem in the reallocation of national resources. Meanwhile, the attractiveness of new locations in the South was reduced by a broad extension of incentives in central and northern Italy (the so-called "depressed areas" of Law 614/1966), and proposals for disincentives for congested areas of the industrial triangle were abandoned between the first and the last versions of the Five-year Plan.

The mid-1960s were characterized by missed opportunities for a common start to, and close links between, national and regional planning; nonetheless, the regional committees considering studies and proposals (CRPE, the Regional Committees for Economic Plans) were the first experiment in joint work by planners, economists, and pressure groups in the analysis of the growth paths of each region, with particular attention to the intraregional imbalances and territorial basis of regional development (see Indovina, 1965; Carabba, 1977, pages 112–116; Meini et al, 1978). Also during this period a major debate developed about subregional planning as an appropriate level for the integration of economic and physical planning; the first moves in this direction were the designation of fifteen ecological areas in Piemonte and the first spatial plan at the metropolitan area level in Milan (see section 5.1).

In the early 1970s the crisis of the centre-left coalition in Parliament (which arose not because of a lost majority, but because of the coalition's increasing inability to cope with the changing social attitudes and the emerging opposition of the PCI) coincided with the abandoning of planning methods and issues. During the years of 'democratic solidarity', of cooperation between the opposition and government (1976–1978), there were many laws of reform and planning for each sector (Law 173/1976 on regional policies for the Mezzogiorno; Law 675/1977 on the restructuring of industry; Law 984/1977 on agriculture; Law 457/1978 on housing; Law 833/1978 on health services), but no general planning framework except for a very advanced reform of the state budget (Law 468/1979) which could become a very powerful planning tool if it was taken seriously by the political powers in the government and Parliament (see Spaventa, 1981, pages 74–77).

All this has meant that the working of the new regional bodies was handicapped and largely diverted by this long-lasting crisis and transition in the central state, and the lack of a coherent planning approach in national laws and expenditures. This is a conclusion confirmed by the recent Parliamentary Inquiry referred to in section 3.

2.3 Physical planning

The physical planning system in Italy is still regulated by the Planning Act of 1942 (Law 1150/1942), which has been only partially modified by subsequent laws and still stands as a fundamental national law, together with the new Regional Planning Acts[4] produced in the last few years. This system is based upon a hierarchy of plans (Italian initials are given[5]):
PTC territorial plans of coordination, a basic level for strategic planning;
PRG (or *PRI*) plans of one (or more than one) commune translating PTC strategies into more detailed statements about policies and land allocation;
PPPP and *PdL* (detailed allotting plans) executive plans on action areas, proposed by public authorities or developers;
PdF building plans, an alternative to PRG, eliminated by recent regional acts.

The system does not work satisfactorily at present because a planning decision cannot be changed in 'real time' unless a whole series of alterations and reviews is introduced up and down the hierarchy of different plans affected by it. A second problem is the lack of a temporal dimension in plans prepared under the 1942 Act. Regional acts now tend to overcome this by specifying a time horizon within which they apply, and a recent national law (10/1977) introduces this dimension via three-year general executive plans at the commune level. A third problem is the indefinite character of planning on a broader than local scale.

The 1942 Act gave the Ministry of Housing and Public Works the authority to prepare PTC. The functions of these plans were to identify special areas and restraints and to locate new large developments, special plants, and major infrastructure. They were merely intended as indicative plans representing the regional impact of central government policies,

[4] Fourteen regions have adopted regional planning acts, the most outstanding examples being Piemonte (Regional Law 56/1977, modified by Regional Law 50/1980) and Emilia-Romagna (Regional Law 97/1978, modified by Regional Law 23/1980).
[5] Corresponding Italian names are: PTC, Piano Territoriale di Coordinamento; PRI, Piano Regolatare Intercomunale; PRG, Piano Regolatare Generale; PPPP, Piani Particolareggiati; PdL, Piano di Lottizzazione; PdF, Piano di Fabbricazione.

without any evaluation of resource allocation. No local authority was responsible for their preparation and implementation, and only a few such plans were drawn up during the 1950s (those for Campania and Molise, Lombardia, and Emilia–Romagna, for example), with strong opposition from local authorities. The turning point was the devolution to regions in the 1970s. Recent regional planning acts give more detailed functions to these plans and define their specific role in the wider framework of regional and subregional planning.

Under the 1942 Act, the Ministry, on request of at least one local council, defines the area of an inter-commune plan and devolves the preparation of the plan to a local authority. The aim of such plans was to solve problems arising from the new scale of cities; but the 'compromise' of a wider local plan in the absence of new tools such as a structure plan, the lack of a planning authority at the new scale, and the complicated procedures of approval were the main reasons for the failure of this planning tool.

The acceleration of urban growth, following the economic growth of the 1950s, led to widespread enlargement of urban centres and suburbanization. Inter-commune planning practice in Turin, Milan, Florence, and Rome prompted debate which led to the first proposals for a new intermediate institution between regional and local councils. The 1956 conference of the National Institute of Planners (INU) was the first forum for this debate, and the 1960 Planning Reform Bill proposed by this Institute identified the *comprensorio* as a definite subregional unit with primary planning functions. A common element in various bills on planning reform in the 1960s was the agreement on two levels of strategic planning, regional and subregional, the latter requiring a corresponding planning authority.

The setting up after 1971 of Mountain Communities, groupings of communes established under Law 1102/1971, was the first large-scale experiment in subregional planning and policies. Although restricted to the most peripheral mountain and valley areas, the value of this practice depends upon the existence of a definite institution (intermediate between regional and local authorities) endowed with comprehensive powers and with socioeconomic and physical planning tasks. The statutory goals of the intermediate authorities include preservation of the environment, hydrogeologic policies, and an end to underdevelopment and out-migration.

From the beginning of their legislative activity in the 1970s the statutes approved by regional councils (see Pini, 1979) have anticipated the creation of wider subregional planning levels, denoted by different terms (circondari, comprensori, inter-commune associations) and characterized by lack of precision as to their roles. Without statutory regulation at national level, regional attitudes swing between the alternatives of the comprensorio as a decentralized body of the region or a voluntary association of local authorities. In 1976, at the end of the first legislature, the regions of Emilia–Romagna, Lombardia, Piemonte, Umbria, Veneto, and Lazio had set up comprensori; Sardegna and Liguria have done so subsequently (see Balbo, 1978; Lombardi, 1979; Bellagamba et al, 1981; Pubusa, 1981; Tazzer, 1981).

The different emphases of these regional laws originated in the different weights given to two problems: (a) to define functional areas for regional planning, mainly with reference to the planning goals of overcoming social, economic, and territorial imbalances and of equalization of access to urban life; (b) to overcome the limited scale of communes for the provision of social services by organizing most of them on a wider scale. The current approach is to divide these two problems between distinct bodies: the 'new province' (created by a reform of the boundaries and powers of an existing province) as a subregional planning authority; and the 'inter-commune association' as a smaller-scale body where common services and technical agencies are concentrated by a number of communes.

A national law of reform of LAs, containing the proposal of these distinct levels, will be submitted to Parliament in the near future, and the last Annual Conference of the INU held at Taranto, 5–6 June 1981, was dedicated to this still controversial issue [for an account of the research promoted by the INU before the conference, see Bellagamba et al (1981)].

3 General hypotheses concerning regional and subregional planning

Many interpretations have been proposed to explain the failure of national economic planning in Italy (see, among others, Amato, 1972; Ruffolo, 1973; Salvati, 1975; Allione, 1977; Carabba, 1977; Lunghini, 1981). Recent years have also witnessed the spread of the new 'free-market' ideology, mainly in the form of an overvaluation of the ability of the moonlight economy and small entrepreneurs (the so-called 'Brambillas') to conquer stagflation, and a related belief that regional problems had been overcome independently of state regional policies (see Arcangeli and Vitiello, 1981). While this kind of debate was going on and a comprehensive approach to national economic planning was neglected, the new regional bodies found it very difficult to direct their own new statutory paths towards more decentralized forms of planning.

An authoritative statement on these difficulties is contained in the conclusion drawn by the Parliamentary Commission on Regional Problems at the end of an inquiry into the relationship between state, region, and local authorities in planning. The Commission concluded that three negative factors emanating from the central state affected regional planning (Senato della Repubblica, 1980):

"(a) It is evident that until now, partly because of the short term of governments, the central bodies of the state have not declared general planning goals for regional planning as they should have done, following article 11 of the Presidential Decree 616[6]. Moreover, no planned reform linked with Decree 616 has been implemented:

[6] The Decree of Devolution to the Regions, issued in 1977 (for a detailed discussion, see Barbera and Bassanini, 1979).

no reform of local authorities, of local finance, of social subsidies, of historical properties, of the chambers of commerce, of national parks, of public works administration, and so on. The aim of the Decree was to build up a new coherent system of laws, to be implemented step by step. But the government and Parliament have taken decisions in an opposite direction, modifying or delaying that system (eg in the fields of water management, maritime property, housing), in spite of the great political relevance of the above mentioned Decree and of its constitutional function. (b) Sectoral plans have filled the gap in general planning goals. These plans have played a fundamental role in priority fields, but without a common framework they gave rise to inconsistencies. We must therefore argue for their change and for a step-by-step move toward a system of intersectoral links in 'horizontal' planning, where the regions could have an autonomous role and achieve their own development goals within general guiding rules, following Article 11 of Decree 616. For this purpose it would be better if not only the government but also Parliament examined the regional development plans ... . Within this framework, the regions must share in the national decisionmaking process—with clear guarantees on procedures and information—and not simply be consulted. Regions should also be allowed to coordinate investments and plans by local authorities, with subregional levels of coordination to be outlined in the intended reform of local authorities, following and generalizing previous experiences of 'agreement committees' between regions and local authorities. (c) The evaluation of the present situation cannot ignore the fact that regions at best only have real control of 10-12% of their total budgetary expenditure. Everything else is tied up by national laws or government's decisions, sometimes in a very detailed form. This is the reason for the marked dependence of regional finance, which is in contradiction to the statement of Article 119 of the Constitution and is another negative factor affecting not only regional development planning, but also the efficiency and timing of regional expenditures".

The Parliamentary Inquiry added something more to these elements—a critique of the way regions used their own powers:

"... But the three negative elements mentioned are not enough to explain why regions agreed to use the allocated resources in such a passive way and became more and more bureaucratic. Regional governments and offices broke up into separated centres of decisions, thanks to the closer and closer vertical links between national ministries, the members of regional government, and their staff in the same field: all this clashes with the constitutional and statutory principle of the collective character of regional executive committees".

After this interesting analysis, the Parliamentary Inquiry did not draw radical conclusions, but limited itself to the recommendation of some minor changes in the planning system and in the relationship between regions and central government. This implies that this Inquiry into the planning programme of the government will lack meaningful effect. So, in a climate of new attempts to reopen the way toward economic planning in Italy, no organic connection has been created between the new proposal of the Medium-term Plan (see Ministero del Bilancio, 1981) and regional planning.

Now, given the new monetarist, free-market, and 'new economics' wave and the present phase of crisis of the 'social state', it is difficult to justify growing state intervention unless it shows high productivity in terms of goals achieved and use of resources. Without the inclusion of a detailed discussion of the nature of planning in a capitalist economy, it is suggested that only a shift toward decentralization could possibly give a new social efficiency to planning systems; this is the first hypothesis of this paper.

It is true that regional planning has not yet produced any satisfactory results in Italy, ten years after the creation of regional councils, but we must remember the context of this slow and difficult start:
1. the change of scenarios during the 1970s, with few analytical tools useful for planning in a 'zero-sum' society;
2. the deep crisis of national economic planning, which gave no framework to the regions as far as national priorities, accounting, allocation of financial resources, and so on are considered (see Parliamentary Inquiry above);
3. the limits of regional devolution until 1977;
4. the limits of the theoretical background of planning, both as a national system (neoclassical paradigms but also the limited usefulness of their neo-Ricardian critique) and as a regional one (regional problems in Italy are generally identified only with the Mezzogiorno as an area of special state intervention);
5. the limited effort to define the precise role and particular goals of regional planning, with the participation of different social groups (on the one hand, the new regional institution has been loaded with operative functions in a wide range of fields; on the other hand, economic and local pressure groups do not perceive it as an authoritative and fully endowed planning institution).

Besides this, inefficiency and a negative attitude to innovation by the new regional bodies has produced very bad results: no reform of the planning system is possible unless state and regional administrations are modernized.

The second hypothesis of this paper is that new approaches to regional planning can be developed if:
(a) this new institution is more fully integrated into a (reformed) system of LAs, so as to develop the ability of such a system in the field of strategic planning and the link between development goals and budget policies;
(b) participation in regional planning ceases to be ineffective; a much deeper involvement of regional social and economic forces in the plan formation would give the region much stronger support in negotiations with central government. In this case, bringing consistency to regional plans would not be a purely theoretical exercise, or a result of power relationships within the state, but also a much larger social and political process of selecting priorities and evaluating alternatives for *national* development.

My third hypothesis refers to the theme of participation in regional planning. The subregional agencies, often called comprensori, were intended as coordination agencies between regional and local councils and should have contributed to the development of participation. But the results have been very poor, both because methods in regional planning are still inadequate[7] and because no real tools, power, and role have been given to the comprensori. Even when their role in the preparation of a regional plan was exactly defined (see, for example, Regione Piemonte, 1978), they depended for their very existence on the region itself.

This is why it was difficult to promote participation in regional planning in a period when the new regional bodies pressed for more power from the older institutions at higher and lower scales, and the communes were overwhelmed by urban crisis, financial problems, and difficulty in planning and managing a growing number of services (more and more requiring an inter-commune scale). Therefore, the third and last hypothesis is that a new phase of regional planning could be opened if the correct definition were given to the intermediate institution between region and commune— a 'new province' with its own powers (because its existence stems from the Constitution and from direct election of representatives by the people, and not indirectly from local councils and the region, as for the comprensori). Furthermore, the new province should be fully integrated into the regional planning cycle (preparation–monitoring–implementation), not only engaged in the 'translation' of regional plans into subregional ones or in the preparation of separate and incoherent structure plans for each provincial area, but also acting as an autonomous agent in a two-level integrated process of regional planning.

4 Regional planning in the 1970s: problems and perspectives[8]
Regional development in Italy moved toward new patterns in the 1970s, as in other industrial countries (see, for example, Camagni and Cappellini, 1981); this shift is characterized by decentralization of manufacturing activity and steady levels of the different indices of regional imbalance during the earlier years of the 1970s (after a sharp increase until 1964 and a slow decrease in the mid-1960s). Behind this partial 'convergence' there was a strong spatial restructuring which followed general (international)

[7] For example, neither regional nor national authorities have ever tried to reach an agreement on common standards for regional plans, so as to make possible comparison of plans within a common framework (a prerequisite for implementing Article 11 of Decree 616/1977), as proposed by Bianchi (1980, page 38). Consequently, quite different (and often inadequate) techniques and attitudes have been adopted at various stages of the regional plan-making process. These stages include defining aims, identifying major policy options and the relationships between aims and actions; collecting supporting information; generating and evaluating alternative strategies; preparing plans with a continuity between preparation and implementation, monitoring, and review.
[8] More detailed reviews are given by CESPE–CRS (1980), Giunta Regionale Toscana (1979), and Meini et al (1978).

tendencies of competition within industries and new locational patterns
(see Massey, 1979; Lipietz, 1980)[9].

The major features of Italian development in the 1970s can be
summarized as follows.

(1) With the partial overcoming of the North–South dualism, the majority
of northern and southern regions converged toward an intermediate level of
growth, the exceptions being the 'industrial triangle' (Lombardia, Piemonte,
Liguria; now enlarged to include Emilia–Romagna and parts of Toscana
and Veneto) and the most depressed areas of the Mezzogiorno (the internal
areas, Calabria, and the islands).

(2) Interregional migration flows decreased very sharply; and their
evolution became unpredictable, like that of many other spatial patterns.

(3) Long-lasting regional policies in the Mezzogiorno, combined with the
new locational requirements of many manufacturing activities, have created
a diffuse industrialization in almost all the coastal areas, with new
characteristics of 'peripheral development' that are different from the
previous pattern of growth poles and large firms in heavy industries.

(4) The peripheral development of the northeastern and central regions
(see Arcangeli et al, 1980) was still dominant in the 1970s, but with the
rate of growth of output higher than that of productivity, limits of labour
supply began to become evident, and this was one reason for the shift
toward more 'intensive' accumulation in the North and enlargement of the
spatial basis of 'extensive' accumulation to the South.

(5) Regional specialization has not decreased, except in the most dynamic
and innovation-oriented subregional areas. This implies that new 'problem
areas' will arise in the North (owing to sectoral crisis), and that regional
'intermediate' economies are very dependent on trends in international
trade (the favourable conditions for exports in the 1970s for many Italian
goods were a major factor of growth, but it is unlikely that this situation
will persist in the 1980s).

This evolution from North–South dualism towards heterogeneity and
greater regional differentiation would have required much more effective
regional planning, but in present-day Italy regional planning means little in
practice because of the limited power of regions over their own expenditure.
The total budget of regions and LAs is equal to 15% of national income
(see Barbera, 1980), that is, a very high proportion for purposes of demand
management and also for some effect on the supply side of the economy.
But the share that regions can autonomously allocate is no higher than 1%
of national income: state policy and the communes determine the major
financial flows; the regions are 'squeezed' and can decide only the intra-

[9] More recently, in the latter part of the 1970s, regional disparities again widened
owing to the problems of the southern economy; as productivity declined, the growth-
pole strategy failed, and growth fell back, problems were compounded by the closing-off
of the safety valve of migration northward of surplus labour (see Brancati and Zezza,
1981; Arcangeli and Vitiello, 1982).

regional location of sectoral subsidies or investments (among people, social groups, or areas), without real powers on intersectoral resources allocation.

If this minimum financial condition for regional planning is attained in the future as a result of the conclusions of the Parliamentary Inquiry discussed in section 3, new problems will emerge and the difficulties of regional planning will be ascribed to the region itself. In fact, if we consider the first generation of regional plans, we do not find their quality higher than that of the first exploratory studies of the 1960s, before regional devolution; what is worse is that many original ideas and proposals produced in the 1960s are now simply revived without revision [compare Batey and Breheny (1978) on the British experience].

Even though the contents and methods of the various regional plans have been very different, their impact has been similar (see Bianchi, 1980, page 37); very little effect on regional bodies and administrative organization; a very weak effect on the economy, society, and local councils (only indicative planning or mere 'advice'); no effect upon the central state (government and Parliament have ignored regional plans, their implementation, and the resources they require).

The region must qualify and specialize as a body of political direction, legislative power, and budget planning over the whole system of LAs within its boundaries; this is the only way it will avoid being a poor imitation of the central state and play its role as the main centre of 'strategic planning' for the LAs. If this is the choice of the regions, it will be useful for them and for the balance of power between regions and communes if they coordinate their own planning with a stronger system of local powers. This could be the outcome of a reform of the provinces, following the proposals referred to in section 3.

With stronger subregional power, local authorities would be better able to take part in the regional planning process. An example of a correct approach, which could work much better with 'autonomous' subregional powers (a new, reformed province) in place of the actual weaker committees (comprensori), is given by the Regione Piemonte (1978). This example is only concerned with plan preparation, but a precise solution of the problem of the intermediate institution could easily extend this two-level planning system into the level of monitoring and implementation as well. It is worthwhile to stress the following features of the Piemontese planning procedures.
(1) There is a strong link and similarity between the two levels (regional and subregional) in each phase (analysis and goals, alternative spatial patterns, choice between alternatives, first outline, and final version of the plan).
(2) Plan preparation at the lower level is in advance of that at the upper one, so that building up of the regional plan means bringing coherence to the system of urban plans (already in preparation in the meanwhile).
(3) The regional physical plan is initially only a very broad scheme without locational details, although a regional development plan with clear general (aspatial) strategies has been prepared.

(4) At the end of an iterative procedure, regional and subregional plans have been prepared in a homogeneous and consistent form; the regional plan has enough detail as to the spatial projection of regional priorities and policies, whereas a much more detailed spatial structure is described in urban (subregional) plans.

A major objection in the past to a new phase of regional planning has always been the argument of the trade-off between regional imbalance and devolution. This argument is now losing support in the face of the new regional problems requiring differentiated policies and the abandonment of obsolete regional incentive schemes. The comments of one of the most distinguished leaders of the postwar 'nuovi meridionalisti'[10], Professor Saraceno (1981, pages 29-30), are very relevant here:

"The reason for the great innovation of the Southern [meridionalistica] action, an extraordinary regional policy, is still valid. This reason can be summarized in these terms; actions required to set up solutions to the Southern problem:

(a) have no reason in the rest of the country;

(b) require large additional resources ... .

Unfortunately there is no reason to change this direction and to stop extraordinary policies[11].

But another factor affects in a positive way the political thinking in favour of the Southern problem, and the evolution towards more effective regional policies in the South; this is the establishment of Regions; we must ask in this connection if the future historian will see in regional devolution the origin of the obsolescence of the statutory framework of 1950 [which established the Cassa per il Mezzogiorno], and will find explanation of the continuous change, every five years, and inadequacy of new statutory frameworks, in the inability of the legislator to stop this obsolescence".

[10] The term 'nuovi meridionalisti' refers to the current of thought and economic analysis which started in the postwar years, with a marked difference from the approach of the 'meridionalisti classici' of previous decades. The analyses and proposals of these new activists formed the basis for the beginnings of state intervention in the South and the setting up of the Cassa per il Mezzogiorno, even if government policies did not follow them exactly (chiefly because of opposition from the ruling classes, mainly located in the North). For evaluations of their influence, see Rossi Doria (1970); Barucci (1978); Graziani (1979); Barbagallo (1980); Arcangeli and Vitiello (1981); Marzano (1981).

[11] At this point, the following footnote was indicated: "Moreover, the northern part of the country is now much more homogeneous than in the 1950s; in that period, the existence of an industrial triangle divided the three northwestern regions from the rest of the North and Centre. The overcoming of this internal imbalance among central and northern regions makes it more difficult to solve the Southern problem, because the real problems of poor regions become farther and farther from the culture of the rich ones, a phenomenon that we register also at the world scale".

The point is that the new phase of southern industrialization in the second half of the 1970s, with a new cycle of small business (local or northern small entrepreneurs) after the end of investment cycles in the South dominated by large firms and public industry, requires a shift from regional policies decided at the national level, toward more decentralized and 'local' policies. Also if the North–South imbalance still requires a shift of resources toward the South, new areas and new actions must have priority within the South, and it is necessary that southern regions learn by themselves how to manage these new problems, different from the traditional ones of a homogeneous underdeveloped region.

5 Subregional planning: case studies
5.1 Strategic planning in Milan
5.1.1 *Introduction*
The actual area of the Milanese comprensorio includes 106 communes with 3·3 million inhabitants (1·7 in Milan itself). It is the core of the Italian economic and urban systems (see Dalmasso, 1972), mainly because of the relationship it experiences between the most diversified and technologically advanced manufacturing industries and the development of an advanced service sector; and the main decisionmaking centres of the private sector of the economy are located here. For a broader view of Milanese planning practice, see Gabellini et al (1980).

5.1.2 *Aims and features of Milanese planning*
The main features of the planning experience in Milan are as follows.
(1) The initiative of the main town (initially with strong opposition from the other communes), has been decisive in giving support to a very experimental attempt of broad-area planning *without* any body of metropolitan government or any viable statutory framework: the 1976 Plan of the City of Milan is the main act giving force of law and direct effect of broad area policies on development control. The City Plan has force only within the boundaries of the commune of Milan, however, whereas the broader metropolitan policies are dependent on the agreement of smaller communes and their inclusion in regional priorities. (This latter effect has become dominant in the last few years.)
(2) The broad-area 'informal' institution, mainly at the technical level, has been a permanent centre of activity, constituting the most extensive Italian experience in the two directions of monitoring in planning and of a new intermediate level of government between regional and local councils.
(3) The main limitation of this long-lasting experience is that none of the different Plans produced (in 1967, 1975, or 1980) has ever been enacted, in order to have statutory effects upon development control, and local and sectoral public policies.
    New possibilities arise now after the passing of the Regional Planning Acts (Regione Lombardia, Laws 51/1975; 52/1975; 34/1978; 63/1978);

the 1980 Plan could be better placed than its predecessors, and regional policies could be managed so as to favour its implementation. But this has so far not happened; a general hypothesis about the Milanese experience is that vested interests (in this core urban area of the country) have been so strong as to reduce the 'degrees of freedom' of planning—this power relation lies behind the precarious statutory framework of planning practice in Milan.

This specific hypothesis is subordinate to the more general one put forward by Secchi (1974; 1975; 1977) and others about the close alliance between different social groups centred upon the growth of building industry, the large developers playing a dominant role in recent years. The result has been a relative absence of conflict between the advanced manufacturing industries and the building industry (except during short periods at the peaks of the long-term building cycles: 1962–1964 and 1969–1970). The lack of conflict between advanced industrial capital and construction capital means that there is no room for an alliance between the working class, the workers' movement, and advanced industrial capital with the aim of placing urban development under tighter control.

The chief problem to be dealt with in the metropolitan area of Milan changed during the period considered. In the 1960s, planners were concerned with the control of the rate of growth of the main quantitative variables—employment, population—and their internal allocation (urban sprawl with land waste, congestion costs). It was within this planning experience that the concept of 'metropolitan reequilibrium' was formulated and tested for the first time, in connection with the great problems of imbalances at regional and national scales. Later, the emphasis changed to the rationalization of an accelerated process of restructuring of the metropolitan area (at almost zero growth) which spontaneously developed in the 1970s. In this last phase the priority was no longer the imposition of quantitative constraints upon the planning area and more congested zones (the city of Milan, the first suburban belt, and the northern hinterland), but the control of an acceleration of filtering of activities within the metropolitan area (the metropolitan corollary of the restructuring of production within 'diffuse industrialization').

The aims of the planning activity have been mainly: (a) to reduce the spontaneous rates of growth (in labour and land-use terms) of the metropolitan area; (b) to orientate new development in two preferred directions, where existing railway public transport could be developed; (c) to rationalize commuting within the area and between it and surrounding areas[12] (the proposed policy has been the promotion of a regional railway system linked with the underground and other means of public transport).

[12] 496000 people per day commute into the comprensorio and 365000 out of it, a net inward balance of 131000; 279000 people per day commute into the city of Milan and 62000 out of it, a net inward balance of 217000 (data supplied by the Comprensorio Milanese).

As far as the first aim is concerned, actual changes have overtaken the planners' aims of reducing population and employment growth: the humanitarian philosophy of planning as a way of reducing spatial unevenness has been overcome by the real crisis of urban growth.

5.1.3 *Effects of subregional plans*
Let us consider the key variables during the very long period of planning, monitoring, and review, which is the peculiar feature of this case study.

Population The 1967 Plan aimed to halve the migrant flow within the area and the aim has been achieved at the global scale: from 1967 to 1973 the planning area shows a population increase of 314000; the 'neutral' projection was 419000; and the target was 297000. The 1975 Plan aimed to reduce migration further; in fact, population growth from 1972 to 1978 was only half the planned target because of the predominance of out-migration in the second half of the 1970s. The 1980 Plan assumes a natural increase of population, without net migration.

Manufacturing employment The 1967 Plan aimed to slow the rate of increase of new jobs to the projected tendency of 62% over the years 1967–1977, through balanced national–regional locational policies and by reducing the projected new industrial sites (especially in the more congested zone of the city centre and the northern belt). A sharp change of strategy was made in the 1975 Plan, in the middle of the crisis and in a new phase of metropolitan restructuring with relocation of manufacturing and changing land uses. Between the Censuses of 1961 and 1971, the city of Milan lost 74000 manufacturing jobs; this was counterbalanced by an increase of 104000 in the hinterland. In the same period the area of land devoted to industrial use decreased by 370 ha in the city and increased by 1400 ha in the hinterland (although this development mainly followed the lines of motorways and not the planned, preferred directions). The aim of the 1975 Plan was to stop employment decrease in the old industrial sites of the city and the northern belt (the district of Sesto S. Giovanni, for example) and to divert the increase toward the less congested southern and eastern areas. According to this planning strategy, the constraints on levels of employment and existing industrial sites should influence the industrial restructuring in the direction of higher value-added, technologically advanced activities, with lower levels of pollution and congestion. The 1980 Plan warns against the effects of the accelerated industrial relocation process and (as did the 1976 City Plan), argues for the continuation of existing industrial sites, but fails to analyze the changing occupational structure (growing production of services within manufacturing firms, unofficial employment and migration, secondary jobs). The maintenance of industrial land use is a necessary, but not sufficient condition, in order to avoid undesirable changes of urban social structure and the labour market.

In the planning strategy of the comprensorio, manufacturing employment has to be preserved in order to avoid the service sector becoming the only outlet for redundancies created by industrial restructuring.

Service employment Whereas the 1967 Plan was concerned with the great concentration around the city centre, the 1975 Plan took account of the business and service sprawl in the hinterland (with the common interests of developers and local authorities in this development), but did not implement the planned locational priorities because of delays in public transport rationalization.

The 1980 Plan analyses the new situation, but does not draw consistent conclusions about it. It suggests that if past trends continue the next ten years would see an increase of around 150000 jobs, whereas the labour force would only increase by 30000. The gap would be filled by a mixture of increased in-commuting, new migration flows, accelerated decline of manufacturing employment, and increased activity rates. Except for this last factor, these trends are in sharp contradiction with the planning strategy.

The large growth of the service sector must therefore be planned at a regional level, by identifying the most receptive existing urban poles and their growth paths. Growth must also be selective within the metropolitan area, in order to keep the local labour market and the urban structure under control.

The 1980 Plan requires such a regional policy, but the planning board (comprensorio) does not have sufficient authority to control locational decisions made outside of the logic of the area plans (the World Trade Center at Assago, the major new development of recent years, is a prime example of such an external locational decision). The control of the location of workplaces within the city has undergone marked improvements with the introduction of the policies of the 1975 Plan in the 1976 City Plan; the problem is now that of the 'diffuse tertiarization' in the hinterland, which is impossible to control unless stronger and efficient broad-area policies are put forward. This would lead to open conflict with the linkage of interests between developers and local authorities favouring indiscriminate dispersal of activities and new congestion effects in the belt around Milan.

As far as the second aim is concerned, the original aim of two preferential directions of development[13] has not been implemented decisively. A major new development has been the decentralization of the head offices of SNAM–ENI (public industry for energy and infrastructures) to S. Donato, along the preferred southeast axis (where other office developments and a new railway station will be located). The 1980 Plan corrects the strategy, mainly considering these directions of growth over a

[13] East (Linee Celeri dell'Adda) and southeast (Via Emilia); both are served by railways (with a plan to quadruple the lines), the first also by subway (line 2).

wider area than the first belt around the city; here, the problems of coordination with neighbouring comprensori and regional planning become predominant.

5.1.4 *Conflicts and problems in Milanese planning*
In the implementation of the Plans, a major problem has always been the lack of inter-agency coordination. In the transport sector, for example, only after ten years have the ideas of the broad-area plans been finally accepted by the state railways. A whole new system of railway services to commuters is about to start, with a general improvement of services and a new line crossing the city, following the model of the S-Bahn in Munich. But the Subway Agency (owned by the city of Milan) opposes the new railway developments within the city and calls for a third underground line, in opposition to the whole strategy of decentralization of the broad-area plans for Milan (see Degani, 1979).

The conflicts in the planning process evolve from the inter-municipality level—the structure of relationship between the surrounding belt and the city of Milan and the allocation of the surplus metropolitan growth within the belt—to a more fundamental issue: who will decide the priority and the soundness of such very large infrastructure investments? At what level are these decisions to be taken? At the agency (firm) level, or at the urban, metropolitan, regional, or even national level?

The emerging problem is that metropolitan planning in Milan has anticipated and partially occupied the functions of a stronger regional government. This is no longer viable now that the continuous metropolitan area is much larger than the area of the Milanese comprensorio. This means that metropolitan restructuring as a hierarchical organization of spatial subsystems can only be controlled on a broader scale, with a stronger coordination of sectoral policies and of their implementation, which can be achieved only by major improvements in the operation of regional governments. This is a general problem, but in Lombardia it appears in a very acute form, because of the disequilibrium between the new regional board and a long tradition of subregional planning practice. Evidence of this is given by the controversial issue of the third underground line in Milan: the correct level at which such decisions should be taken in the first place is the region, because a regional authority could balance the local pressures for immediate implementation and evaluate the goals and priorities of comparative accessibility to the city centre from other parts of the city of Milan or from other urban centres of the region.

5.2 Strategic planning in Turin
5.2.1 *Regional context*
The outstanding feature of this case study is the supremacy of the regional authorities and offices over the whole planning process (also at the subregional scale): in other words, the traditional Piemontese mix of efficiency and centralization—perhaps closer to French than to Italian style!

The situation is quite different from that of Milan, where metropolitan plans promoted and anticipated the regional planning process, and regional laws gave a statutory framework to the already existing subregional planning practice.

The internal consistency and mutual support of regional, subregional, and metropolitan planmaking in Piemonte is based on a long-standing tradition of high-quality regional studies; outstanding examples of these are the analysis of regional urban hierarchy (Regione Piemonte, IRES, 1977), the advanced use of spatial interaction models (Bertuglia and Rabino, 1975; Regione Piemonte, IRES, 1976), and a textbook (Socco, 1976) on subregional planning methods which is remarkable because of its emphasis on placing methods within the context of their use.

In this specific regional environment, the effect of the second legislature (between the 1975 and 1980 regional elections) has been to produce one of the most interesting attempts to overcome the difficulties and weaknesses of regional planning in Italy. The specific plan for the Turin area (see Socco, 1979) does not appear as an isolated effort but as a piece of an evolving regional mosaic (see also Moretti and Ricciuti, 1981; Regione Piemonte, 1981).

The main critical consideration is that the coordination of the entire procedure from different planning levels up to development control, is unsatisfactory. This is because a contradiction is becoming evident, in this advanced experience, between broad-area planning, which has assumed here the British model of structure planning, but which also takes into account the specific Italian statutory framework and the peculiar unbalanced structure of this region; and spatial planning in the communes and their associations (at lower scale than the broad areas), which follows a more traditional approach (use of land-use allocation maps, for example).

It is true that the Regional Planning Act [see note (4)] gives statutory provisions to deal with the relationship between these two levels, but nonetheless some more satisfactory solution will be necessary in the future. More flexibility of local planning is required, with more commitment to strategic planning at the broad-area level.

5.2.2 The Turin area

Work is currently under way on a plan for the broad area and a new City Plan of Turin. These two plans are closely related: for example, the strategy of relocating the service sector within the city has been developed in both. The Greater Turin area includes now 206 communes (the maximum number in one comprensorio) and 2150000 inhabitants, a percentage of regional population which has grown from 35% in 1951 to 47% in 1977. Figure 2 shows the spatial distribution of population density in the comprensorio.

This area shows a concentration of interregional, regional, and subregional imbalances: strategic planning here is concerned with the simultaneous and distinct solution of these. This means that planning concepts developed in the Milanese case are assumed and further developed, both in planning methodology and in the use of analytical techniques. In this specific spatial framework, a clear priority is given to the decentralization of jobs and housing outside the comprensorio (this follows regional policies).

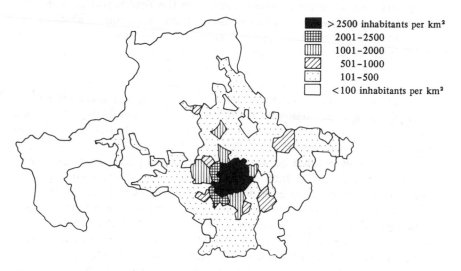

Figure 2. Population density in the Turin comprensorio.

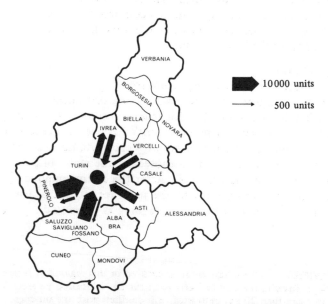

Figure 3. Daily commuting from house to job between the comprensorio of Turin and other parts of the region.

Figure 3 gives an indication of the current situation as regards commuting
into and out of the Turin comprensorio. The strategic aims at the broad-
area level are:
(1) to slow down the growth of the city and to reduce densities and
congestion costs in order to improve environmental quality;
(2) a very restrictive development control in the first suburban belt, in
order to stop urban sprawl and the associated production of absolute rent,
to maintain the agricultural use of fertile land, and to avoid massive new
location or relocation of activities in this very attractive belt where
external economies are high while congestion costs are still low;
(3) the preferential location of new developments of basic production
activities (mainly manufacturing) and urban growth which cannot be
diverted outside the comprensorio in the more peripheral zones of the area
(near the mountain valleys), unless they are necessarily tied up with the
metropolitan environment[14].

The degree of conflict between institutions and public agencies seems
very low compared with that in other regions, even if some kind of
'suppressed' conflict does exist under the disguise of regional centralization
of decisions. The precarious statutory framework of the comprensorio as
a subregional agency of the region is the main limit to this advanced
practice, and this can only be removed via reform at the national level.

Finally, the common framework of socioeconomic and physical planning
is not without problems, mainly because of the interdependence of the
economic structure with the rest of the world. The major event is now the
crisis at Fiat—a very concentrated and specialized economic base has such
large effects upon the whole urban system as to undermine the whole
strategy of rationalization of the local structure.

5.3 Strategic planning in Venice

5.3.1 *A precarious equilibrium of planning authorities*
In the Venetian case the sharpest conflicts, both among institutions and
among social groups, has developed on planning issues. Another outstanding
characteristic is that a vast amount of research work has been concentrated
in the past on the very complex spatial system of Venice, its lagoon, and
its hinterland. All this research has been promoted by the state, but
without coordination with planning practice. After the alarm sounded by
the 1966 flood, subsequent discussion led to the most recent special law
for Venice (Law 171/1973) where broad-area planning is promoted.

---

[14] Special industrial relocation policies have been introduced in this region. A recent
survey found that 70% of firms in the city of Turin with current relocation projects
did not intend to move more than 20 km outwards; this conflicts with the broader-
scale plans for decentralization of the planning authorities (see Ortona et al, 1981,
pages 73–75).

The following special features apply to Venetian planning.

(1) The central government is immediately involved in subregional planning goals and achievements

(2) The broad-area plan has been made the responsibility of the regional authority, after a climate of very sharp contrast between the demand for a 'high authority' (a special agency called for by some newspapers, pressure groups, and parts of public opinion outside Venice) and the local councils' defence of their power.

(3) National and regional statutory requirements give no solution to the problems of monitoring: only a first plan is to be set up; implementation is then to be mainly the concern of regional and local authorities.

Clearly, behind this odd statutory context there is an open conflict between different political forces at the regional and local levels.

5.3.2 *Planning issues and strategies*

The whole range of issues in such a peculiar territory can be defined as an interplay between two subsystems:

(a) an ecosystem characterized by the most anthropocentric lagoon in the world [a synthesis of the very large volume of research work on this subject is given by Ghetti et al (1980)];

(b) an urban system with its centre of gravity in three separate and specialized parts of the city—the historical city of Venice, the urban centre of Mestre, and the urban–industrial district of Marghera. This is not a combination unique in urban history and geography (see Maunier, 1910), but it presents very sharp contrasts in the Venetian case, because of the impact of this century's large-scale industrial and tourist developments on such a large, homogeneous, and beautiful historical city and the whole Venetian urban system (see also Costa et al, 1978).

The interaction of the two preceding systems gives rise to a very peculiar 'artificial environment' (the outcome of a historical process of managing ecological and hydraulic equilibria within the lagoon). Its preservation is of vital importance for the city's survival in the present form; the long-term alternatives would be degeneration into dry land or into the peculiar brackish aquatic environment of the lagoon (a zone of transition between sea and mainland).

The first Plan of the comprensorio of Venice is now in progress (see Comprensorio di Venezia, 1979); the main aim of the plan is to give coherence to the vast demand for a new *quality* of development (giving quality of life for residents without gentrification of the historical city, new forms of tourist enjoyment without consumerism, and so on), in such a way as to overcome the contradiction between or the mere juxtaposition of (and compromise between) the opposing goals of growth and environmental maintenance and improvement. A long-term strategy of change of the structure inherited from the developments of past decades is put forward.

The overall strategies proposed in the past few years have all been rejected, even if many single proposals contained in them have been accepted. The most important of these were: the growth of big industry on the borders of the lagoon; the creation of a large integrated metropolitan area in the regional hinterland (Mestre, Padova, Treviso); and the environmentalist attitude toward decentralization of the manufacturing and basic harbour activities, keeping only the service and tourist activities.

Priority policies of the new Plan are as follows.

(1) The cleaning of the lagoon, together with the implementation of a global strategy of hydraulic management. In the long term, policies of attracting or prohibiting activities will be implemented on the basis of evaluations of the tolerable thresholds for activities located throughout the total area of environmental interaction with the lagoon.

(2) The defence of the social and physical structure of the historical city and the control of urban sprawl in the mainland, via more effective improvement policies for the old housing stock (mainly located in the historical city) and the supply of new housing for the outstanding needs (mainly located in the city of Mestre and its suburbs).

(3) The rationalization of the two predominant activities—manufacturing (mainly chemicals and aluminium) and tourism, together with the diversification of basic activities, including new development of trade (mainly between Central Europe and the East) in the Venetian harbour and the increase of employment in the small and medium-size manufacturing firms of the mainland.

As far as the implementation of such policies is concerned, there is no doubt that only the central and regional governments have the authority, the power, and the resources to meet the very urgent needs of this area.

Finally, if the cases of the major northern cities (Milan, Turin) show the cessation of a first phase of planning before the actual urban crisis, the case of Venice is balanced between this first phase and the next one: there is no problem of urban containment because the growth of the city has stopped in the last few years but demands for a qualitative development of the city are very high, because of the concentration of needs and requirements by very different classes of users (jobs, housing, tourism, and so on).

6 Conclusions

The intention of the paper is not to draw any general conclusion from the analysis of regional and subregional planning in Italy in the 1970s. Among the many problems in the statutory framework and methodology of planning, a very fundamental one is peculiar to the Italian planning system today: the relationship between regions and local authorities. This problem has been tackled differently, but unsatisfactorily, in each individual region. The reform of LAs and the filling of the vacuum between regions and communes has some priority, but it cannot be isolated as a separate reform. Recent debate has been summarized in the forthcoming new version of the Plan for the Comprensorio of Venice (Comprensori di Venezia, 1979), which reaches the following conclusions, themselves very close to those of recent conferences of the National Planning Institute (see Bellagamba et al, 1981).

(a) The region should qualify as a planning agency which will be more integrated within the system of LAs; the communes are inadequate to manage the whole net of social and health services.

(b) The communes should be encouraged to join together in 'inter-commune associations' as intersectoral service agencies; this is a separate problem, with a different spatial extent from that of the necessity of an 'intermediate institution' for planning.

(c) A 'new province', with a wide range of powers orientated toward its role in regional planning, could be the answer to this problem.

(d) This new (reformed) institution could be the synthesis of the experimental comprensori and of fully endowed LAs and could overcome the weaknesses of former attempts in subregional planning. This new institution should not further complicate the working of public administration, but its first task should be to cooperate in the existing regional planning practice.

(e) The planning system could be rationalized to produce correspondence between plans and planning agencies; each level (local, provincial, regional, national) would have specific planning tools and a homogeneous level of government with the ability to implement the planning goals.

After new national laws of reform of LAs and planning procedures, a new generation of regional laws could define precisely the subjects of subregional plans and consequently devolve some regional powers to the new provinces.

References

Allione M, 1977 *La Pianificazione in Italia* (Marsilio, Padua)

Amato G, 1972 *Il Governo dell'Industria in Italia* (Il Mulino, Bologna)

Andriani S, Barcellona P (Eds), 1981 *Sulla Programmazione* (De Donato, Bari)

Arcangeli F, Borzaga C, Goglio S, 1980 "Patterns of peripheral development in Italian regions 1964-1977" *Papers of the RSA* **44** 19-34

Arcangeli F, Vitiello A, 1981 "Alcune riflessioni sulla questione meridionale oggi" paper presented to the Second Italian Conference of Regional Science, Naples, 19-21 October 1981

Arcangeli F, Vitiello A, 1982 "Mezzogiorno tra sviluppo e sottosviluppo" in *Italia: Centri e Periferia. Analisi Regionale; Prospettive e Politiche d'Intervento* Ed. S Goglio (Angeli, Milan) [forthcoming]

Bagnasco A, 1977 *Le Tre Italie* (Il Mulino, Bologna)

Balbo M, 1978 *Comprensori, Ristrutturazione Istituzionale e Territorio* (Angeli, Milan)

Barbagallo F, 1980 *Mezzogiorno Questione Meridionale 1860-1980* (Guida, Naples)

Barbera A, 1980 "Alcuni interrogativi sulla programmazione regionale" in *CESPE-CRS (1980)* pages 11-28

Barbera A, Bassanini F, 1979 *I Nuovi Poteri delle Regioni e degli Enti Locali* (Il Mulino, Bologna)

Barucci P, 1978 *Ricostruzione, Pianificazione, Mezzogiorno: Le Politiche Economiche in Italia dal 1948 al 1955* (Il Mulino, Bologna)

Batey P W J, Breheny M J, 1978 "Methods in strategic planning. Part I: A descriptive review" *Town Planning Review* **49** (3) 259-273

Bellagamba P, Bianchi G, Nigro G, Talia M (Eds), 1981 *Regioni, Programmazione, Pianificazione Territoriale* (Edizioni delle Autonomie, Rome)

Bertuglia C S, Rabino G, 1975 *Modello per l'Organizzazione di un Comprensorio* (Guida, Milan)

Bianchi G, 1980 "L'esperienza di programmazione in Italia: una breve rassegna critica" in *CESPE-CRS (1980)* pages 29-38

Brancati R, Zezza V, 1981 "Divari regionali e ciclo economico" *Politica ed Economia* **12** (10) 33-40

Cacciari M, 1971 "Problemi del mercato e della organizzazione del lavoro" *Contropiano* (3) 491-576

Camagni R, Cappellini R, 1981 "Policies for full employment and efficient utilization of resources and new trends in European regional development" paper presented at the XXI European Congress of the RSA, 25-28 August 1981, Barcelona, Spain

Carabba M, 1977 *Un Ventennio di Programmazione 1954-74* (Laterza, Bari)

Cassese S, 1973 "Tendenze dei poteri locali in Italia" *Rivista Trimestrale di Diritto Pubblico* (1) 283

Cassese S (Ed.), 1981 *Annuario per le Autonomie Locali 1981* (Edizioni delle Autonomie, Rome)

CESPE-CRS, 1980 *La Programmazione Regionale* (Centro Studi Programmazione Economica, Rome)

Comprensorio di Venezia, 1979 *Proposta di Piano Comprensoriale* (Comprensorio dei Comuni della Laguna e dell'Entroterra di Venezia, Venice)

Costa P, Foot D, Piasentini U, 1978 "The Venice problem: an approach by urban modelling" *Regional Studies* **12** 579-602

Dalmasso E, 1972 *Milano, Capitale Economica d'Italia* (Angelli, Milan)

D'Antonio M, 1973 *Sviluppo e Crisi del Capitalismo Italiano—1951-1972* (De Donato, Bari)

Degani R, 1979 "Politica dei trasporti e programmazione territoriale: l'area metropolitana milanese" *Città e Società* **3** 6-8

Del Monte A, Giannola A, 1979 *Il Mezzogiorno nell'Economia Italiana* (Il Mulino, Bologna)

Dente B, 1977 "Il governo locale in Italia" in *Il Governo Locale in Europa* Eds R Mayntz, L S Sharpe, B Dente (Comunità, Milan) pp 201-326

Gabellini P, Morandi C, Vidulli P, 1980 *Urbanistica a Milano 1945-80* (Edizioni delle Autonomie, Rome)

Ghetti R, Passino R, Avanzi C, Gatto P, Rabagliati R, Rosa Salva P, Zitelli A, 1980 *Ripristino, Conservazione ed Uso dell'Ecosistema Lagunare* (Municipality of Venice)

Giunta Regionale Toscana, 1979 *Programmare, Amministrare, Confronto con l'Esperienza Britannica* (Edizioni delle Autonomie, Rome)

Graziani A, 1979 "Il Mezzogiorno nel quadro dell'economia italiana" in *Investimenti e Disoccupazione nel Mezzogiorno* Eds A Graziani, E Pugliese (Il Mulino, Bologna) pp 7-65

Graziani A, Pugliese E (Eds), 1979 *Investimenti e Disoccupazione nel Mezzogiorno* (Il Mulino, Bologna)

Guida per le Autonomie Locali 1978-1980 (Edizione delle Autonomie, Rome) published annually

Il Piano del Lavoro della CGIL 1949-1950 1978, Proceedings of the Conference held in Modena, 9-10 May 1975 (Feltrinelli, Milan)

Indovina F, 1965 "La pianificazione regionale in Italia" in *Pianificazione Regionale* Ed. F Indovina (Marsilio, Padua)

Lipietz A, 1980 "The structuration of space, the problem of land and spatial policy" in *Regions in Crisis: New Perspectives in European Regional Theory* Eds J Carney, R Hudson, J Lewis (Croom Helm, London) pp 60-75

Lombardi F (Ed.), 1979 "Il comprensorio e l'ente intermedio: storia, istituzioni, politica" *Urbanistica Ipotesi* (3) Florence

Lunghini G (Ed.), 1981 *Scelte Politiche e Teorie Economiche in Italia* (Einaudi, Turin)

Marzano F, 1981 "Scelte politiche e teoria economica nell'ultimo trentennio, con particolare riferimento alle politiche d'intervenzione nel Mezzogiorno" in *Scelte Politiche e Teorie Economiche in Italia* Ed. G Lunghini (Einaudi, Turin) pp 203-244

Massey D, 1979 "In what sense a regional problem?" *Regional Studies* 13 233-243

Maunier R, 1910 *L'Origine et la Fonction Économique des Villes (Étude de Morphologie Sociale)* (Franklin, Paris) [reprinted 1968]

Meini M C, Naef S, Cucchi M, 1978 "Materiali di documentazione sulla esperienza di programmazione nelle regioni a statuto ordinario" paper presented to the Conference *Ricerca e Programmazione Regionale* (IRPET, Florence; IRER, Milan)

Merloni F, Urbani P, 1977 *Il Governo del Territorio tra Regioni e Partecipazioni Statali* (De Donato, Bari)

Ministero del Bilancio, 1967 *La Programmazione Economica in Italia* (Ministero del Bilancio e della Pianificazione Economica, Rome)

Ministero del Bilancio, 1981 "Piano a medio termine 1981-83" *Mondo Economico* (Ministero del Bilancio e della Pianificazione Economica, Rome) number 4, pp 60-64

Moretti A, Ricciuti F (Eds), 1981 "Piemonte" *Edilizia Popolare* XXVIII (160) 4-60

Ortona G, Parodi L, Santagata V, 1981 "Problemi della rilocalizzazione nel Comprensorio di Torino" *Quaderni di Ricerca IRES* (6), Instituto di Ricerca Economica e Sociale, Turin

Pallante M, Pallante S (Eds), 1975 *L'Italia Contemporanea: Dal Centro Sinistra all' Autunno Caldo* (Zanichelli, Bologna)

Pini R, 1979 *Procedure di Programmazione e Ordinamento Regionale* (CEDAM, Padua)

Pubusa A, 1981 "Comprensori" in *Annuario per le Autonomie Locali 1981* Ed. S Cassese (Edizioni delle Autonomie, Rome) pp 93-103

Regione Piemonte, IRES, 1976 *Linee di Piano Territoriale per il Comprensorio di Torino* (Guida, Naples)

Regione Piemonte, IRES, 1977 *Le Gerarchie Territoriali nella Strategia della Programmazione* (Giardini, Pisa)

Regione Piemonte, 1978 *Primo Schema della Metodologia per la Formazione di Piani Territoriali di Comprensorio* (Regione Piemonte, Turin)

Regione Piemonte, 1981 *Rapporti sulla Pianificazione e Gestione Urbanistica in Piemonte: 1975-1980* (Regione Piemonte, Turin)

Rossi Doria M, 1970 "Saraceno e la politica economica del dopoguerra" *Nord e Sud* (August-September) 48-51

Ruffolo G, 1973 *Rapporto sulla Programmazione* (Laterza, Bari)

Salvati M, 1975 *Il Sistema Economico Italiano: Analisi di una Crisi* (Il Mulino, Bologna)

Saraceno P, 1981 *Rapporto 1980 sull'Economia del Mezzogiorno* (SVIMEZ— Associazione per lo Sviluppo Industriale del Mezzogiorno, Rome)

Secchi B, 1974 *Squilibri Regionali e Sviluppo Economico* (Marsilio, Padua)

Secchi B, 1975 "Il ruolo dell'edilizia nello sviluppo economico italiano" *Economia e Territorio* 4 4-18

Secchi B, 1977 "Central and peripheral regions in a process of economic development: the Italian case" in *London Papers in Regional Science 7. Alternative Frameworks for Analysis* Eds D B Massey, P W J Batey (Pion, London) pp 36-51

Senato della Repubblica, 1980 *Documento Approvato dalla Commissione Parlamentare per le Questioni Regionali* nella seduta del 12/2/80, a conclusione dell'indagine conoscitiva sui rapporti tra gli organi centrali dello Stato, le regioni e gli enti locali ai fini della programmazione (Senato della Republica, Camera dei Deputati, Rome)

Socco C, 1976 *Teorie e Modelli per la Pianificazione Comprensoriale* (Giardini, Pisa)

Socco C, 1979 *Contributo alla Formazione del Piano Territoriale del Comprensorio di Torino* (Regione Piemonte/F Angeli, Milan)

Spaventa L, 1981 in *Sulla Programmazione* Eds S Andriani, P Barcellona (De Donato, Bari) pp 74–77

Tamburrano G, 1971 *Storia e Cronaca del Centro-Sinistra* (Feltrinelli, Milan)

Tarantelli E, 1978 *Il Ruolo Economico del Sindacato. Il Caso Italiano* (Laterza, Bari)

Tazzer M, 1981 *Lo Strumento di Pianificazione Territoriale di Livello Intermedio nei Sistemi Regionali di Pianificazione e di Rapporto alle Proposte di Riforma del Governo Locale* graduation thesis, Istituto Universitario di Architettura, Venice

Strategic Choice and Uncertainty: Regional Planning in Southeast England

P DAMESICK
Birkbeck College, University of London

1 Introduction

This paper examines the evolution of regional planning in southeast England with special reference to developments during the 1970s. It focuses particularly on the impacts on the planning strategy for the region of changing economic and demographic circumstances and of shifts in policy concerns and objectives. It aims to show how the development of the regional strategy in the South East reflects the weaknesses and problems inherent in the British style of regional planning and also the difficulties of devising a viable strategy to cope with uncertainty. To provide the necessary background for this examination, some salient features relating to the development of British regional planning are outlined initially.

2 The nature and context of regional planning in Britain

In their introduction to the *Strategic Plan for the South East*, the South East Joint Planning Team (SEJPT, 1970, page 4) observed that, in comparison with local land-use planning,

"The role of regional planning is much less clearly defined. Its aims and methods are neither fully worked out nor generally agreed. On the one hand it is an extension of local planning, dealing particularly with those matters—the movement and distribution of employment, the complex interaction of social and economic needs, the provision of major recreational facilities and the main communications network, for example—which can only be decided for areas much larger than the areas of existing local planning authorities. On the other hand it is concerned with inter-regional flows of population and employment, with the availability and use of resources, and with long-term economic prospects which cannot properly be decided except in the context of the balance to be achieved between growth in one region and growth in other parts of the country, on which only the Government can decide. A further complication arises from the difficulty of isolating and assessing problems at the regional level as distinct from the local and national levels".

Two dimensions of regional planning are outlined in this statement: the intraregional ('bottom-up'), and the interregional ('top-down'). These reflect the two separate stimuli to the development of regional planning in Britain. One was a concern with the primarily physical planning problems of environment and land use in and around large metropolitan areas. In essence, this dimension of regional planning focussed upon regulating and moulding the form of urbanisation within metropolitan regions. Its principal themes have been the containment of the physical extension of large urban areas and the planned dispersal of population and economic activity to smaller, physically distinct settlements. This strand of regional planning received its most forceful impetus and achieved its fullest

development in southeast England, although containment of the outward
spread of conurbations and planned overspill arrangements, including New
Town developments, have featured in the planning strategies for other
regions (Hall et al, 1973).

The second main stimulus to regional planning in Britain was a concern
to achieve a more balanced pattern of regional economic growth and
development within the country as a whole. A 'regional problem',
classically identified in terms of interregional disparities in unemployment,
has been recognised in Britain since the 1920s (McCrone, 1969). Initial
policy responses to the regional problem, from the Industrial Transference
Scheme of 1928 (designed to assist labour mobility from areas of high
unemployment) through the Special Areas Acts of 1934 and 1937 (Pitfield,
1978) to the Distribution of Industry Act of 1945, were very largely based
on concern with the social consequences of localised high unemployment
in the depressed regions of northern and western Britain. A Royal
Commission on the Distribution of the Industrial Population, set up in
1937, drew attention in its report in 1940 (known as the Barlow Report,
after the Commission's chairman) to wider considerations relating to the
national economic and strategic interest arising from gross regional
disparities in economic development and the overconcentration of growth
in and around Greater London (Barlow, 1940). The Barlow Report argued
that the problems of the depressed regions were an inseparable complement
to the growth and prosperity of the London metropolitan region. Both
aspects of the changing national space-economy should be encompassed in
a coherent policy framework designed to restrain growth in the South East
and West Midlands and to redistribute it to the depressed areas.

After a brief period of active policy in line with the recommendations of
the Barlow Report in the immediate postwar years, Labour and Conservative
governments from 1948 until the late 1950s both allowed regional policy
to lapse (McCrone, 1969; McCallum, 1979). In part, this was due to the
preoccupation of central government with national economic affairs,
especially demand management and the balance of payments. This
emphasis was reinforced by the quite widespread view that the regional
problem had been substantially solved, and by the Conservatives' dislike of
intervention in the location of industry.

In the late 1950s and early 1960s, a number of factors combined to
reawaken political interest in regional policy and to generate new interest
in regional economic planning. One was the reemergence, or rediscovery,
of the regional problem. Regional disparities in unemployment worsened
in the cyclical economic downturns of 1958–1959 and 1962–1963. The
immediate government response was to reactivate regional policy through a
resumption of the advance factory-building programme in the depressed
areas and by a tightening of controls on industrial development in the
South East and West Midlands. At the same time, the government was
becoming increasingly concerned with the poor growth rate of the national

economy and the recurrent balance of payments crises. The two were related by the so-called 'stop-go' policy of successive reflation of the economy and subsequent deflation as imports outstripped exports. In seeking a way to break out of this 'stop-go cycle', and thus avoid the dampening effects of short term economic expedients upon the national growth rate, government policymakers were impressed by the apparent success of the French mode of 'indicative' economic planning (Leruez, 1975; Budd, 1978). In 1961, the National Economic Development Council (NEDC) and Office were established to assist in the promotion of a higher and stable rate of economic growth.

In 1963, the NEDC published a report on *Conditions Favourable to Faster Growth*, which was designed to show how the 4% annual growth rate established as an aim in its first report might be achieved. The report on *Conditions* contained considerable discussion of regional issues and argued that regional policy should not be seen simply as a response to a 'social' problem, but as a means of drawing into productive use the unemployed labour reserves of the depressed regions and thus contributing to national growth. Equally, regional policy could help to alleviate the social costs, including general inflationary pressures, generated by the concentration of growth in the more prosperous regions, especially the South East. Hence the report (NEDC, 1963, page 29) argued that

"A national policy of expansion would improve the regional picture; and in turn, a successful regional development programme would make it easier to achieve a national growth programme".

Also in 1963, there appeared two government White Papers setting out development proposals for central Scotland and northeast England, the two depressed areas worst affected by the economic downturn. These were not regional plans as such, but they did present strategies intended to regenerate the economies of their respective areas. Both papers stressed the importance of environmental and infrastructural improvements, especially in communications, for regional development. In the North East, the key 'trigger' mechanism for generating economic expansion was to be a massive road-investment programme (Board of Trade, 1963).

A Labour government was elected in 1964, largely through voting shifts in Labour's favour in the less prosperous regions. It was firmly committed to economic planning and regional development, and among its first acts was the establishment of a new Department of Economic Affairs (DEA), headed by George Brown, then the deputy Prime Minister. The first task of the DEA was the preparation of a National Plan, which was presented in September 1965 with the aim of achieving a 25% increase in national output in five years. The Plan carried further the ideas of the 1963 NEDC report on the interdependence of national and regional economic planning, particularly with regard to the role of regional planning in the achievement of faster national growth whilst avoiding inflation (DEA, 1965, page 85):

"A policy of stimulating economic growth in regions with under-employed resources will ... help to avoid regional concentrations of excess demand which set the pace in driving up costs and prices".

The Plan also emphasised the need for improvements in the social and economic infrastructure of the less prosperous regions and for spatial selectivity in development strategies (DEA, 1965, page 85):

"... regional policies will not be concerned with bolstering up small areas which have no economic future; they will be concerned with developing those parts of each region where there is real growth potential".

To facilitate the integration of regional planning into national planning, the government established new regional planning machinery, centrally in the DEA and at the regional level in the form of Economic Planning Councils (EPCs) and Boards (Wright and Young, 1975). The EPCs were composed of part-time members drawn from local government, business, the trade unions, and the academic field. Their role was purely advisory, concerned with the formulation of regional strategies and the articulation of the implications of national economic policies for their regions. The Boards consisted of senior civil servants from the government departments with regional responsibilities. They were intended to service the EPCs and provide them with an 'executive' arm through the coordination of activities in different government departments. Along with these institutional innovations, the Labour government also embarked upon a major intensification of regional policy, extending the areas eligible for assistance and increasing expenditure on regional aid (McCallum, 1979).

The high aspirations held by the Labour government for its new regional planning system are revealed in the following statement from a DEA publication of 1966 (DEA, 1966, page 4):

"... because regional planning is now taking its proper place as an integral part of national planning, it has become possible for problems within individual regions to be tackled against a background of national objectives and to be supported by co-ordinated national policies in such a way as to promote the sound growth of each region as a whole".

The mid 1960s thus marked a high point in the scope and expectations given to regional planning by central government. However, in July 1966, the growth objectives of the National Plan were abandoned under the impact of deflationary policies to meet a sterling crisis. The sacrifice of growth to defend the exchange rate was in fact to be in vain, for, in November 1967, the government was forced to devalue the pound. The abandonment of the National Plan dealt a severe blow to regional planning, as, perforce, the subsequent development of regional strategies lacked a coordinating framework of national objectives and policies with regard to regional development.

The Labour government attempted to revive a form of indicative planning in 1969 in a statement of revised economic aims, *The Task Ahead (Economic Assessment to 1972)* (DEA, 1969). This document reaffirmed that an improvement in 'regional balance' was a condition for achieving a satisfactory growth rate. However, in October 1969, the government dispensed with an already-diminished DEA and transferred its regional planning functions to a new Ministry of Local Government and Regional Planning, which subsequently became the Department of the Environment (DoE). Throughout its relatively brief life, the effectiveness of the DEA as a planning ministry was highly constrained by the fact that the key decisions concerning fiscal, monetary, and public expenditure policy largely emanated from the Treasury, where a different set of perspectives on economic priorities, generally short-term and almost wholly lacking in any spatial dimension, prevailed. The disappearance of the DEA and the absorption of its regional planning responsibilities by the DoE very substantially diminished the *economic* component of regional planning. Administration of industrial location controls and regional development incentives remained in a separate ministry, which later became the Department of Industry.

At the regional level, the machinery of Economic Planning Councils and Boards remained, although they had lost their role of translating national objectives into regional strategies. A distinctive feature of the institutional framework for regional planning in Britain which has persisted throughout its development is its lack of a political or statutory base comparable with that possessed by local land-use planning. Initially in the *Strategic Plan for the South East* (SEJPT, 1970) and then in the North West (NWJPT, 1974), East Anglia (EARST, 1974), and the North (NRST, 1977), the preparation of regional strategies took place within tripartite arrangements involving central government departments, the regional planning council, and local authorities. These strategies have been described as beginning to approach "... the (probably unattainable) ideal of a corporate plan for the region concerned" (Powell, 1978, page 8).

However, regional strategies have no statutory basis in themselves; they depend entirely for implementation upon other planning machinery and agencies. These agencies include not only central government departments and local authorities, but also transport and public utility undertakings. Without a consensus and commitment involving these agencies, regional strategies can have only a very tenuous reality. As Manners (1977a, page 5) observes: "Regional planning of the non-executive British variety is not, and cannot be, an activity whereby understanding and priorities developed at one particular scale of geographical generalisation are imposed upon component sub-regions and localities". Rather, regional planning comprises "... an activity whereby intelligence and understanding are exchanged between activities that operate at different geographical scales". Ideally, such exchanges should occur 'downwards', 'upwards', and laterally within the spatial hierarchy. In practice, however, the flows have operated with highly variable effectiveness, and in certain cases particular dimensions of the network of exchanges have been virtually nonexistent. The highly centralised nature of policymaking power within the British governmental

machine has contributed greatly to this problem, particularly through
the sectoral character of public expenditure planning and its ultimate
determination in Whitehall by the Treasury and the major spending
departments. Equally, the policies pursued by British Rail on fares and
electrification of lines, for example, derive from a decisionmaking process
in which regional planning considerations are frequently excluded.

As a consequence of the dual stimuli to its development, regional
planning lies at the interface of physical and economic planning. However,
as already indicated, the administrative arrangements for regional planning
in Britain have not been conducive to a proper integration of these two
elements. Moreover, the practice of regional planning has suffered from
the absence of an adequate theoretical framework incorporating the inter-
relationship between regional economic performance and regional spatial
structure (Parr, 1979).

Much regional economic analysis treats the region either as a dimensionless
point or as undifferentiated territory (see, for example, Brown, 1972). On
the other hand, the physical planning approaches which have prevailed in the
formulation of regional strategies tend to neglect the role of economic and
social forces both in their diagnosis of the problems and in their proposed
solutions. It is, nonetheless, in the sphere of physical planning that
regional planning in Britain has recorded perhaps its most significant and
certainly its most tangible achievements, chiefly through the containment
of conurbation sprawl and the accommodation of overspill populations in
new and expanded towns (Manners, 1980). The successes of regional
planning should not be underestimated, but the 1970s saw increasing
questioning of the adequacy of the prevailing, physically biassed form of
regional planning in meeting the needs for economic regeneration in certain
regions (NWJPT, 1974; NRST, 1977). At the same time, the traditional
remedy of planned dispersal as a solution to the problems of large urban
areas was being associated with the emergence of a new 'inner-city'
problem (Eversley, 1972).

3 Regional planning in southeast England
3.1 Regional profile
The South East is the most populous and prosperous region of Britain,
containing 31% of the country's population on 12% of its land area and
with an average personal disposable income 10% above the UK average in
1978. The postwar unemployment rate of the region has been consistently
below the national figure. In the current recession, the unemployment rate
in the South East had risen to 5·2% by October 1980, compared with rates
of 7·7% in Britain as a whole, 10·6% in the North, and 10·8% in Wales.

Although the South East is the country's leading industrial region, with
26% of the national manufacturing work force in 1977, the structure of
employment within the region is strongly biassed towards the service
sector. Services accounted for no less than 72% of total employment in

Greater London in 1977 and 61% in the rest of the South East (RoSE), compared with 53% in the rest of Britain. The South East contained 38% of national service employment in 1977, and individual service industries in which it is especially dominant include insurance, banking, finance and business services, legal and accountancy services, research and development, national government, air transport, and cinemas, theatre and broadcasting. The region is also the overwhelmingly dominant focus of corporate control in the national economy. London headquarters controlled just over three-quarters of the total turnover of the leading 1000 companies in the country in 1977 (Goddard and Smith, 1978). In 1971, the South East accounted for 43% of all office employment in Britain, with 27% in Greater London alone. Office occupations comprised 38% of all jobs in Greater London and 25% in the RoSE, whereas the comparable figure was less than 20% both in Wales and in the North.

For most of this century up to the mid 1960s, the South East region recorded increasing shares of national population and employment (Lee, 1971). Since then, however, the region has shown relative decline, and from 1972 the population of the South East fell absolutely. This relative decline has been almost entirely due to massive losses of population and employment, especially in manufacturing, from London, whereas the RoSE continued to record major growth (Keeble, 1980). The experience of London provides the most striking instance of the 'deindustrialisation' process affecting the major British cities since the 1960s (Massey and Meegan, 1978; Thrift, 1979), and occurring in the context of a national loss of $1 \cdot 3$ million (-15%) manufacturing jobs in the period 1966–1977.

Some commentators have attributed the relative decline of the South East partly to the intensified impact of regional policy from the mid 1960s, and considerable evidence has accumulated on the success of regional policy in diverting manufacturing investment and employment to the peripheral depressed regions (Moore et al, 1977; Ashcroft and Taylor, 1979; Mackay, 1979). Significant spatial shifts in employment also occurred in favour of the new 'growth regions' of East Anglia, the East Midlands, and the South West; at least part of this expansion may be seen as a 'spillover' from the adjacent South East region. Recent trends in the interregional pattern of employment have also been interpreted as deriving from inherent, market-based forces producing a new spatial division of labour (Massey, 1978; 1979). Thus, uneven development between regions based on regional industrial specialisation by *sectors* is being replaced (or supplemented) by regional differentiation in terms of economic *functions*. Within this system, peripheral regions are characterised by growing dependence upon branch plant, assembly-type production operations. In contrast, the leading metropolitan region (that is, the South East) is distinguished by the 'tertiarisation' of its employment structure, underlain by the concentration of financial and commercial services and its specialisation in planning and control and in research and development functions.

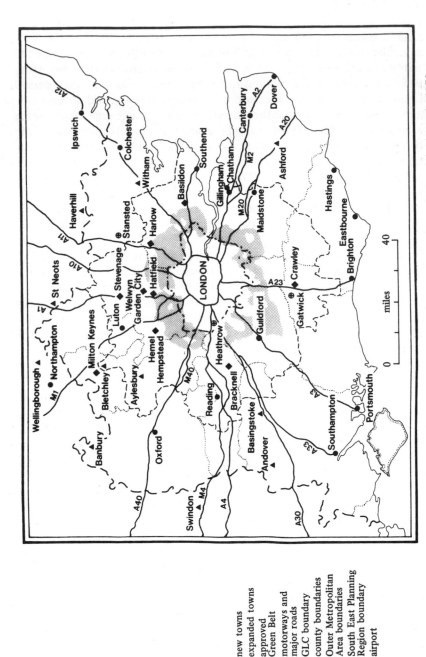

Figure 1. The South East Planning Region. Regional boundaries and the road network are those obtaining in the early 1970s.

new towns
expanded towns
approved
Green Belt
motorways and
major roads
GLC boundary
county boundaries
Outer Metropolitan
Area boundaries
South East Planning
Region boundary
airport

3.2 *The Greater London plan, 1944, and its impact*

The basis of regional planning in the South East in the postwar period up to the mid 1960s was the 1944 *Greater London Plan* prepared under the direction of Professor Patrick Abercrombie (Abercrombie, 1945). The impetus to this plan had developed over a long period and essentially stemmed from concern over the physical extension of the built-up area of London and the problems of the overcrowded and unsatisfactory residential environment of the core of the conurbation. These issues formed the basis of two of the main elements of the Plan: containment of outward growth through the establishment of a 'Green Belt', and the redevelopment of Inner London at lower residential densities. To facilitate these two objectives, the plan proposed the dispersal of one million persons from London to new and expanded towns beyond the green belt.

These proposals met with the approval of the postwar Labour government, and by 1949 eight new towns had been designated in the South East outside London, under the 1946 New Towns Act. Subsequently, under the Town Development Act of 1952, twenty-eight expansion schemes for towns in the South East and adjacent regions were agreed on, in order to accommodate London overspill. The London Green Belt proposals were given force through local development plans during the 1950s, resulting in a statutorily approved belt extending about fourteen kilometres from the suburban fringe of London (Thomas, 1970).

The development of the London New and Expanded Towns and enforcement of green belt controls has undoubtedly had a significant impact upon the spatial structure of the South East in the last three decades. By 1980, the eight 'first-generation' New Towns accommodated a total population of 520000, of which four-fifths represented growth since designation. The towns were all located within 50 kilometres from central London, and varied in size from 91000 in Basildon to 26000 in Hatfield (figure 1).

3.3 *The South East in the 1960s: issues and responses*

It had become apparent by the early 1960s that the Abercrombie plan was no longer adequate to meet the strategic planning needs of the South East region. In the main, this was because the 1944 plan had been founded on two key assumptions concerning trends in the South East, which subsequently proved invalid. One was Abercrombie's assumption of a static regional population; the other was that the controls on industrial development in the South East recommended by the Barlow Commission (of which Abercrombie had been a member) would successfully hold down regional employment.

The sharply rising birthrate from 1955 to 1964, helped by significant immigration, undermined the first of these assumptions. Despite the net out-migration of almost one million persons from Greater London in the period 1951–1966, the net population decline of the conurbation in this period was only 0·35 million (−4·5%). In Inner London, the population did not decline sufficiently to allow the extensive redevelopment and improvement envisaged by Abercrombie. Even in 1971, some 2·3 million people in Inner London lived at residential densities of more than 85 persons per hectare, compared with only half a million in the whole of the rest of the country (SEJPT, 1976, page 35).

In the RoSE, population growth of more than two millions was recorded in the period 1951–1966, with three-quarters of the increase concentrated in the Outer Metropolitan Area (OMA) immediately surrounding Greater London. The bulk of this population growth occurred outside the new and expanded towns, and movement to these towns never accounted for more than 14% of the net population inflow in the OMA during the 1950s. Thus, not only had Abercrombie not foreseen the postwar population growth of the region, but he had also underestimated the strength and volume of movement arising from spontaneous decentralisation within the South East.

Total employment in the South East grew by 1·35 million jobs (20%) during the years 1951–1966, of which no less than 0·84 million were accounted for by the rapid expansion of office occupations. Outside Greater London, although the new towns were important foci of industrial expansion, the pattern of manufacturing growth during the 1950s and 1960s was, contrary to Abercrombie's recommendations, a highly dispersed one (Keeble and Hauser, 1971). Within London, the growth of office activities in the central area during the 1950s was, by the end of the decade, seen to be creating problems of congestion, overloading of the public transport system and the displacement of other land uses from the central area (Marriott, 1967; Cowan, 1971). In 1957, the London County Council produced *A Plan to Combat Congestion in Central London*, advocating, *inter alia*, restrictions on office growth. A government White Paper on London in 1963 proposed a tightening of planning control on office development, a programme of government office dispersal, the development of office centres outside London, and the establishment of the Location of Offices Bureau, in order to encourage decentralisation from central London (Ministry of Housing and Local Government, 1963). To these measures, the Labour government of 1964 added the Office Development Permit, supposedly complementing the government controls on industrial floorspace which had existed since 1947. However, comparable financial incentives for office movement to the assisted areas were not introduced until 1973.

In 1959, A G Powell, an official from the Ministry of Housing and Local Government, presented a paper to the British Association for the Advancement of Science which made clear the Ministry's recognition that Abercrombie's plan had been overtaken by events (Powell, 1960). A new regional plan was urgently required to avoid "great new rings of urban development" being "welded onto the core of the London conurbation".

The pressures created by population growth and movement within the region prompted the local authorities affected to form a Standing Conference in 1962, in order to review regional planning issues and coordinate action. The 1963 White Paper on London reaffirmed the need for a new regional plan and the resulting report, *The South East Study, 1961–1981* (Ministry of Housing and Local Government, 1964) proposed the development of a second generation of new and expanded towns to facilitate the dispersal of a further one million Londoners by 1981. The distinctive feature of the report was its recommendation of a series of major expansion schemes on the periphery of the South East and in adjacent regions, thus creating centres which could act as 'counter-magnets' to London.

The proposals of the Ministry of Housing and Local Government (1964) were given substance through the designation, in 1967–1968, of Milton Keynes, Northampton, and Peterborough under the New Towns Act. The most innovative and impressive scheme was that for Milton Keynes. This was to be a new city of 250000 people on a site in Buckinghamshire which, in 1968, housed 40000 people in the three existing settlements of Bletchley, Wolverton, and Stony Stratford. By 1980, the population had more than doubled to 90000, 20000 jobs had been established, and 'Central Milton Keynes' had been opened as a regional shopping centre. The plans for Peterborough and Northampton, both located outside the South East, involved the expansion of existing towns with populations of 81000 and 133000, respectively, to 160000 and 230000, respectively, by the mid 1980s.

While the *South East Study, 1961–1981* thus made an important contribution to the regional planning framework for southeast England, it left unresolved the problem of accommodating growth in the OMA around London. In 1967, the newly formed South East Economic Planning Council (SEEPC) published *A Strategy for the South East* (SEEPC, 1967), which proposed that growth in the region outside London should be sectorally concentrated along a number of major radii of communication. In putting forward this strategy, the Council noted that it had been impressed by several recent plans for metropolitan regions in other countries, including Paris, Stockholm, Copenhagen, and Washington, which had opted for the concentration of growth in corridors or axes along main communication lines. However, except for Paris, the metropolitan regions cited were hardly comparable in scale with the London city region, and the relevance of their planning experience to a regional strategy for the South East was thus questionable. Moreover, the strategy of the SEEPC could be criticised for the emphasis it would give to intraregional radial movement centred on London, as opposed to the promotion of greater orbital and cross-regional mobility.

The local authorities' Standing Conference on London and South East Regional Planning (SCLSERP) put forward its own separate and rather limited proposals for development in the RoSE in 1968 (SCLSERP, 1968).

The government response to this and to the strategy of the SEEPC was to invite the Standing Conference and the Council to cooperate with it in a joint study to prepare a new regional plan. A joint planning team was formed in 1968 and its report, *Strategic Plan for the South East* (SPSE), appeared in July 1970 (SEJPT, 1970).

3.4 *The Strategic Plan for the South East*

The Strategic Plan drew quite heavily on the earlier attempts to devise a new regional plan in the 1960s; like them, it was largely in the Abercrombie tradition. It both strongly reflected and projected the experience of the South East in the 1950s and 1960s, and thus was a strategy designed to accommodate growth in an 'optimum' framework, while continuing the themes of urban containment and redevelopment and population redistribution. The Plan anticipated regional population growth of 3 million over the period 1966–1991. It expected that labour demand in London would remain high, while the resident work force declined, and that strong development pressures would be felt in the OMA.

In essence, the Plan sought to provide a framework within which the volume of decentralisation in the region could be increased and its spatial pattern controlled and directed. At the same time, the Plan recognised the implications of London's status as a 'world city', and accepted the need to promote and sustain the specialised role of central London as a national and international centre of administration, finance, commerce, tourism, and culture. Inner London surrounding the central area was seen to be the major locus of social problems in the region, in need of improvement in environmental and living conditions. The Plan recommended a programme of rehabilitation and redevelopment in this area which would be facilitated by the dispersal of economic activities not essential to the specialised role of central London.

In the region outside London, the Plan proposed that new development should be concentrated in a limited number of Major Growth Areas, located both in the OMA and in the outer South East (see figure 2). Five Major Growth Areas were identified: Milton Keynes/Northampton, South Hampshire, South Essex, Reading/Basingstoke, and Crawley/Burgess Hill. The scale of growth in these areas envisaged in the strategy was such that they would accommodate over half the total population increase of the South East to 1991. Indicative population figures for the five areas by the end of the century ranged from around 0·5 million in Crawley/Burgess Hill to almost 1·4 million in South Hampshire. The Major Growth Areas were to be supplemented by the expansion of certain medium-sized centres, in order to provide both flexibility and variety in the restructuring of the region's urban system. The strategy of concentration was rationalised by the desire to reap economies of agglomeration and to preserve extensive rural areas from development. Overall achievement of the Plan was held to depend on stimulating a high level of employment mobility from London, of perhaps 15000–20000 jobs per annum both in the manufacturing sector and in the office sector.

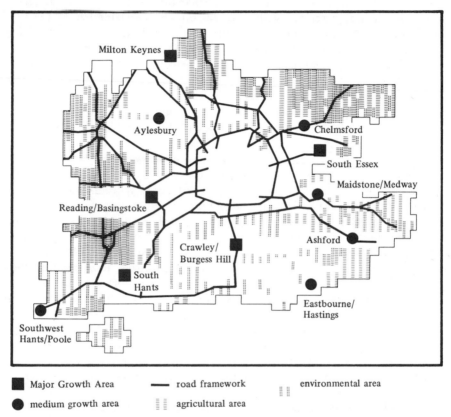

Figure 2. Strategic Plan for the South East, as approved in 1971.

3.5 Problems for SPSE

The Strategic Plan was approved by the government in 1971 with a few modifications, notably the removal of the Bishops Stortford/Harlow medium growth area. The avowed aim of the Plan was to provide a 'framework' for the development of the region, and it explicitly eschewed the 'master plan' approach. However, the framework did have certain deficiencies. One of these concerned the feasibility of its proposals for dispersal from London to the RoSE. The required level of employment mobility in manufacturing of 15000–20000 jobs per annum was considerably greater than the rate of industrial dispersal from London to RoSE in the period 1945–1965, when an average of 11000–12000 jobs per annum was recorded (Keeble, 1971, page 72). In the period 1966–1971, the level of movement from London to the RoSE fell to 5000 manufacturing jobs per annum, no doubt partly as a result of the diversionary effect of a much more active regional policy (Sant, 1975; Keeble, 1976). The Plan's aim of spatially concentrated growth within the RoSE can also be seen as being at odds with the prevailing locational trend of widespread dispersion of manufacturing activity within the region. By the later 1960s, the majority of the largest manufacturing centres in the RoSE were recording declines in industrial employment, whereas the small centres experienced growth (Keeble, 1980, page 174).

Largely as a result of its timing and the style of regional planning, SPSE was unable to take proper account of certain matters of major regional significance. A Commission on the siting of the third London airport (TLA) was appointed in 1968, but had not reported when SPSE appeared in 1970. The SEJPT were not able to make any assumptions about the eventual decision on the airport, despite the fact that it was likely to be the largest single investment decision in the region in the next decade. The deliberations on the TLA are a subject for study in their own right. The key point here is that they largely proceeded independently of regional planning considerations and have been responsible for a substantial element of uncertainty in the regional strategy, creating the need for the strategy to be contingent upon that uncertainty. The feasibility of a Major Growth Area in south Essex was held by the county authority to depend on the provision of a large new employment base. For a short time it seemed that an airport at Maplin would fill this role, but the abandonment of this option left the South Essex Growth Area proposals in considerable uncertainty. The eventual choice of Stansted was much less satisfactory from a regional planning perspective, because "Development here would be contrary to the intentions of SPSE as approved following Government deletion of the proposed Harlow/Bishops Stortford medium growth area" (SEJPT, 1976, page 49).

A further major weakness of SPSE was its lack of integration with strategic planning policies for Greater London. SPSE was primarily a plan for the management of growth in the RoSE, and thus made relatively brief references to London itself. It had, in the view of one commentator, "a gaping great hole in the middle" (Jay, 1974, page 185). The diagrams illustrating the plan seem literally to demonstrate this. Responsibility for strategic planning within London lay with the Greater London Council (GLC), established in 1965. The Greater London Development Plan (GLDP), the 'proto-structure plan', appeared in 1969 and differed significantly from the SPSE with regard to proposals for the continued dispersal of people and jobs from the conurbation. Both plans accepted the need to maintain the specialised role of central London, but GLDP rejected a policy of accelerated and undifferentiated dispersal of manufacturing from London. Instead, it argued for the retention of those industries which contributed to London's economic vitality and which, it claimed, exhibited significantly higher average labour productivity than elsewhere (GLC, 1969; Keeble, 1980). This implied the maintenance of an adequate labour supply within the GLC area, and hence population decline would have to be limited. The GLC 'projection' of a London population of 7·3 million in 1981, which was accepted in the SPSE, was in fact a 'target' based on housing stock estimates.

From the outset, therefore, GLDP and SPSE occupied divergent positions on the dispersal of people and jobs from London. The scale and rate of decline in population and employment in Greater London increased sharply in the later 1960s, in the context of a falling national birthrate from 1964 and a national decline in manufacturing jobs from 1966. As the accelerating loss of people and jobs became apparent in the early 1970s, the GLC began to argue more forcibly for the need to restrain the decline. In their submission to the Layfield Panel of Inquiry on GLDP, 1970–1972, the GLC claimed that 'over-rapid' decline of population and employment was leading to selective out-migration, reductions in average incomes, labour-market mismatch and unemployment, and rising unit costs of public services.

One of the most important contributions to the debate over the consequences of the policy of decentralisation from London was made by David Eversley, who had been appointed Chief Planner (Strategy) at the GLC. Eversley (1972, pages 363, 365) summarised the problem thus:

"London's burdens are not reduced because population and employment decline. Given its growing international, national and regional role, the need to maintain the social infrastructure continues. Tourism adds to the load. The remaining population includes a higher proportion of people needing subsidised housing, special education facilities, welfare services and public services provision of all kinds ..."

"... If nothing is done, and differential migration continues, combined with restriction on economic expansion, maintenance of the present administrative boundaries and continued rises in urban construction costs, a very unpleasant situation may develop".

By itself, this was not an attack on the policy of decentralisation as such, but an attempt to draw attention to its consequences within the existing administrative framework. Eversley accepted that London was still growing, both in real extent and in wealth, but the growth was occurring outside the boundaries of a 'Greater London' defined by the London Government Act in 1963. One possible solution to London's resources problem was to define a wider 'Greater London' area for fiscal purposes. A second potential remedy was for the national exchequer to bear a greater share of the costs of running the capital. Thirdly, London itself could be allowed greater powers of local taxation.

In presenting its case to the Layfield Panel of Inquiry, the GLC argued that the population of London should not be allowed to decline too far or too fast. This received short shrift from the Panel (DoE, 1973, page 627):

"We emphatically recommend rejection of the GLC view that there is any particular danger in either a lower level of population ... or in the particular rate of change. The arguments put forward in support of the view ... are, in our view, either illogical or unsupported by the evidence. In any case, we see very little likelihood that policies could be successful in restraining any particular rate of change".

It was the Panel's view that employment and incomes were not the concern of planners and, even if they were, they could not influence them. This did not prevent the GLC arguments gaining wider currency and support as they crystallised around the emergent issue of London's 'inner city problem'.

3.6 Background to the 1976 Review of SPSE

As the 1970s progressed, the divergence between the SEJPT and the GLC in their positions on the dispersal of people and jobs from London widened and assumed greater significance for the future of the regional strategy. At the same time, more general economic and demographic changes seemed to question the continuing validity of SPSE.

As the birthrate continued to decline after 1970, there was a sharp downward revision in official population projections for the South East. The previously expected increase from the mid 1970s to 1991 all but disappeared, while London's population was declining much faster than expected and had already fallen to 7·3 million by 1973. The 1973-based projected population increase to 1991 in the RoSE was only one-half of that expected in SPSE.

The 1973 rise in oil prices brought in its wake a sharp deterioration in the national economic climate, with rising energy costs, inflation and unemployment, and balance-of-payments problems. As the most prosperous region in the country, the South East was cushioned against the worst effects of the recession, but the SPSE assumptions on the region's growth prospects in the 1970s were undermined. Public expenditure was entering a period of severe restraint at a time when the allocation of resources between London and the RoSE was emerging as a significant issue.

These changed circumstances underlay the decision in late 1974 to commission a study to review and update SPSE. The study was to be addressed particularly to the implications of London's decline for developments in the region in the context of a new economic uncertainty and financial stringency.

3.7 The 1976 Review

The study was undertaken by a new Joint Planning Team of officers from the DoE and the SCLSERP with some contributions from other government and local authority departments. The examination of the existing regional situation and the forces underlying current trends took the form of seven reports on major issues, for example: Population, Housing, Resources, the Economy. An Interim Report (DoE, 1976), attempting to assess the strategic implications of these studies, revealed the differing opinions on the need for realignment of the regional strategy. The view of the GLC was clear: a major redirection of policy and resources was required to stem London's decline. The current situation was very different from that at the time of SPSE: London's economic and resource base was being seriously weakened and social problems were becoming acute, especially in the inner city. The GLC thus favoured slowing down or ending the New and Expanded Towns (NETs) programme and diverting resources to urban renewal. Special attention for the London Docklands and reconsideration of the Growth Area proposals were also sought.

The GLC view, however, received little support in the report of the Economy Group of the new Joint Planning Team. This took a distinctly neoclassical, noninterventionist line, concluding that the South East had a robust and flexible economy with significant growth potential which, in the regional and national interest, should not be impaired. The SPSE Major Growth Areas varied in their economic performance. Milton Keynes and South Hampshire were both growing rapidly and were proving attractive to mobile manufacturing. Service employment had shown vigorous expansion in the Reading/Basingstoke area, which had been a popular destination for decentralised London offices. Substantial office movement to South Essex had not been matched by the attraction of manufacturing to the area envisaged in SPSE. Local labour shortages and local authority reticence were appearing as checks on further expansion of Crawley/Burgess Hill.

Elsewhere in the RoSE, however, there was relatively little difference in performance between the medium growth areas and certain other parts of the region (East Hertfordshire, for example) which appeared to have considerable growth potential. The Economy Group observed that an objective of maximising economic growth might imply easing restraint in these areas. The now well-known research findings of the Department of Industry (Dennis, 1978) showed that manufacturing decline in London since the mid 1960s was attributable far more to straightforward plant closures than to industrial movement. The capital's manufacturing decline was not seen as a direct cause of hardship or unemployment. A high proportion of the unemployed in Inner London had last worked in construction, distribution, or transport, rather than manufacturing, and lack of skill was the dominant characteristic of those out of work. A recent decline in manufacturing jobs in the OMA had been more than offset by growth in service employment. Thus the characteristics of economic change in London were now spreading over a wider area, and the apparent striking contrast between the decline of London and growth in the RoSE was largely a function of existing boundaries.

Their findings led the Economy Group to conclude that there was not a particularly strong case for intervention in order to slow down existing spatial trends in the region. The Resources Group were more cautious, however, and much concerned with the problem of uncertainty. Rehabilitation was offered as the best compromise solution to this problem. At a strategic level, this implied that there was a case for devoting more resources to viable renewal in London and for not trying deliberately to stimulate growth in the RoSE.

The new Joint Planning Team accepted that, although much less than the SPSE expectations, population growth in the RoSE could still amount to 1·6 million persons by 1991. Equally significant was the expected growth in the numbers of households, especially those of one person. Whereas SPSE had assumed that average household size would remain fairly stable, it now appeared that household fission and the growth in the numbers of single-person households would contribute greatly to a possible increase of one million new households in the RoSE by 1991. Even in Greater London, where the total number of households was expected to decline by 188000 by 1991, there could be an increase of 125000 one-person households. Aggregate demand for dwelling units would therefore be comparable with that expected in SPSE, although, of course, its composition would be different.

The Team therefore concluded that the region would still experience substantial demands for new development, and that SPSE remained an appropriate framework for accommodating these demands. With regard to London, the Team recognised that "the accelerating loss of London's population and manufacturing employment has adverse consequences in the short term", but it was "not wholly convinced that in the longer term the adjustment may not bring substantial benefits. Reduction of pressures in London has, after all, been a main objective of national policy since the time of the Barlow Report and the Abercrombie plan" (DoE, 1976, page 5).

The Team's final report, the *1976 Review*, presented a somewhat modified but similarly equivocal view on the issue of London's decline (SEJPT, 1976, page 36):

"The extent to which the decline or rate of decline in population or employment poses threats to London's future is debatable. In some ways the trends can be regarded as a desirable process of adjustment to changing circumstances. Nevertheless, very real problems do exist in London. Where trends and problems appear to be related the connection seems to be due to the speed of change rather than the actual process".

In these circumstances, the Review concluded that it would be appropriate to attempt to slow the decline and ease the process of adjustment.

However, the Team also reaffirmed an earlier conclusion that cutting back on planned migration to the NETs, as proposed by the GLC, would have little effect on the total population outflow from London, as most movement was 'unplanned'. It observed that "... the motives behind migration seem to be abundantly clear. People are moving in search of better housing conditions" (SEJPT, 1976, page 36), and the private outflow "will be very difficult to stop so long as London does not or cannot produce private housing of the quality and density, in the type of environment and at the prices which private buyers seek" (SEJPT, 1976, page 15).

The Review was also extremely cautious in considering possible policy modifications designed to alter existing trends. It sought clarification of what particular aspects of the current London situation were undesirable, and therefore what policies to modify trends would be aiming to achieve. It also warned that if efforts were focused solely on modifying trends, problems in Inner London which were not related to the trends would be ignored. Such caution now appears well-founded in the light of the growing appreciation of the fundamentally structural, rather than spatial, origins of urban deprivation and the associated limits on area-based policies.

In the face of a growing clamour for a shift in policy, it would clearly have been politically unacceptable for the Review to advocate a *status quo* position. It therefore proposed a carefully balanced contingent approach whereby, for an initial period up to about 1981, London should be given a 'breathing space' in order to get to grips with its problems, during which developments in the RoSE should not be allowed to jeopardise such efforts. In proposing this strategy, the Team were also influenced by the uncertain economic outlook and likely resource availability in the context of a perceived risk of overcommitment to housing development in the RoSE. Although arguing that applications for industrial and commercial development in the RoSE need not be subject to the same restraint as housing, the Review did not favour any substantial loosening of industrial controls in the RoSE, because of the likely effects on London and the Green Belt. It recognised that this meant that the objective of maximising economic growth, considered to be in the national and regional interest, would not be realised. There thus arose the possibility of conflict with the Labour government's industrial strategy (DoI, 1975), initiated in November 1975 and designed to find means of improving the performance of particular 'growth' industries. Had the strategy succeeded, the South East would have been the main regional beneficiary, as it had a relative concentration of the selected industries (Cameron, 1979).

The Team's concern with uncertainty underlay its rather neutral and cautious approach, deferring choices as much as possible. This was perhaps justifiable with regard to the general economic outlook, but much less so with respect to London, inasmuch as the revised strategy was to be contingent on London-based policies which were not fully worked out either in their aims or in their methods. This must be considered a serious weakness in the revised strategy, and one which compounded the problem of uncertainty. It reflects a weakness in the regional planning system and the difficulties faced by the advisory Joint Planning Team in confronting the electorally-based power of the GLC. The latter authority also flatly opposed the recommendation of the Lambeth Inner Area Study (DoE, 1977) that more balanced population dispersal was essential in a policy of inner city renewal.

The Review's proposals for tighter development controls in restraint areas and for a 'holding operation' in 'nonrestraint' parts of the RoSE were not unwelcome among certain planning authorities outside London, of course. Some of these authorities also appreciated the opportunity of a 'breathing space'. As well as showing an understandable reluctance to plan for growth in the face of uncertain future resource availability for the provision of infrastructure and local services, some authorities were also influenced by local aspirations for the preservation of communities and environments from development. The Review itself noted that there had been "much opposition to development" within the Reading/Basingstoke Major Growth Area. In Hertfordshire, a county with a record of strong economic growth and considerable further potential for expansion, the Structure Plan authority took the view that the designated Growth Areas in the South East (or other parts of the country) should absorb the development pressures which it did not want. The Hertfordshire Structure Plan (1980) explicitly aims to restrain economic development within the county, especially if it would create significant employment growth, and divert it elsewhere; this policy is seen as consistent with the county's 'proper role' within the South East region. Whether this type of restraint on employment generation, manifest in the plans of certain other authorities in the RoSE, is indeed in the current regional or national interest seems questionable. It may, of course, be misguidedly perceived by the GLC to be in *its* interest as it attempts to erect an 'economic planning wall' around London.

The contingent 'strategy' of the Review thus left planning authorities in the region largely free to pursue policies geared to the perceived needs of their own areas of responsibility and, despite avowals to the contrary, it tended to endorse the separation of London from its surrounding region. The failure to define a wider regional interest, and to ensure that component areas have regard to this interest and to each other's welfare, has direct parallels at the level of individual strategic planning authorities within the region. For instance, to improve the residential environment of Inner London, whilst retarding the overall loss of population from Greater London, requires a significant intrametropolitan redistribution of population. The Review recognised this (SEJPT, 1976, page 58):

"The outer London boroughs have an important part to play in relieving housing pressures within the inner boroughs".

The outer boroughs have consistently shown a marked reluctance to subscribe to this objective, and the GLC itself has now substantially abandoned its housing role. Constrained by the power of the London boroughs, the GLC has steadily relinquished its strategic planning responsibilities and confined itself to promoting the sectional interests of a Greater London area with boundaries which must be considered as being in many senses artificial.

The need to arrive at proposals which would command the required degree of consensus within the region was an obvious problem for the 1976 Review. Its 'neutral and cautious' proposals in the face of uncertainty attempted to reconcile the demands of London with the requirement to maintain the overall economic potential of the region and accommodate likely pressures for development. It was purely an advisory document, primarily designed "... to be instructive and helpful in pointing to the decisions that need to be taken in government investment programmes and in structure plans". It was not "... in any sense a 'decision document' dealing in resource-allocation terms with specific development programmes"

(SEJPT, 1976, page 52). Indeed, the Review implicitly acknowledged that regional planning does not exist in the sense of there being any power or machinery at a regional level to determine the allocation of resources in support of strategic objectives.

3.8 *The Government Statement, 1978*

The government's response to the 1976 Review (DoE, 1978) took over two years to appear. During that time, and prompted particularly by worsening unemployment in Inner London, a series of significant policy shifts and initiatives with regard to the country's inner cities was introduced. The Inner Urban Areas Act was passed, inner-city 'partnerships' were formed, government controls on industrial and office development in London were adjusted, the remit of the Location of Offices Bureau (LOB) was revised (Manners, 1977b), and there was a substantial shift in financial subventions to London, through the Rate Support Grant. The New Towns programme was scaled down, with an aggregate cut of 140000 in the target populations of Milton Keynes, Peterborough, and Northampton, and through a government refusal to grant boundary extensions to Harlow, Bracknell, and Stevenage.

The Government Statement on SPSE purported to be a "free-standing document" setting out strategic planning policies for the South East. As a unilateral declaration of policy, it brought to an end ten years of cooperation and consultation on the regional strategy involving the Standing Conference of local authorities and the Planning Council. The Statement made little overt response to the 1976 Review and indeed claimed to be comprehensible "... without reference to the Report of the Team or the original Strategic Plan".

Interpretation of the document in these terms is virtually impossible. The Statement carried further the process whereby the prescription of policy becomes independent of information or analysis, and the regional strategy was effectively moved into the realm of 'planning by good intention'.

The government reaffirmed the diversity and resilience of the South East's economy and pronounced that its potential "must not be stifled" (DoE, 1978, page 4). Nowhere in the Statement is there a serious attempt to consider whether the prescribed policies for the region accord with that objective. The government expected that its inner-city initiatives and revised New Towns policy "... will have a significant effect on the net movement from London" (DoE, 1978, page 10). However, it recognised that only a small proportion of such movement was attributable to planned dispersal: "The remainder is susceptible only to more tenuous and indirect control" (DoE, 1978, page 10). The disparity between intention and likely outcome is reflected in the conclusion that "... continuing provision must be made against the possibility of population growth in the region outside London even though the needs of Inner London must now have priority" (DoE, 1978, page 10).

The Statement recorded that major growth in population and employment in the London Docklands was proposed in the 1976 *Docklands Strategic Plan* for the area, and the Docklands were included in the Major Growth Areas in the regional strategy. The Docklands Plan had in fact proposed a larger increase in population and employment in a shorter time-span than had been planned or achieved in any of the NETs. The 1976 Review had stated (SEJPT, 1976, page 57):

"The Docklands hardly seem able to compete with other growth areas or, for that matter, with other 'green field' sites in the rest of the region. [A] 'growth area' label would not in itself change the situation".

The Statement's lack of comment on the feasibility of the Dockland proposals may be contrasted with the assertion (DoE, 1978, page 11) that the new population target for Milton Keynes was

"... a realistic assessment of how best to balance the requirements of Inner London and the changed attitudes towards outward movement from the conurbation with the need to build upon the proven ability of new towns to stimulate and encourage modern industrial development".

The basis for this "realistic assessment" was not discussed. Where the 1976 Review was an exercise in coping with uncertainty, the essence of the Government Statement was an attempt to 'balance' objectives and priorities in response to "changed attitudes". For the latter, one is tempted to read 'political expediency', notably the need for government to be seen to be attending to the demands of London. Having committed itself to a more pronounced change of direction on policy for the inner city than the 1976 Review had advocated or envisaged, the government faced the problem of fitting this revised policy into a coherent regional strategy for the South East. The 1978 Statement signally failed to achieve this.

In the cause of promoting the impression of 'balance', the Statement avoided all hint of conflict in objectives and priorities. It thus left unresolved such issues as how the priority of Inner London's needs was to be balanced against the need for continuing provision for population growth outside London. On several topics, the Statement offered little strategic guidance of specific relevance for the South East, relying instead upon the recital of broad government policy. This "lack of clear strategic thinking" drew strong criticism from the Standing Conference (SCLSERP, 1979, page 6) which was also concerned that the Statement "... unaccountably lacks any sense of time—juxtaposing current spending, future plans, and timeless hopes" (SCLSERP, 1979, page 7).

The Standing Conference dismissed the Statement as inadequate for regional planning needs and called for a return to the contingent strategy approach as proposed in the 1976 Review. The SEEPC also found the Statement unsatisfactory and favoured a new strategy which would be geared to the positive promotion of economic growth in the region, building especially upon the industrial potential of the five Major Growth Areas. Both these proposals, however, were made to a new Conservative government, elected in May 1979, which showed considerable reservations on the role and process of regional planning and was committed to public expenditure reductions and less intervention.

3.9 *The Conservative government and the regional strategy 1979–1980*

The Conservative administration lost little time in acting upon its reservations over the value of regional planning and policy. During 1979, it abolished the Economic Planning Councils, dispensed with the Location of Offices Bureau, and announced its decision to cut projected expenditure on regional aid by 38% over a three-year period and reduce the areas eligible for assistance (Townsend, 1980). Local authority finances were placed under major pressure by constraints on public expenditure, and new government initiatives to regenerate depressed urban areas were confined to proposals for two Urban Development Corporations (for the London and Merseyside Docklands) and for a number of so-called 'enterprise zones'. The latter were to be small areas with streamlined planning procedures and offering tax and rate exemptions with the intention of stimulating development and employment. The Isle of Dogs in East London was selected as the location for one of the zones.

In the South East, the SCLSERP stood firm in its view that a revised government statement on the regional strategy was required. Its representations to the DoE on the need for clarification of the strategy ultimately bore fruit in the form of a 'statement' contained in a three-page letter from the Secretary of State in August 1980. The Conference itself undertook to prepare a document to amplify the implications of this statement (SCLSERP, 1981).

The avowed purpose of the statement was "... to set out strategic guidance for land use planning in the region". Objectives for the region's development were defined as the improvement of London's attractiveness; achievement of "orderly development" in the RoSE, which safeguarded the Green Belt and other rural areas of restraint; and improvement of some regional transport links. With reference to the first objective, the statement offered little strategic guidance beyond the assertion that "London is no longer regarded as a source of population and jobs for other areas", and a call for "favourable conditions" to be created in London "... so that private individuals and firms will once more choose to live and invest there".

The statement clearly implied that the government was looking for the private sector to provide the motive force for the regeneration of London, and local authority policies were to be geared towards providing the necessary planning support and achieving the government's wider aims of stimulating the private sector, sweeping away obstacles to commercial enterprise, and achieving more home ownership and private house building. Underlying this approach is an implicit presumption that past planning policies, rather than market forces, were responsible for the decline of London.

With regard to the region outside London, the statement (SCLSERP, 1981) affirmed the government's support for rural conservation and endorsed "... the strategic policy of concentrating a large part of future development in carefully selected 'growth areas' ". The statement did not consider any implications for development in the RoSE likely to arise from the completion of the M25 orbital motorway around London nor from the decision on the siting of a third London airport at Stansted. The official DoE view of the M25 as being primarily a 'bypass' route seemed to overlook the signs that it would generate substantial development potential in some parts of the OMA and that county and local planning authorities were already responding differently, and perhaps not coherently, to this potential. The pressures and opportunities created by the M25, along with the Stansted proposal, the problems of selective restraint policies in favour of 'local needs' in parts of the RoSE (Healy, 1980), and, of course, the complex question of London, look set to remain outstanding issues that may at some stage persuade central government that there is a real need for a clear and feasible regional strategy for the South East.

4 Conclusions

The confusion and uncertainty surrounding the regional strategy in south-east England at the beginning of the 1980s contrasts markedly with the heady aspirations for regional planning manifest in the mid 1960s. The primary reason for the disappointment of expectations was that, from the outset, the aspirations for regional planning were not compatible with the constraints exerted by the political and administrative system. This meant, as Wright and Young (1975, page 25) observe, "... that the advent of regional planning was more apparent than real".

The conception of regional planning as the natural and necessary complement to national economic planning, ensuring that all regions' resources were used fully and effectively to promote national growth whilst avoiding inflation, disappeared with the abandonment of the 1965 National Plan. The assumption of responsibility for regional planning by the Department of the Environment, which, like its predecessors, was strongly orientated in its concerns and expertise towards intraregional physical planning, also helped to stifle the development of the economic interregional dimension of regional planning. Integration of the economic and physical dimensions of regional planning was further frustrated by the separate administration of the regional *policy* response to the problems of the depressed areas. Whereas regional policy has involved the diversion of resources to particular areas, there has been little, if any, regional dimension in the resource-allocation procedures of central government departments generally, nor in other agencies such as the nationalised industries. Moreover, regional strategies have exerted very little direct influence on resource allocation within the existing system. Regional strategy reports, such as those for the North West (NWJPT, 1974) and the North (NRST, 1977), which attempted to exert such influence were received antipathetically in Whitehall as "... another thick book from region X asking for money" (comment by a DoE Official at a Regional Studies Association conference on regional planning, London, November 1980).

The institutional and administrative context for regional planning thus reduced it to a process of study and discussion of factors, problems, and possibilities in individual regions, combined with efforts to communicate the implications to the bodies which exercise power and allocate resources. It is not denied that much valuable work has been undertaken through this process. The primary failing has been that such work has not been matched by an adequate *political* commitment to regional planning. The failure of the Labour government to lay down a clear strategy for the South East in its 1978 statement was indicative of the low priority given to regional planning. The present Conservative administration's abolition of the EPCs, and its own profound disinterest in regional planning, means that the onus for regional planning initiatives in England has shifted to regional associations of local authorities, such as the Standing Conference in the South East. As local authorities are the statutory instruments of land-use planning, in contrast to the purely advisory role of the former EPCs, this is not inappropriate in one respect. The crucial and missing component is an overall integrated and coherent approach to the issues of regional policy and regional planning on the part of central government.

Acknowledgements. The author would like to thank Mr Brandon Howell, formerly of the Standing Conference on London and South East Regional Planning, and Professor Gerald Manners for their helpful comments in discussions on the subject of this paper. The author is, of course, solely responsible for the interpretation and views contained in the paper.

References

Abercrombie P, 1945 *The Greater London Plan, 1944* Report prepared for the Standing Conference on London Regional Planning (HMSO, London)

Ashcroft B, Taylor J, 1979 "The effect of regional policy on the movement of industry in Britain" in *Regional Policy: Past Experience and Future Directions* Eds D Maclennan, J B Parr (Martin Robertson, Oxford) pp 43-64

Barlow M (Chairman), 1940 *Report* Royal Commission on the Distribution of the Industrial Population, Cmnd 6153 (HMSO, London)

Board of Trade, 1963 *The North East: A Programme for Regional Development and Growth* Cmnd 2206 (HMSO, London)

Brown A J, 1972 *The Framework of Regional Economics in the United Kingdom* (Cambridge University Press, Cambridge)

Budd A, 1978 *The Politics of Economic Planning* (Fontana Books, London)

Cameron G C, 1979 "The national industrial strategy and regional policy" in *Regional Policy: Past Experience and Future Directions* Eds D Maclennan, J B Parr (Martin Robertson, Oxford) pp 273-294

Cowan P, 1971 "Employment and offices" in *Planning for London* Ed J Hillman (Penguin Books, Harmondsworth, Middx) pp 64-76

DEA, 1965 *The National Plan* Department of Economic Affairs, Cmnd 2764 (HMSO, London)

DEA, 1966 *Economic Planning in the Regions. The Work of the Regional Economic Planning Councils and Boards* (Department of Economic Affairs, London)

DEA, 1969 *The Task Ahead (Economic Assessment to 1972)* (HMSO, London)

Dennis R, 1978 "The decline of manufacturing employment in Greater London, 1966-74" *Urban Studies* **15** 63-73

DoE, 1973 *Greater London Development Plan, Report of the Panel of Inquiry, Volume I: Report* Department of the Environment (HMSO, London)

DoE, 1976 *Development of the Strategic Plan for the South East. Interim Report* (Department of the Environment, London)

DoE, 1977 *Inner London: Policies for Dispersal and Balance* Final Report of the Lambeth Inner Area Study (Department of the Environment, London)

DoE, 1978 *Strategic Plan for the South East, Review. Government Statement* Department of the Environment (HMSO, London)

DoI, 1975 *An Approach to Industrial Strategy* Department of Industry, Cmnd 6315 (HMSO, London)

EARST, 1974 *Strategic Choice for East Anglia* East Anglia Regional Strategy Team (HMSO, London)

Eversley D E C, 1972 "Rising costs and static incomes: some economic consequences of regional planning in London" *Urban Studies* **9** 347-368

GLC, 1969 *Greater London Development Plan, Written Statement* (Greater London Council, London)

Goddard J B, Smith I J, 1978 "Changes in corporate control in the British urban system, 1972-1977" *Environment and Planning A* **10** 1073-1084

Hall P, Thomas R, Gracey H, Drewett R, 1973 *The Containment of Urban England* (two volumes) (Allen and Unwin, London)

Healy P, 1980 "Regional policy in the South East" *Town and Country Planning* **48** 406-407

Hertfordshire Structure Plan, 1980 *Hertfordshire County Structure Plan. Alterations 1980* (Hertfordshire County Council, Hertford)

Jay L S, 1974 "Regional policy and sub-regional planning: the confused state" in *Regional Policy and Planning for Europe* Ed. M Sant (Saxon House, Farnborough, Hants) pp 171-187

Keeble D, 1971 "Planning and South East England" *Area* **3** 69-74

Keeble D, 1976 *Industrial Location and Planning in the United Kingdom* (Methuen, Andover, Hants)

Keeble D, 1980 "The South East" in *Regional Development in Britain* second edition, Eds G Manners, D Keeble, B Rodgers, K Warren (John Wiley, Chichester, Sussex) pp 101-176

Keeble D E, Hauser D P, 1971 "Spatial analysis of manufacturing growth in outer South East England 1960-67. I. Hypotheses and variables" *Regional Studies* **5** 229-262

Lee C H, 1971 *Regional Economic Growth in the United Kingdom since the 1880s* (McGraw Hill, Maidenhead, Berks)

Leruez J, 1975 *Economic Planning and Politics in Britain* (Martin Robertson, Oxford)

Mackay R, 1979 "The death of regional policy—or resurrection squared" *Regional Studies* **13** 281-296

Manners G, 1977a "The 1976 Review of the Strategic Plan for the South East—some outstanding economic issues" *Planning Outlook* **20** 2-8

Manners G, 1977b "New tactics for LOB" *Town and Country Planning* **45** 444-446

Manners G, 1980 "Intra-regional development and planning" in *Regional Development in Britain* Eds G Manners, D Keeble, B Rodgers, K Warren, second edition (John Wiley, Chichester, Sussex) pp 71-100

Marriott O, 1967 *The Property Boom* (Hamish Hamilton, London)

Massey D, 1978 "Regionalism: some current issues" *Capital and Class* **6** 106-125
Massey D, 1979 "In what sense a regional problem?" *Regional Studies* **13** 233-244
Massey D, Meegan R A, 1978 "Industrial restructuring versus the cities" *Urban Studies*
    15 273-288
McCallum J D, 1979 "The development of British regional policy" in *Regional Policy.*
    Past Experience and Future Directions Eds D Maclennan, J B Parr (Martin Robertson,
    Oxford) pp 3-42
McCrone G, 1969 *Regional Policy in Britain* (Allen and Unwin, London)
Ministry of Housing and Local Government, 1963 *London—Employment; Housing;*
    Land Cmnd 1952 (HMSO, London)
Ministry of Housing and Local Government, 1964 *The South East Study, 1961-81*
    (HMSO, London)
Moore B, Rhodes J, Tyler P, 1977 "The impact of regional policy in the 1970s" *CES*
    Review **1** 67-77
NEDC, 1963 *Conditions Favourable to Faster Growth* National Economic Development
    Council Report (HMSO, London)
NRST, 1977 *Strategic Plan for the Northern Region* (Northern Region Strategy Team,
    Newcastle upon Tyne, England)
NWJPT, 1974 *Strategic Plan for the North West: Report 1973* (HMSO, London)
Parr J B, 1979 "Spatial structure as a factor in economic adjustment and regional
    policy" in *Regional Policy. Past Experience and Future Directions* Eds D Maclennan,
    J B Parr (Martin Robertson, Oxford) pp 191-211
Pitfield D E, 1978 "The quest for an effective regional policy—1934-37" *Regional*
    Studies **12** 429-443
Powell A G, 1960 "The recent development of Greater London" *Advancement of*
    Science **17** 76-86
Powell A G, 1978 "Strategies for the English regions" *Town Planning Review* **49** 5-13
Sant M, 1975 *Industrial Movement and Regional Development. The British Case*
    (Pergamon Press, Oxford)
SCLSERP, 1968 *Framework for Regional Planning in South East England* (Standing
    Conference on London and South East Regional Planning, London)
SCLSERP, 1979 *Strategic Plan for the South East: Government Statement. Report by*
    the Technical Panel SC1150 (Standing Conference on London and South East
    Regional Planning, London)
SCLSERP, 1981 *South East Regional Planning: the 1980s* SC1500 (Standing
    Conference on London and South East Regional Planning, London)
SEEPC, 1967 *A Strategy for the South East* (HMSO, London)
SEJPT, 1970 *Strategic Plan for the South East* Special Consultative Report of the
    South East Joint Planning Team (HMSO, London)
SEJPT, 1976 *Strategy for the South East: 1976 Review* Special Consultative Report
    of the South East Joint Planning Team (HMSO, London)
Thomas D, 1970 *London's Green Belt* (Faber and Faber, London)
Thrift N, 1979 "Unemployment in the inner city: urban problem or structural
    imperative? A review of the British experience" in *Geography and the Urban*
    Environment. Volume 2 Eds D Herbert, R J Johnston (John Wiley, Chichester,
    Sussex) pp 125-226
Townsend A R, 1980 "Unemployment and the new government's regional aid" *Area*
    12 9-18
Wright M, Young S, 1975 "Regional planning in Britain" in *Planning, Politics and*
    Public Policy. The British, French and Italian Experience Eds J Hayward, M Watson
    (Cambridge University Press, Cambridge) pp 237-268

Issues and Tendencies in Dutch Regional Planning

H VOOGD
Delft University of Technology

1 Introduction

In the past, the Dutch physical planning system has received considerable attention from various foreign authors (see, among others, Bigham, 1973; Burke, 1966; Dunham, 1971; Dutt, 1970; Hamnett, 1975; Heywood, 1970). Most of these express some admiration for the formal separation of planning functions and the symmetry of the arrangements for coordinating various levels of government. However, practice teaches us that this apparent neatness of the Dutch system also embodies a number of weaknesses. This paper attempts to illustrate those weaknesses by discussing some current issues and trends in Dutch regional planning.

In section 2, there is a brief examination of the administrative structure which constitutes Dutch regional planning. In addition, attention is paid to regional planning both from a national perspective and from a provincial perspective. Section 3 outlines how the central government copes with regional planning problems, whereas section 4 is devoted to the provincial point of view.

Currently, regional planning practice is mainly focused on three major problem areas: the location of building places; the protection of environmental qualities; and the struggle against regional unemployment. These key issues will be discussed in detail in section 5. The last section is devoted to some final remarks and conclusions.

2 The administrative structure

The organization of regional planning in The Netherlands is mainly based on two levels of government—the central government and the eleven provinces. The central government sets out the main lines of regional planning policy in various reports. In addition, it exercises supervision over the policies of provinces and municipalities and settles differences between them. Planning at the national level in The Netherlands is the responsibility of various Ministers, depending on the issues to be tackled. The main responsibility for physical planning rests with the Minister for Housing and Physical Planning, who is assisted by the National Physical Planning Agency (Rijks Planologische Dienst, or RPD). Coordination with other departments of central government is partly maintained by the National Physical Planning Committee, which is a monthly meeting of top civil servants. Another rather influential committee on a national level is the Physical Planning Advisory Committee. This Committee, on which scientists, businessmen, and representatives of other interest groups sit, produces advisory reports and organises public participation on draft plans published by the RPD.

As has been mentioned before, planning on a national level is not the sole responsibility of the RPD. Regional economic policy, for instance, is mainly based on directives issued by the Ministry of Economic Affairs. This Ministry currently produces a triennial report on regional economic planning, in which guidelines and directives are presented on economic development and control. Another very powerful Ministry is that of Transport, Waterways, and Public Works (Rijkswaterstaat), which is responsible for water engineering and road construction and maintenance. Although much of the work of this Ministry is delegated to the provinces and municipalities, it retains direct responsibility for the construction of motorways and the maintenance of the larger waterways. If The Netherlands were to lose the protection of its dunes and dikes, the most densely populated part of the country would be flooded. The Rijkswaterstaat fulfils an important role in preventing this. Consequently, this Ministry has possessed great power throughout the course of Dutch history and even today is often referred to as 'the state within the state'. It will be evident that this limits the effectiveness of physical planning proposals brought forward by the RPD and by other related Ministries, such as that of Health and Environmental Protection. This latter Ministry was created in 1971 to try to ensure more effective protection of the quality of the physical environment. At that time, a separate Ministry was chosen for this task, rather than its integration into the Ministry of Housing and Physical Planning, in the belief that an independent position between the RPD and the Rijkswaterstaat would benefit environmental interests.

The main political decisionmaking bodies in the provinces are the Provincial Councils. Each of these councils is technically assisted by a provincial planning service (Provinciale Planologische Dienst or PPD). There is also a committee on which various interest groups and experts are represented. This committee functions almost on similar lines to the National Physical Planning Advisory Committee. The main task of the Provincial Councils is to draw up regional plans (streekplannen) for (parts of) their territory. They also exercise supervision over the policies of the municipalities. Coordination between regional planning of the provinces and the central government is attained through inspectors who represent the Ministries at provincial level. With regard to provincial–local relations, the province must consult municipalities likely to be affected by its policy [for an extensive overview of the rules governing physical planning in The Netherlands, see Brussaard (1979)].

This organization of regional planning, which in itself is effective, also has its drawbacks. A major disadvantage is that, because of lack of cooperation between the various planning bodies, there is often a corresponding lack of coherence in the various policies. Regional plans can fulfil an important role in arriving at a better integration of the various policies (see Van Meel, 1977). This issue will be considered in more detail

in section 4. Another point of discussion, which some see as a drawback
of the Dutch planning system, is the size of the provinces (see figure 1).
Regional scale is generally thought to be somewhat smaller than provincial
scale. In the last decade, several proposals to extend the number of
provinces have been discussed in the Dutch parliament. The debate is still
continuing. At present it looks as if the final outcome of these discussions
will be rather modest, and that in the next few years, only the Rijnmond

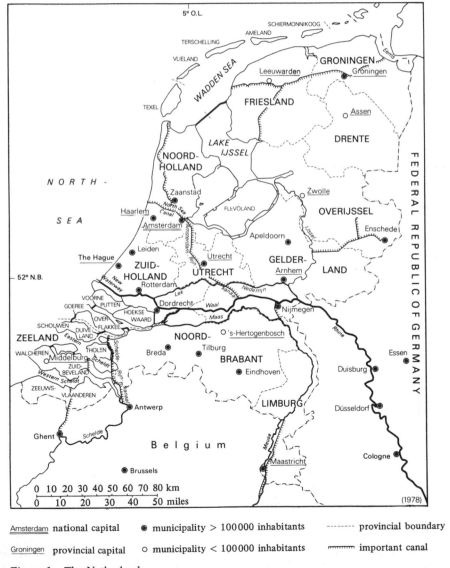

| Amsterdam national capital | ⊕ municipality > 100000 inhabitants | -------- provincial boundary |
| Groningen provincial capital | ○ municipality < 100000 inhabitants | ﹏﹏ important canal |

Figure 1. The Netherlands.

area, which includes Rotterdam and twenty-three municipalities of the Rhine estuary area, will receive provincial status.

3 Regional planning and development in the national perspective
Regional planning in The Netherlands is to a large extent guided by measures, documents, and guidelines from the central government. For example, the various reports produced by the RPD are very important documents. The First Report on Physical Planning was published in 1960, followed by the Second Report in 1966. Both reports are very descriptive, and clearly reflect a 'blueprint' approach to planning. However, the failure of this approach was soon realized. This resulted in the decision to produce a Third Report on Physical Planning, which was to be more 'process-oriented'. This report was published in three parts. The first of these, the *Orientation Report*, contains the objectives of the national physical planning policy. It was published in April 1975 as government policy. The principal aims of this report were the achievement of a balanced distribution of population and employment, dispersed from existing centres, and the protection of open (rural and natural) areas. The major objectives relate to environmental protection, control of economic growth, reduced mobility, and the reduction of inequalities both within and between the Dutch regions. In order to implement these resolutions, various regulations were announced, such as Selective Investment Rules and the dispersal of public services from the Randstad (literally 'Rim city', that is, the urbanized part of the western Netherlands) to other parts of the country.

The second part of the Third Report; the *Urbanization Report*, was published as government policy in February 1977. This part mainly concentrates on the urbanized areas in the western Netherlands. This is the area where the greatest urban problems are found, the strict dispersal policy of the First and Second Reports having been largely abandoned as a solution to these problems. In the *Urbanization Report* it was stated that further urban growth must be accommodated within or in the vicinity of the Randstad wings, and that large-scale migration from the Randstad to the provinces of Noord Brabant and Gelderland must be restrained. Also, the displacement of part of the urban growth to peripheral areas in the northeast and southeast of the country was advocated less emphatically than previously (see Nijkamp, 1977; Witsen, 1977a). A policy directed at reinforcement of urban functions was proposed, in order to combat urban decline and sprawl and to prevent a further deterioration of small towns and villages around the big cities. In addition, greater emphasis was placed on concentration in a limited number of growth towns and centres, in order to control the diffusion effects of urbanization from the Randstad area (see figure 2).

The third part of the Third Report on Physical Planning, the *Report on Rural Areas*, was published in 1978 as government policy. The underlying

philosophy of this report is that the nonurbanized part of the country
may no longer be regarded purely as an area for agricultural production.

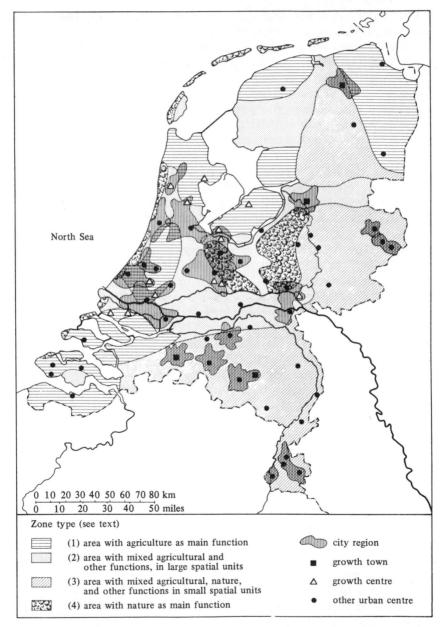

Figure 2. Regional economic policy, as outlined by the RPD Third Report on Physical
Planning.

Joint use by the nonagricultural population, care for nature, and landscape conservation are becoming increasingly important. For this reason, the report introduces a system of zoning, upon which a regional policy can be based. The following zones are distinguished (see figure 2):

(1) areas where the agricultural interests have the highest priority;

(2) areas with mixed agricultural and other functions in large spatial units, where the regional planning priorities should depend on the particular circumstances of each area;

(3) areas with mixed functions in smaller spatial units, where the highest priority is given to landscape preservation;

(4) areas with nature as their principal function, where the highest priority is given to the preservation of environmental quality.

The national physical planning policy laid down in these three reports is further elaborated in the so-called *Structural Outline Sketches* and *Structure Schemes* (see Wiggerts, 1979). It was aimed to review these sketches and schemes every five years, thus emphasizing the process character of planning. However, there appear to be so many documents to be reviewed that at present, a review period of five years appears to be very optimistic: it is questionable, for instance, whether the review of the *Urbanization Report* will be ready by 1982. It will be evident that this is a real problem, as apart from the *Structural Outline Sketches* of the Third Report there are also a large number of *Structure Schemes.* Structure schemes relate to the long-term policy for a sector. They have a strong physical planning emphasis, which means that the RPD will be involved in their production to some degree. Many such schemes are already ready or in preparation, and include those dealing with drinking and process water supply; electricity supply; navigable waterways; traffic and transport; housing; civil airports; seaports; outdoor recreation; nature and landscape conservation; land reconstruction; military training grounds; and pipelines. It will be very difficult to review these reports every five years. In addition, there are many complaints from the lower-tier authorities about the huge amount of paper that they have to read and interpret. In some circles, there is already talk of the 'report dictature' of the central government.

Another important regional planning document originating from central government is the *Report on Regional Socioeconomic Policy*, published in 1977. It is intended to update this report every three years, and a new report is expected at the beginning of 1981[1]. This report aims at an integrated spatial and socioeconomic policy. In order to remove undesirable regional differences in employment and income, a socioeconomic dispersal policy is pursued, whereby a number of regions are designated as development areas. In the growth centres (see figure 3), the establishment of firms—not only those in the service sector—is encouraged by means of financial and other measures. A distinction is made between the incentive

[1] *Note added in proof*: this report has now appeared (RPD, 1981).

area in the Northeast and the restructuring area in the South. In the southern province of Limburg, all the coal mines were closed between 1966 and 1975, so that the already existing industrial structure had to be altered. The western provinces—Noord-Holland, Zuid-Holland, Utrecht, and western Gelderland—form the so-called restriction area. In this area, the establishment of new industries can be prevented—if they do not meet certain environmental standards, for example. At present, this regional economic policy can neither be considered a success nor rejected as a failure. A judgement is very difficult because of the effects within The Netherlands of the recession in the world economy. Nevertheless, the deterioration of the national economy has its influence on the policy in the restriction area, in the sense that the constraints are interpreted less severely now than a few years ago.

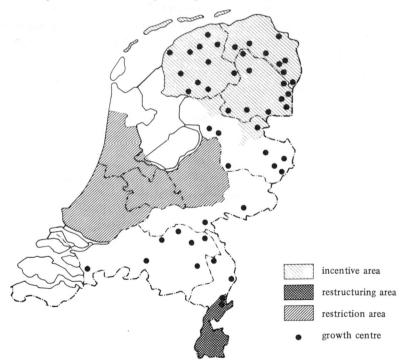

incentive area

restructuring area

restriction area

● growth centre

Figure 3. Regional economic policy 1977–1980, according to the 1977 *Report on Regional Socioeconomic Policy.*

4 Regional planning and development in the provincial perspective
Almost the entire country is now covered by regional plans (streekplannen). Regional plans, as laid down in the Physical Planning Act of 1965, have three functions:
(a) a spatial development plan for the area of the regional plan;
(b) a yardstick against which to judge the municipal allocation plans;

(c) the means whereby provincial and central government may use directives to affect the contents of municipal allocation plans.

The regional plan has no binding character; rather it can be considered as a flexible programme which is not linked to particular prescriptions. It is principally directed towards a progressive and developmental elaboration of the specified goals and the means and guidelines to achieve these. Recently, a fourth function of the regional plan has gradually become more evident: that of an integrative framework (see Van Meel, 1977). In this case, the regional plan is seen as an outstanding opportunity to promote the mutual cohesion of the various individual developments and to attune the policies of the central government, the provinces, and the municipalities to each other. Thus the regional plan will be increasingly used to coordinate all government measures of importance for the development of an area. This includes all government authorities—central government, provinces, municipalities, and water boards. Consequently, provincial regional planning will involve progressively greater vertical and horizontal coordination of activities. Until recently, practical experience had shown that, in these two respects, the regional plans did not exactly function optimally. According to Van Meel (1977), the practical preparation and, in particular, the implementation of regional plans more closely resembled a constantly interrupted hurdle race than a balanced physical planning policy. It is first necessary to clarify and harmonize the various policy lines for the principal sectors (such as those of economic, sociocultural, and environmental policy). However, many sector policies are almost entirely conducted at national level, which implies that provincial physical planning policy depends to a large extent on central government. At the moment, the main difficulty in this respect is that the central government policies are not operationalized in such a way as to be capable of being satisfactorily integrated into regional plans in accordance with their spatially relevant aspects.

Currently, there is a strong tendency to solve these coordination problems by means of a 'commitment-generating' approach to planning, whereby bargaining and negotiation are the keywords. For instance, for the regional plan for Twente, in the province of Overijssel, an organization structure has been chosen in which representatives of all governmental levels are actively participating (see Dekker, 1980). The basic idea behind the Twente planning process is that, for instance, a new road is not included in the plan if the representative from the Ministry of Transport, Waterways, and Public Works is unable or unwilling to guarantee future funds for this project. According to the participants in this process, this planning strategy works reasonably satisfactorily.

However, it must be mentioned that the approach of Twente is not (yet) accepted by all other provinces. To some degree, this reflects the fact that the various provinces have to deal with different problems. In the western provinces, the major problem is the allocation of land for building; this is often a very emotional political issue which cannot be solved solely by negotiations between civil servants. In the northeast and south of the country, environmental and economic problems are more important; the latter type, especially, are heavily related to the finances available to attack them. These finances are mainly controlled by central government, which means that provincial regional planning in concert with the central government may be very advantageous.

5 Some important issues

With an average of 411 inhabitants per square kilometre of land, The Netherlands is the most densely populated country in Europe. The total population has now reached fourteen million people, living in approximately 4 800 000 dwellings, of which 60% were built after World War II. However, in the most densely populated areas in the west of the country there still remains an acute housing shortage (figure 4).

These housing needs arose not so much because of demographic expansion, but rather because of the growing share of small households (elderly people, young workers, students, divorced persons, and others) and because of the large number of foreign migrants who arrived after World War II (for example, a few tens of thousands of Netherlands nationals arrived from Indonesia; subsequently, a quarter of the population of

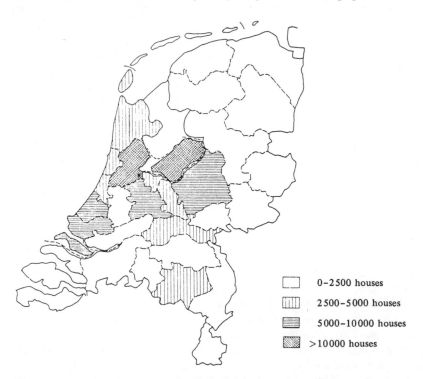

Figure 4. Housing shortage in The Netherlands, by region. (Source: Houben, 1980.)

Surinam has migrated to The Netherlands since the territory achieved
independence in 1975). The housing shortage is also partly caused by the
qualitative housing policy: urban renewal, slum clearance, and related
processes tend to contribute to the loss of available dwellings.

All this implies a continuing need for building space which, however, is
increasingly more difficult to find in the western Netherlands. This is
illustrated in figure 5, which shows that the scarcity of space is felt very
acutely here. The expansion of urbanized areas is, therefore, a matter for
careful consideration. There is also a great lack of recreational space in
and around the Randstad area. The agricultural 'Polder' landscape of the

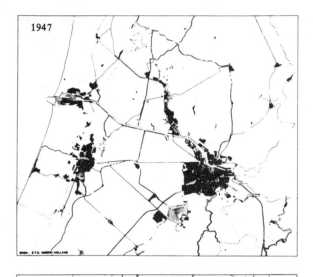

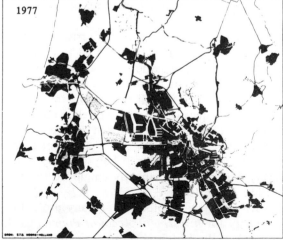

Figure 5. The agglomeration of Amsterdam, 1947-1977.

'Green Heart' inside the Randstad—apart from a number of lakes—does not lend itself to mass recreation. Furthermore, the damage to the environment (water, air, and noise pollution) is becoming serious in some areas. The main policy is to concentrate expansion in a limited number of growth towns and nuclei, most of which are located in overspill areas outside the 'Green Heart', such as Noord-Holland (north of Amsterdam), the southern Ijsselmeer Polders (that is, Almere new town), and western Noord-Brabant.

This policy has some disadvantages. The concentration of expansion in the growth towns has resulted in a large increase in the number of commuters. This is giving rise to great traffic problems, particularly during the rush hour. Another, longer-term, problem concerns the employment of the 'second generation' in the growth centres. It appears that the children of the commuters only look for work in their immediate environment, and not in the cities as their parents do. This is increasingly becoming a problem which is not yet solved.

Regional economic problems are seen as very important, especially in provinces outside the western Netherlands. However, provincial policy is mainly based on the financial instruments proposed by the central government. Two such important instruments should be mentioned here: Investment Premium Regulations (*Investerings Premie Regelingen*) and the Investment Account (*Wet Investerings Regeling*). The former are intended to promote the establishment and extension of enterprises in the economically weaker regions of the country. There are three forms of premium provided under the regulations.

(1) *Investment premiums for industrial enterprises* There are three ways in which such enterprises may qualify for an investment premium: first, by establishing themselves in a designated area (see also section 3); second, by moving from the Randstad into a designated area; and third, by extending inside a designated area. The premium amounts, at most, to 25% of the investment costs.

(2) *Investment premiums for 'booster enterprises' in the services sector* These are enterprises which are not, by their nature, bound to a specific place and the activities of which are at least regional in scale. The premiums for these projects are the same as those for industrial projects.

(3) *Premium regulations for Lelystad* The special regulations that apply to this new town in Flevoland are intended to improve the relatively weak economic structure of the town. There is one important difference between these and the first two types of regulations, in that an entrepreneur who establishes an industrial or service enterprise in Lelystad may obtain a premium of £10000 for every employee permanently employed in the enterprise who has gone to live in the town.

Any entrepreneur who is liable to pay income or company profit tax in The Netherlands may also qualify for *Investment Account Premiums*. In the 1978 Investment Account Act, the Dutch government earmarked a

very large sum of money to encourage investment in operating assets by business. It appears that this premium offers greater possibilities for the promotion of investment, and thus for combatting unemployment, than had been provided by the traditional tax measures before 1978. The Investment Account provides for a general basic premium and a number of additional premiums. The latter are paid over and above the basic premium when a business investment fulfils certain conditions. The following additional premiums are currently available:
an additional premium for small-scale enterprises;
an additional premium for investments necessitated by the removal of business activities to certain growth towns and nuclei;
an additional premium for investments in incentive and restructuring areas (see figure 3);
an additional premium for major projects involving relatively large investments.

In general, the system of additional premiums makes it easier to 'steer' investments to desired locations, thus making it possible to give an extra stimulus to those business investments which are seen as important in relation to improving the regional economic situation.

Another issue which has recently received much attention in regional planning is the natural environment. Recent regional plans in The Netherlands show a growing concern for environmental preservation and protection. This is partly due to the specific geographical situation in The Netherlands. Its maritime character, for instance, together with the low-lying situation of the coastlands, gives rise to a serious salt-seepage problem. The great European rivers, the Rhine, the Meuse, and the Scheldt, transport many waste products to The Netherlands. The high population density and associated intensive use of land also adversely affect levels of all forms of pollution. The prevailing southwesterly winds carry air pollution inland from the industries established in the coastal areas.

There is one province in The Netherlands, however, where the environmental problems are particularly noticeable. This is Limburg, where already a large part of the natural environment has been lost because of the extraction of gravel and marl. Since these are important raw materials for the building industry, for which no alternative materials are currently available, it is reasonable to expect that environmental deterioration of this area will continue for at least a few more years. However, opposition to this idea is becoming increasingly strong. As a consequence, the province has only been willing to produce a very global regional plan for the area, in which no verdict is given on this subject.

Another very important area from an environmental point of view is the Waddensee region. A major part of the Dutch Shallows is still hardly influenced by human activities. The area has a unique natural scenery. This is caused by its situation on the interfaces between water and land on the one hand, and between salt and fresh water on the other hand.

Its physical structure is composed of islands, sandbanks, gullies, mudflats, and estuaries. As such, it is the only large natural tidal area left in Western Europe. The Dutch Shallows also perform an important role from an international point of view by functioning as a nursery for shrimps and many fish species from the North Sea. It also serves a very important ornithological function, by providing a habitat for various species of geese, ducks, and gulls, for example. Recently, a joint plan has been developed for the Waddensee by the three provinces of Noord-Holland, Friesland, and Groningen. This plan is based on the goal of maintaining the high environmental and ecological qualities of this region. Consequently, various land-use regulations have been made, and intentions have been expressed to keep certain 'unfriendly' human activities, such as sailing and draining of effluent water, under control. However, in order to secure these intentions, many additional pieces of legislation, permits, and controls are needed. It is questionable whether the present Dutch legislation is effective in the prevention of environmental deterioration, as it only deals with primary effects, without taking into account the spatial distribution or cumulation of these effects. One important weapon to protect the environment may be the Environmental Impact Statements (see In't Anker and Burggraaf, 1979). However, these are also only project-oriented, and not region-oriented. This is an important shortcoming, as neglect of the spatial interrelation of various effects might lead to a hidden deterioration of the environment.

6 Concluding comments
Dutch regional planning can be considered to be in a transition stage from a 'blueprint' to a 'process' type of planning. Whereas the Dutch Physical Planning Act of 1965 was based on a 'blueprint' approach, the central government and the provinces are more and more inclined to adopt a more flexible, process-like approach. This sometimes leads to incompatibilities: for example, public participation on a national level is regulated by means of the so-called *Crucial Planning Decision Procedure* [Planologische Kern Beslissings Procedure; see Witsen (1977b)]. This procedure involves a rather time-consuming set of activities in order to arrive at an insight into the objections of the public to a proposed plan. However, this participation procedure is hardly compatible with other proposals of the central government to review their plans every five years and also to adapt their contents in the intervening period on the basis of monitoring results.

A similar picture can be seen in provincial planning. However, in this case the situation is even worse, because the regional plans only have to be reviewed every ten years. Thus the plans should contain guidelines for at least ten years ahead. That this is an impossible task is clearly illustrated in some provinces, where the recently approved regional plans already deviate from actual developments. Some provinces try to cope with this problem by using the power to elaborate plan details in accordance with article 4, clause 8, of the Physical Planning Act, which allows the detailed development of the regional plan by disaggregation into smaller plans that form part of the overall regional plan. This implies that, at present, there exists a tendency to make the regional plan more and more global, and to use clause 8 as a means of dealing with expected adjustments.

In section 4 it was pointed out that regional plans are increasingly becoming a means to coordinate the policies of the various levels of government. Consequently, the present tendency in Dutch regional planning is that provinces adhere more and more to a 'commitment-generating' bargaining approach to planning. As a result, some provinces have already abolished their research departments, and have integrated researchers with policymaking departments. This implies that the role of research is becoming far more limited than previously. A 'commitment-generating' approach without research support will almost always result in a satisfactory plan for those parties concerned. However, there will also be a high probability that the plan itself is intrinsically inconsistent; this will undoubtedly be revealed in the implementation phase (see Voogd, 1980). It is therefore necessary to shape new conditions under which a more planning-oriented type of research may be accepted as a useful activity, on a level with administration, bargaining, communication, and so forth.

Acknowledgement. The various maps are derived from a publication of the Dutch Ministry of Foreign Affairs, entitled *Compact Geography of The Netherlands*.

References
Bigham A, 1973 "Town and country planning of Britain and the Netherlands—a short comparison of law and administration" *Journal of Planning and Environment Law* (May) 15-32
Brussaard W, 1979 *The Rules of Physical Planning in the Netherlands* (Ministry of Housing and Physical Planning, The Hague)
Burke G L, 1966 *Greenheart Metropolis* (Macmillan, London)
Dekker A, 1980 "Analysis and integration in strategic planning: the case of the regional plan Twente" in *Strategic Planning in a Dynamic Society* Ed. H Voogd (Delft University Press, Delft) pp 35-47
Dunham D M, 1971 "The process of spatial planning in the Netherlands" in *Issues in Regional Planning* Eds D M Dunham, J Hilhorst (Mouton, The Hague) pp 115-123
Dutt A K, 1970 "A comparative study of regional planning in Britain and the Netherlands" *Ohio Journal of Science* 70 33-41
Hamnett S, 1975 "Dutch planning—a reappraisal" *The Planner* 61 (3) 102-105
Heywood P, 1970 "Regional planning in the Netherlands and England and Wales" *Journal of the Town Planning Institute* 56 178-195
Houben J M J F, 1980 "Regional uitkomsten R. W. B. O. 1977" *Stedebouw & Volkshuisvesting* 61 (11) 598-603
In't Anker M C, Burggraaf, 1979 "Environmental aspects in physical planning" *Planning and Development in the Netherlands* 11 128-145
Nijkamp P, 1977 "Urbanization policy: plans and possibilities" *Planning and Development in the Netherlands* 9 115-134

RPD, 1981 *Report on Regional Economic Policy* (Staatsuitgeverij, The Hague)

Van Meel W A S, 1977 "Regional plans" *Planning and Development in the Netherlands* **9** 169–185

Voogd H, 1980 "A plea for planning-oriented research" *Planologisch Memorandum 1980/12* Department of Urban and Regional Planning, Delft University of Technology, Delft

Wiggerts H, 1979 "Coastal management—the Dutch experience" *Planologisch Memorandum 1979/7* Department of Urban and Regional Planning, Delft University of Technology, Delft

Witsen J, 1977a "Some general aspects of the urbanization report of the Netherlands" *Planning and Administration* **2** 76–85

Witsen J, 1977b "Crucial physical planning decisions" *Planning and Development in the Netherlands* **9** 99–114

The Role of the State in Regional Development, Planning, and Implementation: The Case of Denmark[†]

H TOFT JENSEN
Roskilde University Centre

1 Introduction

In the post-1945 period the Danish state has exerted a growing influence on the Danish economy. For example, state expenditure increased from 20% of Gross National Product in 1955 to more than 45% in 1980 (Danmarks Statistik, 1966, pages 8 and 52; 1981, page 111), indicating the growing importance of the public sector in the mixed Danish economy. At the same time, the state has increasingly intervened in a number of ways in society. This growing intervention has become a focus of attention both in day-to-day political life and in debates about the character of the state, especially in relation to the ability of the state to secure the implementation of its plans for the economy in general and for regional development in particular.

In the literature, attention is increasingly drawn to the significance of state planning and regional policy for regional development and changes in the location of population and production (see, for example, NordREFO, 1978a). Emphasis is placed upon the influence of the central state and the local authorities on the levels of public service provision and living conditions in different parts of Denmark.

Despite the long-standing debate on uneven development ("imbalanced Denmark") in relation to living conditions, job opportunities and the availability of public services vary between regions (figure 1 shows the division into regions or 'counties'; figures 2–4 provide graphic examples; see also Guttesen et al, 1976; NordREFO, 1978b; Bogason and Villadsen, 1979; Friis, 1980; Jensen-Butler, 1980). For example, although manufacturing employment in Copenhagen fell both absolutely and as a proportion of the Danish total over the postwar period, in the mid 1970s almost 30% of all Danish manufacturing employment was located there (Friis, 1980, table 2A). However, the highest concentrations of manufacturing employment in relation to population were and still are to be found in parts of Jutland (see figure 3), and generally regions outside Copenhagen showed increases in absolute and relative levels of manufacturing employment over the postwar years. In contrast, state employment is concentrated most heavily in Copenhagen, with the lowest levels of state employment in proportion to population being found in south and west Jutland (see figure 4); moreover, these differences are also

† Translated by David Etherington, with assistance from Ray Hudson.

Note. The Region of the
Capital is made up of three
counties (Copenhagen,
Roskilde, and Frederiksborg)
and two cities (Copenhagen
and Frederiksberg)

0   50 km

Figure 1. Location of counties within Denmark.

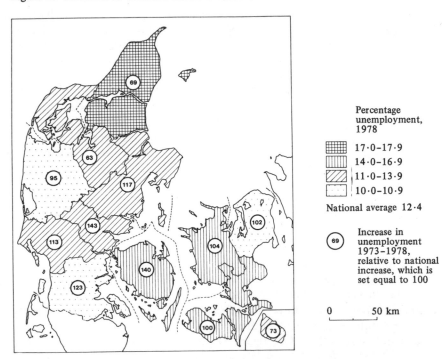

Percentage
unemployment,
1978

17·0–17·9
14·0–16·9
11·0–13·9
10·0–10·9

National average 12·4

Increase in
unemployment
1973–1978,
relative to national
increase, which is
set equal to 100

0   50 km

Figure 2. Unemployment rates, 1978, and percentage increases in unemployment
1973–1978. Source: Planstyrelsen (1980).

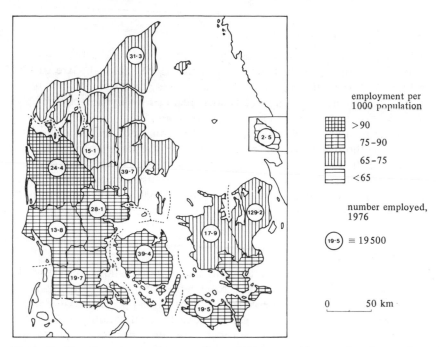

Figure 3. Manufacturing employment (in establishments with more than five employees) per 1000 population, 1976. Source: Planstyrelsen (1978).

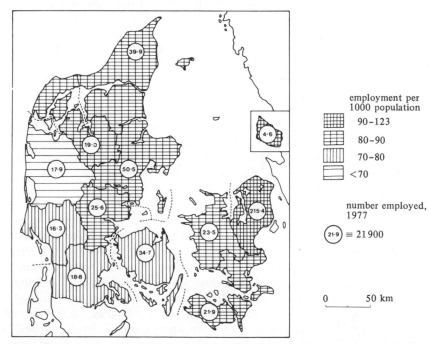

Figure 4. Central and local state full-time employment per 1000 population, 1977. Source: Planstyrelsen (1978).

indicative of the variation of accessibility of various medical and social services over the different regions (see Friis, 1980, table 7). Are such imbalances due to the fact that the state cannot or does not want to redress the balance? A study of Danish regional policy will perhaps give an indication as to how to answer this question.

An examination of regional policy and regional political strategies is difficult without a discussion of the nature of the state which is carrying out such policies and without an evaluation of the possibilities for planning and regional policy in advanced capitalist society in general. Thus, the following questions can be posed: what are the limits to policy implementation? Has the state a free hand when intervening in the economy, production, and regional development?

2 Bourgeois theories of the state
When capitalist economic development and resource allocation via market forces in themselves cannot secure balanced economic growth, this is because (according to orthodox bourgeois theories) profit maximisation by individual capitals does not necessarily lead to ideal conditions for accumulation in the economy as a whole or for expansion of capital in general. Alternatively, this absence of smooth growth is attributed to crises—the oil crisis, for example. Ultimately the results of such a pattern of development make it necessary for the state to intervene in order to counter the worst inequalities in society, for such imbalances are socially undesirable as well as unfavourable to continuing accumulation. This theory therefore conceptualises the state as an external force intervening within society.

One of the most influential theoreticians to point out the necessity for state intervention in a capitalist society was Keynes (1936). He emphasised the necessity for intervention through an economic policy designed to counteract cyclical fluctuations in the economy. Thus the state is to take an active part in the economy and these interventions are not simply determined by obvious social inequalities. There are two tendencies in the Keynesian conception of the state: "left" Keynesian and "right" Keynesian (see, for example, Scase, 1980).

Left Keynesianism (see, for example, Robinson, 1962) emphasises the role of financial policy through which the state has to take measures to control economic activity in periods of boom and slump. Left Keynesians maintain that intervention should take the form of planning and control— that is, should be aimed directly at influencing the economic structure of society by regulating the market mechanism. Left Keynesians hold that crises are primarily a result of "underconsumption". The possibility of counteracting crisis via increased consumption is primarily to be achieved through wage demands conducted by the unions, but the state, through a progressive redistribution of income, can also stimulate consumption and demand for investment goods, if necessary by means of an incomes policy.

The introduction of such a policy may, however, lead to real wage cuts, increasing income disparities, and a reduced level of effective demand.

Right Keynesianism emphasises more that the state should limit itself to policies that are directed at private industry and which encourage investment without the state's intervention in the structure of society (see, for example, Hansen, 1941).

There is, however, another school of bourgeois theory of the state and the economy: monetarism. The proponents of this view (for example, Friedman, 1969) argue that crises arise because the state has intervened too heavily in the economy and limited the free play of market forces. The state must ensure the free establishment of competitive conditions so that all kinds of monopolies (first and foremost the union monopoly over labour power) are abolished. The state should primarily control the money supply, and the market mechanism will guarantee the right direction of economic development.

3 Economic policy in Denmark

The question of which type of policy is implemented in Denmark is clearly relevant to understanding the attempts of the Danish state to influence regional development. It is characteristic of the Danish state that there has not been investment directly in productive industry and that its industrial grants policy has displayed little selectivity. Accordingly, it has no control over the development of industry in terms of sectors, and only limited control in terms of regions. Clearly there is a pro-industry policy which promotes investment (through low levels of taxation on profits, for example, or even through writing off investment against profits[1]) but it can be stated without exaggeration that no industrial policy exists in Denmark. The Danish state is one of the most liberal in Western Europe as far as industrial production is concerned. Production may be *regulated* to a certain extent, by means of environmental legislation, for example, but there is very little real *control*. This indicates that policy has a right-Keynesian character in terms of industrial policy, but there are left-Keynesian elements in social policy and provision of public sector services. Furthermore, to a very limited extent, there have been left-Keynesian features in a few of the attempts to formulate an incomes policy which have been made in recent years. It is important to bear this in mind in relation to the following analysis, in which the measures regulating private production will be outlined in order to throw light on the influence of the state on regional development and differences in Denmark.

[1] The general arrangement is that one-third of the value of an investment can be offset against profits in the first year after the investment is made, the remaining two-thirds in succeeding years. In specific cases, however, it is possible to reach a special arrangement whereby investments can be written off against profits *before* the investment is actually made.

However, before this analysis it is important to stress the necessity of challenging certain variants of bourgeois concepts of the state which deny the class character of the capitalist state [notably those of functionalist and systems theory, see, for example, Easton (1965)]. We shall therefore first consider Marxist theories of the capitalist state.

4 A Marxist theory of the capitalist state

The Marxist theory of the state emphasises the point that the state in a capitalist society must first and foremost guarantee accumulation by establishing conditions for continuous surplus-value production (for a review of the variants of Marxist theory, see Jessop, 1977). The state is not a neutral organ, but must act to ensure the reproduction of these conditions in order to maintain the capitalist mode of production. To ensure the existence of these general conditions of production, the individual state must continually create an environment in which capitals can maximise profit. The following six areas are important components of state intervention.

(1) *General conditions of production* These conditions are utilised by more than one individual capital and are not specifically designed to fulfill any single capital's needs. Another characteristic feature of the provision of general conditions of production is that it involves large-scale investments which are necessary for continuing accumulation but unprofitable in themselves to the individual capitals—thus the state, either partially or wholly, assumes financial responsibility for them. Often this type of investment is used up in production over a number of years. The classic examples of general material conditions of production are the transport network and infrastructure.

(2) *Natural resources* The recent rapid development in technology has meant that the provision of the general conditions of production has become far more complex than it used to be. The increase in the number of chemical products—by about 500 new products per year in Denmark— has resulted in the problem of the environment becoming a central issue. It has become increasingly necessary for the state to step in to regulate the relationship between individual capitals, because pollution arising from one capital's production process can adversely affect the profitability of other capitals, should access to unpolluted resources be made difficult.
    Another development which has led to the state being given new tasks is the recognised shortage of raw materials. As a result, it has assumed the role of regulator to a hitherto unprecedented degree. In this case it is not a question of profit but of access to resources. Given the anarchic character of capitalist production, the state has been forced to further the interest of capital in general in future surplus-value production by regulating the rate of depletion of raw materials, such as chalk and gravel in Denmark.

(3) *Labour power* The state must ensure the existence of a labour force which can be of use to capital both in general and specifically in the development and operation of new technology. It must thus ensure that the labour force possesses the necessary general qualifications, as regards both skill and discipline to production. Furthermore, it is important for the state to make sure that the required amount of labour power is available generally as well as in relation to the demands of specific sectors. Consequently, it must be responsible for the socialisation and reproduction of labour power and be able to establish the conditions for the mobilisation of an 'industrial reserve army'.

(4) *Law and judiciary* The state must ensure that private property relations—the basis for the possibility of surplus-value production—are not threatened. It must enforce law and order and thus be able to intervene when private property and free-market conditions are threatened. This applies in a variety of circumstances, ranging from a simple case of burglary to situations when mass class conflict gives rise to factory occupations.

(5) *National capital interests* Through its defence, currency, and trade policies, the state ensures that the interests of national capital are maintained and can expand further in the world market. In other words, the state pursues a foreign policy which furthers the interest of capital at the national level. It is therefore difficult to undertake a course of action which to any significant degree threatens general profitability.

(6) *Crisis management* The state intervenes when crises threaten the continued production of surplus value and thus attempts to implement economic stabilisation policies.

The six areas outlined above demonstrate the necessary functions of the state in capitalist society. There is a continuing debate within Marxist theory as to which of these six areas is actually most central and as to whether some of the areas discussed above can be combined together. However, the most important point is to stress that the prime function of the state in a capitalist country is to guarantee the conditions necessary for the production of surplus value and that it therefore has a clear class character. However, these various functions cannot always be successfully fulfilled. Law and order can be threatened by class conflict. Although the state may use direct force in repressing such actions as factory occupations and strikes, it has been known for the whole basis of state power to be successfully challenged by the working class. The state can also implement a short-term or long-term stabilisation policy, but the crisis nevertheless cannot be avoided as it constitutes an inherent and integral feature of capitalism. Nor is it always possible to make available the right quantity of labour power with the required qualifications, as the educational system cannot necessarily guarantee this as its output. It is also possible that the state's infrastructure policy has not been adequately adapted quickly enough to the general needs of capital.

Furthermore, the state can not automatically maintain these various functions. There are many barriers which must be overcome if overall economic and social stability is to be enforced: for example, the existence of a militant class conflict, class consciousness within state employees, and many more factors.

However, it is important to make clear that the state cannot ignore the fact that it must always seek successfully to intervene in these six areas if required, as well as to be aware of the fact that the state apparatus has considerable power and resilience and, at times, can reveal violent tendencies when conditions for surplus-value production are threatened. It is in this context that the following analysis of regional policy must be understood. It contains a short summary of the objectives of regional policy, a comprehensive introduction to the workings of regional policy and concludes with a brief summary of the essential elements of the analysis.

5 Regional policy in Denmark
5.1 The possibilities for regional policy
Peripheral areas, uneven regional development, and areas possessing significantly high rates of unemployment are topics that have been frequently discussed in the debate on the aims of Danish regional policy over the last twenty years. The aim of regional policy has repeatedly been stated[2] as an attempt to counteract the concentration of industry and employment in the Copenhagen region and in east Jutland, and at the same time to encourage industrial development and the creation of employment in the peripheral areas. Few people would disagree with objectives stated at this level of generalisation. A more precise definition of them requires clarification as to the means of implementation and the priorities of the objectives of regional policy in relation to other objectives of state policy.

In general, regional policy initiatives must be such that they do not contradict the requirements of capital accumulation. There are limits to the amount of tax revenue that can be used to pursue regional policy aims—the burden of taxation must not be increased to the point at which it threatens profitability of private capital. Furthermore, regulative measures must not be so extensive as to limit profit maximisation. Finally, the representatives of capital oppose the nationalisation of production in circumstances where there is the slightest chance of establishing private production and trade. In Denmark there is particularly strong opposition to any form of state intervention in manufacturing industry, so much so that state intervention is opposed even in those branches where it is not, at the time, possible for individual capitals to produce profitably.

[2] See, for example, the various *Annual Reports* of the Danish Regional Development Council, Copenhagen.

This opposition is orchestrated by the Federation of Danish Manufacturing Industry (Industriradet) and the Employers Association (Arbejdsgiverforeningen).

In a number of other European countries, for example Italy, France, Sweden, and the United Kingdom, the state has selectively supported industries experiencing difficulties and taken over industries that have not yielded sufficient profit. In the United Kingdom the state took over the unprofitable parts of the important basic transport, coal mining, and steel industries in order to preserve them. In Sweden iron ore mining and parts of the timber and paper industries have been taken over by the state. In recent years extensive financial support has been given to those shipyards in Western Europe which have not been directly taken over by the various national states. In Denmark the organised interests of industry and the centre and right-wing political parties have prevented state activity being extended into the sphere of production. There is even great opposition to giving special grants to industries and sectors which are experiencing difficulties, owing to a desire to maintain a clear division between the public and private sectors. Consequently such special grants are very limited—the two examples to date being the Burmeister and Wain shipyard, and Denmark's only steel works, at Frederiksberg.

In the long run, however, it is difficult to imagine that the Danish state is really incapable of implementing a coherent industrial policy, even if this should require sectoral and regional regulation of investment. Such a policy is feasible without limiting the possibilities for producing surplus value and realising profit by private capital. State subsidies to, or investment in, specific sectors would thus allow the release of private capital for more profitable investments.

5.2 Regional policy and regional political objectives

Regional policy is an expression of state policies directed towards the objectives of influencing the structure of industry, living conditions, and consequently the distribution of population in different regions. The desired direction of the development of industrial structure and living conditions is apparent from the objectives of regional policy. In discussion of these, the question of improved conditions for industry in the peripheral regions is of central importance. Uneven regional development has been a central issue in the debate. A frequently stated goal is to counteract the concentration of industrial development in the Copenhagen and east Jutland regions. More detailed regional policy objectives can be seen both in the legislation and in the *Declarations of Intention* which appear in the summary reports from the Environmental Ministry, especially in the annual National Planning Statements from the Environment Minister (Miljøministeriet, 1975–1980).

In recent years it has repeatedly been emphasised by central government that opportunities and resources are not available for development of services and job opportunities in all parts of the country. Therefore, the emphasis must be on so-called growth centres or regional centres if a more balanced regional distribution of service and jobs is to be achieved (see, for example, Miljøministeriet, 1979, page 7). Therefore the aim of official policy has been defined as counteracting regional inequalities in such a way as to further the development of industry and supply of services in growth centres of about 5000 inhabitants. In the discussions of regional policy objectives, it has been said that the strategy of growth centres enables the rationalisation of resources through the channelling of state subsidies, public investments, and the zoning of areas for investment in the peripheral regions. However, the improvement of services in towns with a population of 5000 takes place at the cost of public service provision in rural areas and in the smaller urban areas, as the level of service provision in the former is planned for a population of 20000.

Recently energy supply has become an issue of importance for the objectives of regional policy. In the National Policy Account of the Minister of Environment of December 1978 (Miljøministeriet, 1978, page 4) the supply of energy is emphasised in connection with the discussion of the various regional plans. The supply of natural gas means, according to the Minister, that decentralised growth is unacceptable. The growth of towns must be centred around natural gas pipelines so that investment can be optimally utilised.

So far we have pointed to the issues which have received special attention in the debate, without attempting an evaluation of the concrete importance of these for the policy that has been implemented. It has briefly been shown how general objectives of counteracting uneven regional development in Denmark have been drawn up so that an efficient use of resources could be achieved through a growth-centre strategy. This strategy can further be seen as a policy which primarily concentrates the efforts of regional policy on the use of public resources in such a way that industry benefits from them rather than on their use to maintain dispersed population in the peripheral areas. For example, the concentration of public services in towns with population of around 5000 leads to migration to these, mainly from surrounding villages and hamlets, and in this way to the creation of labour reserves in these centres.

5.3 Instruments of regional policy

The means available for influencing population and industrial structure differ between regions. Only some of these appear as direct measures of a regional political character; others have a more indirect regional political aim. Regional political measures are relatively few in number in Denmark. However, in recent years a number of reforms have been implemented which, in addition to their main purpose, have an effect on regional problems or can be used as instruments of control in regional policy. A considerable part of the reforms in the last decade was related to the public sector. Of these, the local government reform, which affected the size of municipal districts, the distribution of finance and responsibilities between the central and local state, and the planning legislation all have a bearing upon regional problems. These reforms have both a direct and an indirect regional political aim. The public sector reforms[3] have all been aimed at simplifying the administration and improving the possibilities for management *within* the public sector, but the possibilities for the state to control the private sector have not been improved.

In the above discussion of the characteristics of the Danish state, attention has been directed to the fairly clear line of demarcation between the private sector (which dominates completely in the sphere of production) and the public sector (which is confined to the reproduction of labour power through education, social, and cultural policy, and to maintaining the general material conditions for production).

The improved possibilities for management *within* the public sector and thus for influencing the conditions of reproduction in a regional context could possibly explain why this area has received most of the emphasis. In the following overview of regional policy the possible influencing of the location of employment is the point of departure. This is because the location of production and services forms the basic source of labour demand (and thus jobs) and this, in the long term, affects the geographical distribution of population. The growth of private motoring made long-distance commuting acceptable in the 1970s. Distances of up to 100 km between place of work and place of residence are common. This has meant that the definition and concept of the region has been enlarged, although it has *not* meant that residences and the location of production and services have become independent. Influencing the location of employment is therefore among the central preoccupations of regional policy.

A simple and rational means to this end is for the state compulsorily to direct employers to locate in specified areas where there is a shortage of a particular type of job. This policy could be used when a factory owner wishes to establish a new plant or expand or rebuild upon existing premises. Such directives, however, are difficult to make compatible with a capitalist economy which defines the limits to decisionmaking in Danish society. The assumption is that the individual capital has to take the risk involved in investments and that investments are only made when they are likely to make a profit.

There are many arguments put forward against state intervention. For example, why should a small engineering firm not be allowed to expand in the place where the firm is situated rather than having to move to an

[3] Local government reform that was carried out in 1970 reduced the number of municipal districts from about 1250 to 275. Subsequently, other reforms have altered the relations between central and local state (the municipal districts). One of the most important of these is the reform of the planning laws, carried out in 1972 (as it affected municipal districts) and 1973 (as it affected regions).

underdeveloped area such as Lolland (an island south of Sjaelland)? If this was made a condition of the permission to expand, the firm may abandon its plans altogether. The expansion would not take place, and 'society' would thus forfeit the jobs which it could have created. This kind of argument is built upon the assumption that job creation should only be a result of private investment. It fails to take into consideration the question of whether the location of the business would be optimal with respect to macroeconomic conditions. Regulating the location of large businesses by compulsory measures has been used in some European countries such as Italy and France (see Holland, 1977), but it has been possible to avoid such measures in Denmark. This corresponds quite well with a state policy with very few direct selective interventions in the private economy—that is, a right-Keynesian industrial policy. The instruments of state policy are indirect. State initiative is therefore limited to encouraging private capital to locate industry and services in certain regions by making it economically more advantageous to choose these rather than other regions. Conversely, by threatening to withhold investment the larger capitalist firms are able to locate where they like.

6 Analysis of the instruments of regional policy

It is evident from the above that the instruments of regional policy must be related to the location of jobs, as these are the basic condition for the long-term existence of population in a region. This relation can, however, be of a more indirect character. For example, the concentration of housing in certain areas can encourage the establishment of jobs there; likewise, setting up functional childminding facilities can induce the creation of work which uses female labour. Regional policy attempts to influence
(a) the location of employment;
(b) the location of labour power;
(c) the location of public services.
Establishing employment must be seen as the ultimate aim of regional policy. It is difficult to make an unambiguous division of the measures which influence location, according to the three areas above. Most of the subdivisions are made on the basis of regional policy legislation. Here we shall posit a subdivision of regional policy measures which takes as its point of departure the six areas described in the discussion on the Marxist theory of the state (section 4). Of these the first three areas are especially relevant as instruments of regional policy—that is, the general conditions of material production, resources, and labour power. In addition to these three areas there are two types of measures in regional policy which are not immediately related to them—general economic measures and information. We can therefore draw up the following five types of policy instruments:
(1) expenditure on the establishment and use of transport, communication, and infrastructure;

Danish regional development

139

Table 1. Areas and means of state intervention in current regional policy in Denmark.

Areas of intervention	Means of intervention				
	establishment and financing of infrastructure	regulation of land use	provision of qualified labour power	grants and investments	information
Location of workplace	infrastructure, public transport, communications, transport rate policy	regional plans, land-use zoning, preservation legislation, environmental protection laws, legislation on the rate of raw material extraction	regional development laws, subsidies for wages during training periods	Regional Development Act, investment subsidies, EEC Regional Fund, decentralisation of government activities	Industrial Location Bureau, National Planning Directives
Location of labour power		regional plans	work-assignment legislation, migration subsidies		work-assignment legislation
Location of public services		regional plans, local authority structures	technical colleges, specialist worker courses	block grant for local authorities, allocation of costs for state functions and the redistribution of responsibilities between local and central government	forecasts

(2) regulation of land use;

(3) provision of suitably qualified labour power;

(4) financial subsidies and investment grants;

(5) information about the possibilities in and character of different locations, as regards general conditions of production.

A number of different categorisations of regional policy interventions have been used—the classification of such interventions as restrictions, financial incentives, or information provision, for example. However, the restrictive measures are rarely used in Denmark and so are not employed in the classification used here.

This categorisation of measures and topics which are the object of regional policy can be set out schematically (table 1); this includes the legislation and measures related to regional policy. This is, not, however, to suggest that the legislation is in fact used for regional political ends.

The scope of this paper does not permit a proper analysis and evaluation of regional policy measures. In the following sections, however, comments will be made on some of the most important measures. Further information can be found in the sources referenced in the next section.

6.1 Infrastructure

An important precondition for the location of production is that a transport network is provided. Railways, roads, and harbours have played a significant part in the placing of production. Today, access to transport plays an equally important role for services and distribution.

In discussions of regional industrial structure in Denmark, it has frequently been emphasised that the good quality of minor roads (B roads) has been of great importance for the location of production (see Maskell, 1975). Most investments in the Danish transport network do not in fact support this view. On the contrary, where production and employment had been established, the transport network was then developed. In only a few cases was the transport network developed in order to attract industry to the peripheral regions. The good quality of the minor roads was originally a result of the orientation of Danish agriculture towards dairy produce and the consequent need for frequent transportation. Furthermore the political strength of the Danish agricultural sector influenced the establishment of a good transport system in the rural districts. This rural transport system has naturally been a good incentive for the location of various types of manufacturing industries in rural districts. But there are actually only a few examples where it was decided to develop a road system in Denmark with a view to promoting the development of a region. The outstanding example is the building of the road system in the southern part of Jutland after the First World War, although this was primarily a policy to attach to Denmark via promoting its development a region that had been under German government for about fifty years. However, public transport fare policies are to some extent employed in regional policy, so that, for example, location on a remote island does not create too severe an economic strain for local industry.

Other types of infrastructure investments that are important in relation to the location of production are energy supply, water supply, and purification plants. Cheap access to such facilities can be important in Denmark [on the question of infrastructure provision, see Bogason and Villadsen (1978)].

For the location of labour power and public services, access to public transport will probably assume a more important role in the future than it did in the 1970s, because of the changing energy situation. The price of land and houses is significantly lower in commuter villages and rural areas than in the towns and cities[4]. As a consequence, cheap housing outside existing urban areas has formed an important part of the residential pattern in the 1970s. This development presupposed individual transport. In spite of the low price of housing in rural areas, the cost of individual transport may reach such levels that housing in town areas with access to public transport could become characteristic of the residential structure in the 1980s.

Investments in infrastructure form a substantial part of the total public expenditure on construction. These investments could be directed more towards regional political purposes than has been the case in the 1970s. But individual capitals can feel more or less assured that sufficiently good infrastructure will be provided, irrespective of where production is located, as long as it remains within areas zoned for urban land use.

6.2 Land-use regulation

Zoning legislation divides the country into urban, rural, and recreational areas (*By Lov am og Landzone* number 315 of 1969, revised 1978). In rural areas only building for agricultural purposes is allowed. Therefore it is vital for the establishment of employment that areas for housing should be set out. In theory, the designation of land for urban uses in peripheral areas could be used as a means of forcing both employment and population into regions experiencing industrial decline and depopulation. But this is not in fact how zoning legislation is used. A shortage of land zoned for urban development in one region has often led to the designation of extra urban areas in that region. The competition between local authorities and county councils for job opportunities and taxpayers plays an important role in this.

[4] In 1980 the average price of residential building land and housing varied as follows (Danmarks Statistik, 1981):

	Land (DKr per m^2)	Housing (DKr per detached unit)
Copenhagen	230	720000
Towns with population >50000	160	550000
Towns with population <5000	85	400000

Note: £1 ≈ 14 DKr, January 1982.

Regional planning makes it in principle possible to coordinate the planning of public services. Such coordination has only been possible for a decade. The new framework created in the law on land and regional planning (*Lov om Lands og Regionplan*) of 1973, in combination with the planning laws governing sectors of the state such as schools and hospitals, allows regional political considerations to be made more central in the planning decisions of central and local authorities. In practice, decisions seem mostly to be reinforcing existing developmental tendencies rather than counteracting them. Public services are established where there is a preexistent need for them. Only to a limited extent are they provided ahead of demand with the intention of attracting population and industry to specific regions.

Regional planning is a coordinating mechanism for land use and public services for each county (*amtskommune*). Regional plans must be approved by the Ministry of Environment, which takes account of the national planning interest. Until now, these overall national and regional planning interests have largely been ignored.

6.3 The supply of labour power

As a result of the regional development legislation (*Lov om Egnsudvikling*) of 1972, it is possible to obtain subsidies in connection with the establishment and removal of plants. These subsidies can, for example, take the form of the wages paid by industries in regional development areas in a training period of, say, three months. The expenses involved in making the labour force qualified for the work in question are thus borne by the state. The work-assignment legislation (*Lov om Arbejdsformidlnag og Arbejdsløshedforsikring m.v.*) of 1971 makes it possible to give removal subsidies to workers unable to find employment in their regions of residence. This legislation also makes it possible forcefully to remove workers from regions with little employment. Unemployment benefit can be withdrawn if they refuse to take assigned work, even if the place of work is in another region.

The training of semiskilled workers has been of some importance for the requalification of labour power, especially in peripheral regions undergoing rapid changes in industrial structure. Whereas the regional development legislation and the training opportunities are aimed at making labour power fit for use in a specific region, the work-assignment legislation is aimed at facilitating the removal of labour power to the regions where it is needed (see Kirstein, 1974).

6.4 Financial opportunities

The Regional Development Act (*Lov om Egnsudvikling*), first passed in 1958 and since revised, most recently in 1972, is the most important instrument of policy in relation to finance (see Jørgensen, 1979). Several types of subsidies are given which reduce the cost of investment for private capital in regional development areas. Annual expenditure on regional aid in recent financial years amounts to about 350 million DKr (about £25 million), including expenditure through the EEC. This is equivalent to about 5% of total industrial investment in Denmark and about 25% of investment in regional development areas. This sum is, however, only about 0·2% of total state expenditure. Much larger sums are spent on investment in infrastructure and public institutions and, over a number of years, more money has been spent on public grants for house building. Nevertheless, it is still a great advantage to locate industry in areas where it is possible to obtain regional aid.

The most important aspect of the instruments of regional policy is that they are aimed at bringing together capital and labour power. Furthermore, labour power with insufficient qualifications can become qualified via state financial aid. Bringing together capital and labour power is of most importance in periods when there are shortages of the latter in certain regions. The Regional Development Act of 1958 was passed as the first signs of a shortage of labour power in Copenhagen became apparent. Its effect was to reduce competition for labour power in Copenhagen, by making it economically advantageous for industry to move to (regional) development areas. The counterpart of the regional development act is, as mentioned above, the 1971 Work-assignment Act. Characteristically, though, these two laws, which aim to bring together capital and labour power, function in different ways. The Regional Development Act, which is intended to move capital to labour, can offer subsidies, whereas the Work-assignment Act, aimed at moving labour to capital, can employ *coercion* (see Porsborg and Scocozza, 1973). This difference indicates that the state is primarily serving the interests of capital by supplying qualified labour power, with regional political objectives reduced to a subsidiary status.

Decentralisation of state institutions is included in this section because this is a case of investment being made which provides jobs outside of the central regions. Some relocations have taken place—for example, universities have been placed after considering regional political factors—but examples of this are few. In contrast, rationalisation and centralisation of public services (for example, the Danish rail service, the mail service, and customs and excise) counteract the objectives of the regional development plan; as a result, jobs in peripheral areas are lost.

Block subsidies are the grants which the local authorities receive from the central state independently of their expenses[5]. These are given according to 'objective criteria' such as regional area, population, and population age structure. The criteria make allowance for large municipal districts

[5] Local government in Denmark has three sources of finance for its activities. The most important is local rates, mostly raised via local income tax. The level of tax is decided locally and varies with income structure, the age structure of the population, and local activities. In 1975 it varied from 15% to 25% of taxable income. Second, a percentage refund is received from the central state for outgoings such as teachers' wages and expenditure on the road system. The third source is the block subsidies.

which are only sparsely populated, so that these districts receive more subsidies than densely populated districts. Local governments with a small tax base are thus able to establish better public services than their income from taxation would have allowed[6]. The result of this is that the block subsidies tend to promote decentralisation.

6.5 Information

In order to influence the location of industry, it has been suggested by the Danish Social Democratic Party that certain types of industry should receive some guidance about location before new plants were established or existing plants extended or moved. In the liberalist Danish society, this has resulted in industries *being able to* obtain guidance on location if they wish. It is voluntary for the industry to furnish the information which is essential for the provision of guidance to individual firms.

The large number of plans and forecasts being produced in connection with regional and sectorial planning (for a review, see Miljø ministeriet, 1980) contain information which should make it easier for industries to choose a location with access to the necessary material conditions of production, public services, and labour power. No doubt these sources of information are used to a certain degree, but their actual importance in location decisions is unknown.

7 Concluding remarks

In discussing the various regional policy measures, an attempt has been made to estimate the extent to which they are actually being used as regional political instruments with the objective of fulfilling the stated political aim of regional policy as set out in the 1958 Regional Development Act: the equalisation of regional differences in employment opportunities and living conditions.

It is not possible to reach a definitive conclusion on this, but for most measures there are reasons for their existence other than the objectives of regional policy. Regional aid furthers investment in the regional development areas, but other central state expenditure is concentrated in those overdeveloped areas from which a decentralisation of population and industry should take place according to the expressed intentions of regional policy. There are, therefore, a number of contradictory elements in state policy for the majority of state expenditure is in fact in areas where population and industry are already concentrated. This expenditure can be described as reinforcing the existing distribution of population and industry; it could be used for regional political ends, but this only happens to a limited extent. The location of state institutions could be used as part of a regional policy, but because of public expenditure cuts and the

---

[6] In Denmark the total amount of income tax paid to local government is slightly larger than that paid to the central state.

rationalisation of public services, the aims of the official policy are counteracted. A large number of the other measures of regional policy (see table 1) have only a very limited effect in fulfilling the main objective of regional policy. The measures which are mentioned in the table *could*, however, be used in regional policy.

7.1 Indirect instruments of regional policy

A large number of public policy measures which are not mentioned in table 1 also have consequences for the structure of regions without having an overt regional political aim. A few examples follow. When Denmark joined the EEC, the country came within the EEC sugar scheme. Consequently, the sugar works on Lolland-Falster were able to expand production. When restrictions were imposed on the import of ready-made clothing, the clothing industry in Jutland was the beneficiary. The general economic climate also has an important effect on regional development— thus when the price of petrol goes up, it becomes more expensive to live far away from your place of work, even though the price of land is much lower in the country than in the cities. The various housing subsidy schemes could have been used with a regional political effect but there has been no regional differentiation in the possibilities of obtaining public subsidies for house building. Consequently, the subsidies have actually been a centralizing factor in the distribution of population, for they have increased opportunities for establishing working-class housing in the towns.

All things considered, it should be emphasised that state policies which have regional consequences are far more comprehensive than those included in table 1. If Denmark is compared with Norway and Sweden, it can be seen that there is greater expenditure in the latter two countries directed towards actual regional political objectives than is the case in Denmark. This may be a result of the difference between the policies of Denmark and those of Sweden (see section 5.1) and Norway. Regional differences are much bigger in Norway and Sweden, however, than in Denmark. There has, in certain periods, been a danger that large areas in Norway and Sweden would become depopulated if a regional policy which tried to reverse this process was not implemented; one indication of this is the average population density—13 and 18 people per square kilometre respectively, which may be compared with a figure of 120 per square kilometre in Denmark. Furthermore, the two countries are geographically so big that it is more difficult to establish large-scale commuting to a small number of growth centres. In Denmark it is possible to travel very far within the country in an hour's drive.

7.2 Regional imbalances

From an examination of the most recent maps of the spatial distribution of unemployment, it is possible to get a good impression of the actual regional imbalances in the country. Despite the growth in unemployment rates in all areas, it is apparent that drastic changes have taken place within the country over the past ten years: a number of the areas which formerly exceeded the national rate of unemployment are now among those with the lowest unemployment rates, while areas which used to be below the national average now exceed it (see figure 2). Unemployment in the Sønderjylland and western Jutland (Ribe, Ringkøbing) was previously above the national average, today it is below average. The Copenhagen area, which had a rate of unemployment far below the national average, now has a rate very close to the average. Nordjylland, on the other hand, has always had the highest proportion of unemployed. Regional imbalances clearly still exist in Denmark, but they have changed. Figure 3 further illustrates this changing situation, showing the decline in manufacturing employment in Copenhagen with the simultaneous growth in central and local state employment there. Further, it is certain that the overall rise in unemployment has caused regional policy issues to recede into the background, while the debate about the generally high rate of unemployment has become the focus of interest.

7.3 Objectives and limitations

A closer look at the individual measures of regional policy in Denmark reveals three main policy objectives, which can be summarised as follows.

(1) Regional policy tries to bring together capital and qualified labour power. This is made possible via the Regional Development Act, the Work-assignment Act, the education measures mentioned in table 1, and the provision of information. The entire infrastructure is also of importance in this bringing together of capital and labour. Their meeting could be seen as the main objective, whereas the development of regions is a minor one.

(2) Regional policy tries to prevent regional differences of a social character from arising. This objective is pursued, for example, by means of block grants and state reimbursements of local authority expenditures. These schemes function in such a way that the economy of the individual local district does not depend exclusively on the tax income of the local authority. Districts which are economically weak are favoured through these schemes, so that taxpayers' money is actually transferred from districts with a high average taxable income to those with a low income.

(3) Regional policy aims at the more efficient use of resources—land, public expenditure, and raw materials. The entire body of planning law is central in this context, for it is possible by means of this to direct the use of land so that particular activities are prohibited in certain areas. This happens either in order to prevent these activities from destroying the possibilities of other activities in a certain area, or in order to stop large-scale public expenditure becoming necessary as a result of particular land uses in certain areas. In recent years, it has been pointed out that dispersed population growth is too costly because it requires large public investments which can not be fully utilised.

Regional policy measures can be used to fulfill the objectives of regional policy (and will to some extent work in the direction of these goals if the overall development of the economy is working in the same direction). Regional policy measures cannot take precedence over national economic policy which must be implemented in an attempt to manage the booms and crises inherent in the capitalist economy, but the lack of state influence on industrial location should be emphasised as a major limitation on the ability of the Danish state to implement a real regional policy.

References

Bogason P, Villadsen S, 1978 *Regionalpolitikkens Verkmidler og Problemer* Institut for Samsfundsfag, University of Copenhagen, Copenhagen

Bogason P, Villadsen S, 1979 "Regional industrial development: decentralisation or centralisation? The case of Denmark" paper prepared for the EGPA meeting on Regional Industrial Development, Palermo, 15–18 October 1979

Danmarks Statistik, various dates *Statistik Tiasoverigt* (Danmarks Statistik, Copenhagen)

Easton D, 1965 *A Systems Analysis of Political Life* (University of Chicago Press, Chicago, Ill.)

Friedman M, 1969 *The Optimum Quantity of Money* (Aldine, Chicago, Ill.)

Friis P, 1980 "Regional problems in Denmark: myth or reality?" *Dunelm Translations* (4), Department of Geography, University of Durham, Durham, England

Guttesen R, Hansen F, Nielsen B, 1976 "Regional development in Denmark" *Geografisk Tidsskrift* **75** 74–87

Hansen A, 1941 *Fiscal Policy and Business Cycles* (Greenwood, New York)

Holland S (Ed.), 1977 *Beyond Capitalist Planning* (Basil Blackwell, Oxford)

Jensen-Butler C, 1980 "Capital accumulation, regional development and the role of the state" working paper 9, Geographical Institute, Åarhus University, Åarhus, Denmark

Jessop B, 1977 "Recent theories of the capitalist state" *Cambridge Journal of Economics* **1** 353–373

Jørgensen E J, 1979 *Støtte til Brancher og Omrader; Danmark* (Institut for Fremtidsforskning, Copenhagen)

Keynes J M, 1936 *The General Theory of Employment, Interest and Money* (Macmillan, London)

Kirstein P, 1974 *Abejdsmarkedpolitik* (Behlinske Forlag, Copenhagen)

Maskell P, 1975 "Transportsektoren in Danmark 1850–1970 med saerlight henblik pa dens betydring for den regionale udvikling" *Fagligt Forums Kulturgeografiske Haefter* **4** 71–116

Miljøministeriet, 1975–1980 *Landsplanredegørelse* (Miljøministeriet, Copenhagen) [published annually]

NordREFO, 1978a *Målkonflikter i Regionalpolitikken* (Nordic Commission on Regional Policy Research, Stockholm)

NordREFO, 1978b *Information on Regional Policy and Regional Policy Research in Nordic Countries* (Nordic Commission on Regional Policy Research, Stockholm)

Planstyrelsen, 1978, Planstyrelsen, Holbegs Gadi 23, 1057 Copenhagen

Planstyrelsen, 1980, Planstyrelsen, Holbegs Gadi 23, 1057 Copenhagen

Posborg R, Scocozza L, 1973 *Arbejdsløs, Fredløs* (Røde Hane)

Robinson J, 1962 *Essays in the Theory of Economic Growth* (Macmillan, London)

Scase R (Ed.), 1980 *The State in Western Europe* (Croom Helm, London)

Regional Planning—Regulation or Deepening of Social Contradictions? The Example of Fos-sur-Mer and the Marseilles Metropolitan Area[†]

D BLEITRACH, A CHENU
University of Provence

Abbreviations used in this paper

BERIM	Bureau d'Études et de Recherches Industrielles de Martigues
BP	British Petroleum
CFR	Compagnie Française de Raffinage
DATAR	Délégation à l'Aménagement du Territoire et à l'Action Régionale
FDES	Fonds de Développement Économique et Social
FNAT	Fonds National d'Aménagement du Territoire
GSON	Groupe de Sociologie Urbaine de Nanterre
INSEE	Institut National de la Statistique et des Études Économiques
HLM	Habitations à loyer modéré
MAEB	Mission d'Aménagement de l'Étang-de-Berre
OREAM	Organisation pour les Études d'Aménagement de l'Aire Métropolitaine
ORGECO	Organisation d'Études Coopératives
SACILOR	Société des Aciéries Lorraines
SDAU	Schéma Directeur d'Aménagement et d'Urbanisme
SEDES	Société d'Études pour le Développement Économique et Social
SEMA	Société d'Économie et Mathématiques Appliquées
SETEC	Société d'Études Techniques Économiques
SNCF	Société Nationale des Chemins de Fer Français
SOLLAC	Société Lorraine de Laminage Continu
SOLMER	Société Lorraine et Méridionale de Laminage Continu
UDR	Union des Démocrates pour la République
USINOR	Union Sidérurgique du Nord
ZAC	Zone d'Aménagement Concerté

1 Planning and regional development policies in France

The overall policy of regional development in France today is characterised by a fundamental contradiction. On one hand, as an element of the economic policy of the state, regional planning must, as far as possible, satisfy the interests of the fraction of the dominant class which is in power; for this reason, state credits must contribute to the reproduction of the productive forces by maximising the short-term profits of the large

† Translated from a paper originally presented at the Northwest European Multilingual Regional Science Association, Louvain, Belgium, 1974, published in *Environment and Planning A* (1975), volume 7, pages 367–391.

industrial and financial groups. On the other hand, planning must be an element in the support of the existing social structure; hence it must attempt to limit, by ideological means and if necessary by material sacrifices, those political and other protest movements which are liable to question the position of the dominant class.

These two types of demand are contradictory. The reproduction of the forces of production according to the interests of dominant groups tends to reinforce the basic inequalities of the productive forces as a whole: the only sectors which develop are the most competitive in relation to the state of the market. Intersectoral inequalities are reinforced as less profitable sectors are abandoned, while industrial and financial concentration increases. Inequalities within the labour force are also reinforced; workers without professional training, or with training insufficient to meet the needs of the moment, are confined to the most devalued jobs or completely disregarded.

When projected onto the national scale, this uneven development is expressed in sharp contrasts between regions: industrial expansion is concentrated in the few areas which are best equipped in terms of current production techniques; the regions where past industrialisation produced an organisation of production which is no longer competitive (mining areas in particular) are experiencing a serious crisis. The domination of the economy by finance capital (the fusion of industrial and bank capital)—a domination giving rise to a situation of great concentration and which favours further concentration—results in the multiplication of head offices in the big cities (and in France, Paris in particular). Because of this the majority of the rural areas today seem even more abandoned than they used to. Within the labour force this kind of process provokes opposition which, when given an organised expression, threatens the existing social order.

This is why regional planning must be, simultaneously and contradictorily, *action for* the immediate profit of large industrial and financial groups, and *action against* that immediate profit, insofar as the maintenance of the unity of the social formation makes it necessary to satisfy pressing claims by sacrificing credits which might have been more directly profitable.

This contradiction is occasionally reflected in the regional planning documents themselves. Thus one can read in the report by the Commission on 'Aménagement du Territoire' on the direction of the Sixth Plan (DATAR, 1970, pages 95, 96):

> "It is necessary ... to link those actions which promote training and the organisation of modern activities in regions which are already capable of receiving them, with the interventions intended to allow regions, which at present are not yet ready, to eliminate this backwardness within the time available. It seems all the harder to reach this equilibrium, since the principal objective proposed for the French economy by the Plan is international competitiveness, which must be sought by intensifying efforts to adapt regions. Unfortunately, geographical facts and the uneven spatial distribution of the population, which has a very low density in comparison with competitors, have the effect of reducing to a very few the regions which are capable, either at present or within the short period of the Plan, of really effective contributions to this competitive spirit ...".

Massé (1968, page 108) expresses the same contradiction : ral
terms: "One cannot retain the optimistic thesis of natura!
according to which the maximum development of each reg sure
the maximum development of the whole".

Such clear statements of the dilemma at the very heart o: em
of regional planning are, in fact, exceptional in the official te
usual basis for the ideology of spatial planning consists of a de ne
contradictions between the search for 'competitiveness' and the ¿neralised
development of productive forces and of regions. The support given by
the state to the most competitive firms in regional planning, more than in
any other form, must appear as a contribution to the general interest.
Interventions motivated by the desire for profit, which can be designated
schematically as interventions of an *economic* nature, must appear to be
motivated by the desire for general welfare—schematically, as interventions
of a *social* kind. In fact, planning expresses the predominance of the
economic over the social sphere, but at the ideological level it claims a
congruence of the economic and the social—the universal presence of
social preoccupations in economic interventions.

Indeed, this idea of state intervention motivated by general interest
underlies not only the logic of regional planning, but also that of the
whole of state policy, whatever the sector of intervention. However, in
regional development it takes on a special significance: for example,
whereas the theme of competitiveness (and its corollary, the selectivity of
state intervention) can acquire a certain ideological force in the Sixth Plan,
insofar as the accelerated liquidation of unprofitable enterprises appears to
be a public welfare measure, its translation into regional planning terms—
the closure of major enterprises in regions where the redeployment of
workers is difficult or the withdrawal from regions less well-endowed in
terms of the competition between large industrial groups—constitutes, on
the contrary, a dangerous idea, an ill-conceived expression of the law of the
strongest that is too direct and cynical. This is why the prime requirement
of the Plan cannot be expressed in such words in regional development
policies, which must appear more willing to offer help to poorly endowed
regions than the Plan is to assist marginal enterprises. A call for the
abandonment of a region has a more dramatic sound than the prospect of
the failure of a badly run or obsolete business. In addition, at least at the
stage of plans and declarations of intent, regional planning gives greater
prominence to *social* considerations than does the Plan.

Far from revealing a contradiction between competitiveness and
harmonious development of the regions, the explicit logic of regional
planning postulates congruence between these two kinds of aims. We
come across it in all the speeches and official plans and at all the different
stages of regional planning in France. We can follow it in official texts
from the first stages of decentralisation, marking the birth of regional
planning at the beginning of the 1950s, to the current policies of promoting

métropoles d'équilibre (Marseilles, for example) and to the development of highly competitive industrial poles (such as the Fos complex).

The First Plan for Regional Development (Ministère de la Construction et Urbanisme, 1950), associated with the name of Eugène Claudius-Petit, expressed two dominant themes: on the one hand, the insertion of town-planning proposals into wider schemes taking account of the regional and national urban hierarchies; on the other, the encouragement of industrial development in the provinces. The first theme represented a reaction to urban reconstruction activities, then thought of as the simple reproduction of prewar spatial structures. It established a first link between urban and regional planning. The second theme came as a response to the rising criticism of the growing inequality in development between Paris and the provinces. The Fonds National d'Aménagement du Territoire (FNAT), intended in particular to finance industrial zones in the provinces, was created in the same year.

The first decentralisation measures had no practical result in countering the effects of the Monnet Plan of 1946, which, "impervious to an astonishing degree to considerations of spatial order ... contributed greatly to the accentuation of regional disparities by concentrating basic investment in the already developed poles; essentially the Paris basin, Nord and Lorraine" (Labasse, 1966, page 157). In fact, the first Four-year Plan, which arose from the incapacity of the private sector to reestablish the industrial potential of the country, had as its prime objective the *quantitative* increase in the level of industrial production[1], and under these conditions had its greatest effectiveness in the most unequal development of productive forces.

The policy of decentralisation hardly contributed anything to the general development of provincial regions in its first decade. The great majority of job relocations occurred in the Paris basin. So, between 1955 and 1967, the Provence–Côte d'Azur region received 1·3% of the jobs decentralised, although the area represented 8% of the population of the provinces and suffered from a marked underindustrialisation. This was because social considerations—the creation of jobs in regions relatively short of them—which motivated the financial assistance to industrialists, give way in practice to economic ones—the need for a spatial redistribution of sectors of activity. Access to the collective advantages provided by the capital city is necessary to the key sectors in which both research activity and highly qualified personnel are very important. This should not be limited by the cramping presence of too many traditional industries such as engineering and textiles. These very industries are equally concerned to leave Paris, where labour costs are higher than elsewhere. They can also

[1] "France entered the war with an industrial potential inferior to that of Germany, Britain or America, and during the war period this capital was worn out; hence the extreme poverty of France in terms of physical plant and equipment in 1944" (Gruson, 1968, page 39).

take advantage of a transfer to modernise their plant, and the difference in price between sites sold in Paris and those bought in peripheral regions provides an appreciable increase in surplus value. Under these conditions, the 'indicative' credits granted by FNAT only act as supplementary reasons for moving, constituting 'premiums' in the true sense of the word. However, the logic of the system means that these indications only operate within the limit of the maximum advantage which an enterprise can gain from moving, hence the failure of the decentralisation policy in the provinces as a whole and the vast influx into the Paris basin.

Although the effects of the decentralisation policy do not correspond to its objectives, the existence of a limited, but effective, process of 'rationalisation' of state interventions should not be denied. The establishment of a regional planning policy goes hand in hand with the development of the theme, which is first and foremost ideological, of the coherence of state intervention and the ability of the social formation to overcome the problems posed by its spatial distribution. This theme is ideological not because it attempts to substitute the myth of coherence for the reality of incoherence, but because it disguises the nature of the process of 'rationalisation' which takes place.

The plan, as Herzog (1971, page 77) has shown, is an instrument for unifying fractions of the dominant class and results in the effective organisation of a programme for certain activities, an agreement within the dominant class on the principal aspects of general policy; this agreement implies an attempt at analysing the overall coherence of state intervention. It is this partial coherence that is reflected as total coherence in the ideological theme of a planned French economy.

To analyse the 'coherence' of planning practices in a capitalist system, it is necessary not only to compare them with the all-embracing and ideological language of declarations of intent, but also to understand the nature of the state which establishes these planning practices. These two levels— practice and ideology—remain largely phenomenal unless the state is taken as the real object of analysis. In certain respects, state intervention in the economic sector is relatively recent. Most observers are agreed that it goes back to the great crisis of 'overaccumulation'[2] of the 1930s. Since then, it has been possible to observe the development of both industrial and financial concentration to previously unheard-of extents and the role of the state—in the economic sector in particular. State intervention in the economy is no longer a matter of contingency (as in a war economy, for example), but is structural: it has become necessary for the expanded reproduction of the relations of exploitation. In this phase of the capitalist mode of production there is a chronic overaccumulation of capital, which calls for a profound transformation of capitalism: certain

[2] "*The overaccumulation of capital* means the *excessive accumulation of capital* in a given capitalist society, in relation to the limits of the total sum of surplus value, or of profit which can be obtained to valorise that capital" (Boccara, 1966, page 24).

sections of social capital are permanently *devalorised* by the intervention of the state[3].

Public financing represents a devalorisation as.

"public or semipublic funds are lent at rates which are clearly below market rates, or are even given without charge. Public or nationalised enterprises are managed, on the whole, on the basis of very low profit or even deficit, in spite of their material expansion. We say nothing of the nonremuneration of investment in public works in infrastructure for production .... As a matter of fact, at this level the devalorisation of capital seems to be more of a *form of expression*, indicating the common basis of operating rules of the institutions benefiting from public finance or the organisations distributing it" (Boccara, 1966, page 30).

The branches in which fixed capital is extremely important, which are also those where the indivisible and collective character of installations is particularly evident, or those indispensable to national production, will quite naturally be the ones in which the state intervenes preferentially. This is the case, for example, in the infrastructure of exchange or in key sectors such as iron and steel production.

The object of state intervention in the economy is not the 'rationalisation' of growth; the state does not intervene *from outside* to impose the general interest on the sum of private interests of civil society, but its intervention has become necessary for the reproduction of the social relationship of exploitation of the capitalist mode of production. In this framework, the notions of 'coherence' or 'rationality' of planning take on other meanings: they refer to a programming of the state interventions which have become indispensable to the reproduction of capital. This programming presupposes a double process of rationalisation: the first is linked to the establishment of a unity within the dominant class, making it possible to define a general interest of that class; the second is linked to the development of the technical instruments necessary to the effectiveness

---

[3] In the case of overaccumulation of capital, if we have, for example, a capital K giving a global profit ΔK, the accumulation of additional capital K_1 cannot produce any additional profit ($\Delta K_1 = 0$); if K_1 is nevertheless accumulated and attempts are made to valorise it, there is an excess of capital equivalent to K_1. Three solutions are then possible:
1 part of the capital corresponding to K_1 returns a nil profit;
2 part of the capital, eventually less than K_1, is valorised at a negative value;
3 part of the capital, greater than K_1, is valorised at a reduced rate.

These three solutions correspond to what is called the *devalorisation* of capital. This simple example illustrates that state investments in the economic sector which return no profit constitute a devalorised fraction of total social capital, which allows the rest of the capital to go on accumulating. To say that state investments allow the *rest* of the capital to accumulate is partly inexact, as these interventions combine with a transformation of capitalism by concentration and creation of monopolies in certain sectors at the expense of others, through a form of devalorisation.

of this programming (techniques of gathering and processing 'economic and social information').

It is possible to follow the limited, but effective, progress of this double process. In the case under consideration, the desire for coherence in, on the one hand, the territorial distribution of activities and people, and on the other, the growth of productive forces, at first develops separately. We have noted how far the first attempts at regional planning in France were linked to concern with town planning; from this they borrow a Utopian and *social* aspect which is in contradiction with the logic of a national plan. However, we have also seen that it was the same logic that imposed constraints upon regional planning. Convergence is achieved by means of the progressive submission of the objectives of regional planning to those of the plan; there the process of 'rationalisation' is still limited, but effective. Territorial levels had not begun to be considered in the plan until 1955, when "Regional plans for economic and social development and regional planning" appeared, albeit for certain regions only. It was not systematised until 1962 (after the harmonisation in 1960 of regional administrative boundaries), with the creation of regional operational divisions. Once again, this spatial involvement of the plan was less a reflection of the introduction of regional planning considerations into its preparation than of the capacity of the planning apparatus to programme interventions that were differentiated and particularised according to enterprises or groups of enterprises.

Whereas the decentralisation policy of the 1950s and early 1960s contributed to the profitable relocation of numerous enterprises, a balanced assessment would also note the discrepancies between its results and the clear objectives which it had been given. It was not coordinated with major road investments or with rural development policy; and, above all, it took no account of the dynamics of regional units. With the problem fairly crudely conceived as a simple imbalance between Paris and the provinces considered as an undifferentiated whole, the essential result of the policy was a greater spread of industries through sprawl within the Paris basin. It succeeded neither in limiting the disparities of growth between Paris and the provinces, nor in sparking off the development of regional centres of activity with their own dynamism. It thus only partially fulfilled its role of reducing tensions in areas of underemployment. Regions became even more clearly the appropriate foci both for protest movements[4] and for the large industrial and financial groups seeking, within the framework of the European Economic Community (EEC), to obtain more selective support from the state—support which could be centred on a small number of industrial poles where the most powerful firms

---

[4] The abandonment of certain industrial regions, in particular those which have developed close to former coalfields, gave rise to vast protest movements uniting not only workers, but sometimes traders and even agriculturalists as well.

were already largely established or intended to be (the Paris region, Dunkirk, the Rhône–Alps region, and Fos-sur-Mer, for example).

It was under these conditions, from 1962 to 1965, that the two main thrusts of current regional planning policy took shape: firstly, the development of industrial poles capable of being competitive on world markets; secondly, the promotion of *métropoles d'équilibre*. This redefinition of objectives went hand in hand with the increasing importance attached to regional planning as central to the whole range of state interventions. The creation in 1963 of the Délégation à l'Aménagement du Territoire et à l'Action Régionale (DATAR), placed under the direct control of the Prime Minister, meant the movement of regional planning affairs from the Ministère de la Construction et Urbanisme and reflected at the institutional level the all-embracing, and subsequently interministerial, character of regional policy. It came at a moment when effective control of the organisation of space—which, unlike other economic goods, is not indefinitely producible—was becoming essential because of the very precise locational demands of certain industries[5] and the critical situation in traffic, housing, and facilities in the majority of great conurbations.

The policy of developing industrial poles which are competitive on international markets has a relatively modest place in the body of regional planning policies as they are defined in the official texts. The policy of organising 'high-density integrated complexes' which depended on industrial poles (two of which—Paris and Lyons—were nebulous urban areas, and three—Dunkirk, Le Havre, and Fos—were localised coastal industrial zones) appears to be one among a number of others. The priority attached to it became apparent only indirectly, not just from the proposals for regional planning, but through the formulation of the priorities of the Sixth Plan (Ministère de la Planification, 1970, pages 59, 60):

> "There are few fundamental choices on which the Sixth Plan will actually depend:
> 1. *The first priority is undoubtedly the opening of our economy to the outside world*[6]. The government trusts that the Sixth Plan will confirm this decisive choice; not that it seems conceivable to reconsider it but, on the contrary, because it seems vital to deduce all its consequences—in a word, the essential thing is the need for competitiveness".

It would be difficult to express more directly the role of state intervention in reinforcing the inequalities of development: public credits must, as a matter of priority, contribute to the growth of those industries which are best placed in regard to international competition. It amounts to making selective interventions in favour of the strongest of the industrial and financial groups [on the development of the selective nature of state intervention, see Herzog (1971)]. Geographical concentration, to a large

[5] This is the case, for example, of the petroleum industry in the Fos area: well before the creation of the Fos complex, Esso, wishing to establish refineries at Lavéra, ran into the problem of the congestion of that port. Esso was the first enterprise to invest at Fos, as early as 1966.

[6] Our italics, DB and AC.

extent, corresponds to economic and financial concentration: broadly speaking, the location of the plants of the largest enterprises are limited to the industrial poles mentioned above. In terms of regional planning, the requirement of 'competitiveness' takes the form of assigning a privileged development status to the strongest and most modern industrial poles; this is the case in practice, even if in the official texts it is only presented as one option among many.

In fact, if the chapter devoted to regional planning in the report on the options of the Sixth Plan gives a low priority to the organisation of highly industrialised complexes, the introductory chapter defines a very clear difference between the industrialisation of 'high-density zones' and 'the rest of the country' (Ministère de la Planification, 1970):

> "the extensive high density zones, that is, the whole of the Paris region and the lower Seine, the Rhône region and the Mediterranean coast beyond it, and the Nord [region], which in 1965 contained 13 million, 8 million, and 4 million inhabitants, respectively, lend themselves to the establishment of very large-scale, interrelated enterprises, employing a large, diversified work force and using a heavy-duty transport system. In other parts of the country, the industrialisation effort should favour the establishment of medium-sized enterprises, in proportion to the labour available in urban centres and in the surrounding rural area"[7].

The distinction between small or medium-sized centres of industrialisation, which are encouraged in predominantly rural regions, and powerful industrial poles, few in number but receiving massive state aid, was formulated as early as 1965 by the Minister responsible for DATAR, Olivier Guichard:

> "The establishment of these structures (vast industrial sites which have all the facilities and answer the needs of large modern industries) represents an investment which can be very considerable and whose choice can pose a problem, made all the harder by the fact that some of them will be little used for a longer or shorter time, thus tying up financial resources which will not be available elsewhere. This risk must be taken for important industrial operations" (Guichard, 1965, page 44).

This transition from undifferentiated support given to the dominant class as a whole (which is what aid for industrial decentralisation implied) as the main emphasis of regional planning policy, to selective intervention in favour of the most competitive groups (generally speaking the most highly concentrated groups and thus the most monopolistic), which is implied by the policy of encouraging key activities in the high-density zones, expresses the establishment of the monopolistic fraction of the dominant class as politically dominant. To say this means, in this particular case, not only that this dominant fraction is capable of directing the plan—an instrument for the concentration of capital—towards its own fractional interests, but also that it is liable to be supported by state

[7] It should be noted that the Italian government, in its attempt to solve the social problems of the Mezzogiorno, has chosen to encourage the establishment of very large enterprises in this region, a policy which is the reverse of that expressed here.

intervention *as a whole*, even that not *directly* aimed in its favour, to ensure its own development. In fact, regional planning, in conjunction with the plan, in essence represents the programming of state intervention related to the reproduction of fixed capital. The takeover by the state of a large part of this fixed capital encourages investment by large monopolistic groups in sectors which they would not otherwise consider because of the length of time that capital remains tied up (in land or transportation, for example). The scale of the programmes, as we shall see in the case of Fos-sur-Mer, acts in favour of groups which are already concentrated and accelerates this concentration.

At the level of the explicit logic of regional planning, this transition from undifferentiated support for the dominant class to selective intervention was justified with an argument which obviously owed nothing to an analysis in terms of class or of class fractions: intervention made during the first phase of decentralisation resulted in a wave of industrial transfers and this dispersion reduced the effectiveness of the agreed policy, which was unable to give the regions concerned their own dynamism; the policy of concentration of state intervention represented a *rectification* of the earlier policy—it corrected its mistakes. This is the essence of the argument underlying the report "Industrialisation et aménagement du territoire" (DATAR, 1968). It was not a social relationship—the elevation of monopolistic capital to the position of politically dominant fraction within the bourgeois class—which caused the change of policy, but a failure of techniques (prediction, statistical collection, and administrative intervention).

The concrete form taken by the setting up of powerful industrial poles such as Dunkirk, Le Havre, and Fos (which we will analyse more closely in the following section) reveals a very close complementarity between state intervention and the activities of the major firms involved. Initially, the state carried out large-scale works which would not bring immediate returns (harbour installations, railways, motorways, telephone systems, electricity and water supplies, and so on)[8]. In the second phase, the state made massive loans to the large firms which agreed to locate on the infrastructure already established and were therefore assured of short-term profits. In such a process, the principle of freedom of enterprise—the possibility that firms, because of changes of techniques or fluctuations in their markets or their finances, need neither use the infrastructure provided by the state nor respond to public financial incentives—is respected absolutely.

This policy, which took shape in a many-sided and complex way in the regions of diversified activity (Paris, Lyons), was worked out in virtually

[8] This type of public investment is not peculiar to contemporary France: at the time of the first industrial revolution, under Napoleon III, the state assisted the accumulation of private capital by undertaking works whose benefits were made over to it (notably the establishment of rail networks).

experimental conditions in the three French industrial and port complexes recently created or extended: Dunkirk, Le Havre, and Fos. An analysis of the creation of the pole of Fos, which, according to President Georges Pompidou[9], represented "the major regional planning operation of the Sixth Plan in the country", will allow us to see exactly how the links between the state and the large industrial and financial groups involved in the construction of the complex were formed, and how the requirement of competitiveness on international markets was met.

2 The case of Fos-sur-Mer
2.1 The port and industrial area
The possibility of establishing a coastal iron and steel industry at Fos-sur-Mer was first envisaged around 1955 by the authorities of Marseilles Chamber of Commerce and Industry when they were working out plans for the extension of the port to the west of Martigues–Lavéra[10]. In 1962, the combined syndicate for planning and infrastructure of the Gulf of Fos, representing the municipalities of Arles, Fos-sur-Mer, Port-de-Bouc, Port St-Louis-du-Rhône, Marseilles, the General Council of the département (Bouches-du-Rhône), and the Marseilles and Arles Chambers of Commerce and Industry, began to buy sites at Fos.

The participation of local communities and regional employers' organisations, which started with the initial reservation of land—that is, the stage when uncertainties are greatest—quickly took on a symbolic significance, with the state taking over the main controls. In 1964, DATAR entrusted the preparation of the Fos general development programme to a central working party. This party had preliminary studies carried out by large private research institutions, SEMA, SETEC, and SEDES, which submitted their reports to DATAR in 1965 (SEDES, 1965; SEMA–SETEC, 1965). SEMA, which is part of the Métra International group, was under the control of the Banque de Paris et des Pays-Bas, through financial links (Claude, 1969). This big commercial bank, which played practically no part in the iron and steel sector at the end of the Second World War, has since taken shares in several iron and steel enterprises, including USINOR; in particular, it has taken a stake in the coastal iron and steel industry of Dunkirk and Selzaete (Belgium). In 1967, it had a share in the control of production of 11 million tons of steel.

[9] Declaration to the Inner Council of Ministers, 26 November, 1971.
[10] "A harsh blow was dealt to this attempt to raise Marseilles from its relative state of industrial underdevelopment by the decision in 1958 to go ahead with the industrialisation of Algeria under the Constantine Plan. This move indicated the impossibility of promoting other massive investments. Paradoxically, this Algerian effort tended to return Marseilles to exactly the traditional role which it was seeking to escape, and held up still further its entry into the modern industrial era" (Joly, 1971, page 394).

The Fos project took shape, then, under conditions whereby a commercial bank not only had at its disposal the studies that had been made, but was also eventually able to modify these according to its investment programme. In fact, the Banque de Paris et des Pays-Bas, which seemed to have no interest in the Fos iron and steel industry when Wendel–Sidélor had sole control of the Lorraine steel group SOLMER, was called in to play a decisive role when, at the end of 1972, the Lorraine group was forced to take USINOR as an equal partner.

In November 1965 and February 1966, two events took place which were to make it possible to place the complete Fos operation under the direct supervision of the state. First, the law on autonomous maritime ports, passed in June 1965, came into force: the decisive part played until then by the chambers of commerce in port facilities was considerably reduced. The Autonomous Port of Marseilles, as overseer of the port and industrial zone of Fos, thus escaped the control of the local employers' organisation and the elected members of the mixed-economy syndicate. In the second place, the creation of OREAM, a planning organisation heavily dependent on the state, meant that the essentials of environmental plans for Fos (including those for residential areas, transport, research facilities, and a business centre) would be worked out outside the Conseil Général des Bouches-du-Rhône and the municipalities involved[11].

Parallel to this state takeover of the machinery for the establishment of the Fos complex, joint action between the state and leaders of the steel industry was developing, most notably through the Commissions of the Sixth Plan, in which employers were generally in the majority. The steel manufacturers stressed their financial difficulties, the obsolescence of part of their productive capacity, and the severity of international competition. They had a sympathetic audience: the state–steel-industry convention, which came into force on 19 July 1966, granted loans from Fonds de Développement Économique et Social (FDES) of a total of $2 \cdot 7$ million francs. Thus the state fulfilled half the borrowing requirement envisaged by the steel producers (see Laffont, 1971).

While the Fifth Plan was in operation, the conditions of steel production in France were affected by two main changes: the deepening crisis in the Lorraine steel industry and, at the same time, the rising price of steel[12],

[11] The choice of boundaries of the Marseilles Metropolitan Area cannot be justified from either a geographical or an economic point of view. The most plausible hypothesis to explain how they were drawn seems to be the political anxiety not to allow the Metropolitan Area to coincide with the département of Bouches-du-Rhône, so as to avoid control of the former falling into the hands of a Conseil Général with what was then an opposition (Socialist Party and French Communist Party) majority.

[12] This financial change seems to have been a more important determining factor than consideration of the country's steel requirements because, in spite of the prospect of increasing demand, steelmaking groups had asked for—and received—a limit on production targets when the Fifth Plan was being prepared; that is, at a time when steel prices seemed low enough to warrant recourse to imports.

which together led producers to consider increasing their total production capacity by extending USINOR at Dunkirk and creating a new coastal unit. In 1962, Lorraine aroused the enthusiasm of Raymond Cartier, who described it in *Paris Match* as "the French Texas". Today the press speaks of Fos in analogous terms, but cannot refer in the same way to Lorraine, where reconversion is now the order of the day. In spite of the FDES loans, in spite of the infrastructure provided by the state (the Moselle canalisation scheme, new power stations, and so on), reductions in man-power are taking place in steelmaking, and further decline is anticipated. These reductions are in addition to those taking place in the mines and in the textile industry. New jobs for the redeployment of labour are still awaited. The abandonment of a region whose productive capacity is obsolete (economic considerations) prevails over regard for the claims of the population concerned (social considerations).

While this regional crisis was developing, the establishment of a coastal unit in addition to Dunkirk appeared likely to be profitable. Two sites in France had all the necessary requirements: Le Havre and Fos. Technically, they appeared much the same. The choice of Fos was approved by the Interministerial Committee for Regional Planning on 8 December 1969— one year after the adoption by that committee of the white paper issued by the Marseilles Metropolitan Area Organisation (OREAM, 1969), whose employment targets would have become even more 'voluntary'[13] if the Le Havre site had been chosen.

The 'noneconomic' nature of the choice of Fos—that is, the taking into account of the underindustrialisation of the Mediterranean Coast in the decision—was naturally pointed out and stressed by the public authorities. Certain authors have taken up this argument. Thus Joly (1971, page 395) states: "it seems certain that, even though the French steel concerns were anxious to have a coastal plant, voluntary planning considerations played in favour of Fos". Undoubtedly, a plant at Le Havre would have clearly reinforced the imbalance between the industrial concentration of the Nord–Paris-basin area and the rest of France, and an important weapon in the struggle against the political threats provoked by the high level of unemployment and the weakness of industry in the Bouches-du-Rhône would have been lost. But it is unnecessary to resort to these considerations to account for the choice of Fos, as reasons of a strictly economic nature seem sufficient: factory construction costs are appreciably lower at Fos than at Le Havre; raw materials such as limestone and dolomite are available in the neighbourhood of Fos. Furthermore, even if this assessment

[13] The planning proposals of the Marseilles Metropolitan Area (OREAM, 1970, page 139) read: "The economic and demographic targets for 1985 and 2000 set out in the white paper were based on information gathered by the Census of 1962, available in 1966. The first results of the 1968 Census emphasise the *voluntary* nature [italics added] of the targets that have been retained". [The employment rate had been over-estimated in 1966, and it had been possible to make an optimistic extrapolation.]

does not seem to have directly influenced the calculation of the economic advantages of the site, Fos is very well placed for the employment of immigrant labour (the plant envisaged should employ by about 1980, after completion of the second phase, nearly 6000 unskilled workers as labourers, out of a total work force of 11 500), and the impact of this commodity on wage costs can be considerable. In short, the Fos site represents a more internationally competitive position than Le Havre, and this is as true of the steelmakers' specific interests as of the general interests of the state and the industrial and financial groups as a whole, for whom an opening on the Mediterranean is full of promise in the medium and long term. It is expected that by 1980 half the production of the new unit could be exported. In spite of the development of Spanish steel manufacturing with the help of US Steel, the development of Algerian production and the plans for production in several other countries (Greece, Turkey, Egypt), Mediterranean markets are less saturated by competition and offer more potential for growth than those of Northern and Northwestern Europe. In addition, the completion of the Fos complex strengthens the position of the French North Sea–Mediterranean axis in its rivalry with the Rhine–Main–Danube link, which is also expected by 1980–1982[14]. It also improves the position of industrial groups based in France vis-à-vis their competitors in Northern Italy (Turin, Genoa, Milan) and Catalonia (Barcelona). The report on the options for the Sixth Plan is most explicit on this point (Ministère de la Planification, 1970): "We must reply to the challenge of certain particularly dynamic regions on our northern, eastern, and, to some extent, southern borders". The importance of the Fos site for the strategy of industry and of the French government, which is aimed at integrating Spain into the EEC, should also be noted[15].

The industrial group most directly concerned in these development prospects has been the chief steel producing group in France, the Wendel group, which in 1971 accounted for 34% of national production of crude steel. It controls the Fos steelmaking unit, whose trade name is **SOLMER**, through the intermediary of SOLLAC—in 1970, the Wendel–Sidélor group held 65% of SOLLAC capital. If, thanks to the Fos operation, this group seems to be strengthening its dominant position at the centre of French steelmaking, it is actually the role of finance capital which is developing at the expense of the traditional industrial capital represented by the de Wendel family: just as the construction of the Dunkirk plant represented an opportunity for the Banque de Paris et des Pays-Bas to increase its share

[14] "Before 1981, the date by which the Rhine–Main–Danube link is expected to enter service, the link between the Rhône Valley and the Rhine basin will be complete. And the Fos gamble will have come off" (R Ricard, President of the *Association Grand Delta*, in *La Marseillaise* 3 November 1970).

[15] The role played by regional planning in this strategy is very obvious; this is why an industrial zone is now being set up at Rivesaltes near Perpignan, which is likely to be the first link in a chain of Spanish industries established in France.

of USINOR capital, so the building of Fos allowed the Pont-à-Mousson–
Suez group to take an active part in the control of SOLLAC (Damette,
1970, page 34). But in autumn 1972 it appeared that Wendel–Sidélor was
unable to support the finance plan alone, and it was obliged to ask for
fresh assistance from the state. The state agreed to increase its participation
on condition that a freshly constituted group should be operated by
SOLLAC and USINOR together. At the beginning of 1973 an agreement
was concluded between the two steelmaking giants under the leadership of
the finance groups. In 1973 the foremost German steel producer, Thyssen,
took a 5% shareholding.

Second place was taken by the Péchiney–Ugine–Kuhlmann group,
whose main business was in ores and which was already involved in two
ways in the Fos complex: Ugine-Aciers built a factory producing special
steels (employing a labour force of 1 000); Ugine–Kuhlmann were setting
up a chlorine electrolysis unit where production was scheduled to start at
the end of 1975.

In the third place, Fos represented a strategic point of great interest to
the oil and petrochemical industries. Fos and the Étang de Berre form the
starting point for a massive network of pipelines, in which the Lavéra–
Karlsruhe oil pipeline was only the first branch. Esso inaugurated the
industrialisation of Fos with the construction of a refinery which has been
in production since 1966. At Berre and Martigues, Shell, BP, and CFR,
which had been established in the area even earlier, increased their refining
capacity by two or three times and developed their petrochemical plants.
The biggest British chemicals group, Imperial Chemical Industries, set up a
polyethylene plant at Fos.

The possibilities for extension offered by the Fos site are considerable:
although SOLMER expected to produce steel at a rate of 7 million tonnes
of steel per year by 1980, the land it has at its disposal will allow it to
raise production capacity to 20 million tonnes per year, or nearly the
entire 1974 French output. The area usable by industry—at present about
5 000 hectares—could easily be doubled. All the technical conditions for a
massive expansion of productive forces are combined.

Regardless of whether the results anticipated for around 1985 [30000–
45000 industrial jobs, according to the estimates made by SEMA–SETEC
(1965), and subsequently by INSEE] are attained, the state will not have
neglected to provide inducements: the port facilities, power stations,
railways, motorway services, and telecommunications networks are all
being set up, with delays in some cases, but without stinting. The only
real delay will come in the development of waterway services to the north:
financial restrictions have led the Compagnie Nationale du Rhône to put
off, on several occasions, the opening of the Rhône to high-capacity barges;
this will not now be accomplished until the Seventh Plan is in operation.
As well as setting up large-scale installations, the state is directly financing
industrial investments. A sum of 1 850 million francs was loaned to

SOLLAC by the FDES for the construction of the Fos steel plant, plus a supplement of 850 million francs at the time of the Wendel-USINOR liaison. With interest rates of 3% and 4%, and deferment of repayment by five years, these amount not simply to advances of funds but, to some extent, to outright subsidies.

The setting up of the port-industrial complex of Fos is a perfect illustration of the thesis put forward earlier, according to which regional planning represents, above all, a state investment programme in the sphere of the reproduction of fixed capital on behalf of large monopolistic groups. The consultations surrounding this programme are carried on at the highest level, with local representative bodies taking no part. Such consultations thus appear, like a plan and projects depending on it, as a means of procuring the closer unity of the monopolistic section of the dominant class. The state takes charge of nonprofitmaking sectors, which are nonetheless indispensable to the reproduction of capital, and so assures a devalorisation of part of the general capital by making investments which make little or no profit. This allows large monopolistic groups to increase the mobility and profitability of their own funds. However, can such an effort be made without an effect on the needs of other sectors of national activity and without the development of an inflationist policy?

Using the example of the regional planning operation of the port-industrial zone of Fos, we have been able to establish the following points.
1. The state changed from a policy of relatively indiscriminate intervention to selective intervention in favour of the most highly concentrated sectors. Its investments even contribute to the acceleration of this concentration, as in the case of the steel industry.
2. State intervention represented a form of devalorisation of general capital, not only as far as massive investments in land acquisition and infrastructural installations are concerned, but also through aid to the steel industry and loans at very low rates of interest. This devalorisation through public finance was combined with the closure of plants in Lorraine (a negative valorisation of a part of the general capital).

Certain lawyers and sociologists claim to observe in economic or regional planning a modification of the traditional private-public relationship of the capitalist mode of production, which takes place at the expense of the private sector. In this conceptualisation, the state becomes a gigantic machine, making further and further inroads into domains hitherto reserved for the private sector by transforming their usual working. The state, even when acting in favour of large monopolistic groups, imposes upon them a restrictive, bureaucratic investment programme, which profoundly transforms the free play of private interests. This Hegelian or Weberian image masks reality: on one hand, the modification of the play of private interests is the reason for, not the result, of state intervention; on the other hand, if the state does intervene more and more in economic life and if the administration or the law do figure increasingly in the active life of private enterprise, the increase in these interventions does not necessarily mean a submission of the private to the public. The state only retains public property, with the right of management and control, in the sectors which remain unprofitable. If this is not so, the right is relinquished to the advantage of the private sector. The port–industrial zone of Fos provides an example yet again: whereas the construction of the port basins was financed by the state, the construction of wharves reserved for SOLMER was privately financed. One of the first social struggles the zone has experienced, and continues to experience, was that of the dockers prostesting against this private control. The Act of 6 September 1947 reserved public installations for the dockers, and the private control of the wharves makes it possible to take on workers who do not enjoy all the benefits set out in the dockers' statute.

What emerges in regional planning operations which have a bearing on the state investment programme in the reproduction of fixed capital is not therefore a fundamental modification of the traditional public–private relationship, but the innovative role played by the state in the growth of private profits and therefore in the social relationship of exploitation. The state becomes a sort of indispensable catalyst for the generation of these profits, the various modifications of the public–private relationship aiming only at making arrangements for the maximum profit of the private sector. This essential aspect of public intervention characterises not only regional planning or infrastructural operations, but also urban planning, as we shall see in the following section. In fact, as well as carrying out the great investments needed by industry and making loans to the steelmakers, the state is financing—sometimes from its own funds, more often from those of local communities—and organising the surrounding area of the port–industrial complex of Fos. It is here that we will analyse the articulation of the state policy of intervention in favour of powerful industrial poles in the form of the promotion of *métropoles d'équilibre* and the new town policy.

2.2 The urban environment of the Fos complex

In 1964, at the beginning of preparatory work for the Fifth Plan, a definition of the policy of promoting *métropoles d'équilibre* was formulated for the first time by the Commission Nationale pour l'Aménagement du Territoire (DATAR, 1964). This definition was based on the competition between Paris and the provinces: the situation was defined as one of 'imbalance' which, although benefiting the Paris region, where very rapid development was taking place, was at the same time doing harm by the congestion which it was creating. By following the observed tendency, the Plan would only reinforce this imbalance. Such a tendency represented a double threat: the increased congestion of the capital and the increasingly marked relative underdevelopment of the provinces, which had to bear the heavy costs of the development of the Paris region into the bargain.

This was seen as 'morally' inadmissible. It was therefore essential to express the 'will' to break with this process at the national level, and to achieve a state of equilibrium. Quite simple arithmetic then came into play, in which the term 'equilibrium' took its literal sense: towns with population of 50000 or 100000 had insufficient weight to counter the imbalance between a capital city with a population of nearly 9 million and the rest of the country. Only the most important regional centres, with populations of the order of a million or half a million and offering urban advantages in many ways comparable to those of the Paris agglomeration, were capable of reestablishing the equilibrium of the national urban framework, provided that their communications and the level of their services were improved. The eight centres selected were: Lille–Roubaix–Tourcoing; Nancy–Metz; Strasbourg; Lyons–St-Étienne; Marseilles–Aix; Toulouse; Bordeaux; and Nantes–St-Nazaire (see DATAR, 1969).

The principal instrument in the development of *métropoles d'équilibre* was the improvement of the tertiary sector (Ministère de la Planification, 1970, page 61):

"The promotion of *métropoles d'équilibre* implies essentially the development of their tertiary activities, to be exact higher-order services, and ... assumes the need for important infrastructural programmes due to their demographic growth".

The stress laid on higher-order services directly reflects the opportunity for the dominant stratum of big industrial and financial groups presented by the development of the principal towns, resulting in the multiplication of offices and administrative resources in central locations, a high-quality university environment, and efficient transport and communications services. Such an urban reorganisation is currently in progress, to differing extents, in all the eight *métropoles d'équilibre*, but especially at Lyons (with the construction of the Part-Dieu office centre), at Bordeaux (Mériadeck district), at Lille (office centre), and at Marseilles (work on the Sainte Barbe–La Bourse districts). It involves the renovation of town centres and the simultaneous establishment of routes ensuring fact, easy access to them. The new buildings receive offices, businesses, and apartments which are usually luxurious. It is a repetition—on a more reduced scale and slightly later—of the process which has affected Paris, and by which many resident members of the middle and working classes were ejected from the centre and deprived of these new advantages, which were henceforth reserved for the world of business, certain administrative bodies, big stores, and new residents more fortunate than their predecessors. Thus the commune of Lyons, which had 103000 resident workers (41·5% of the active population) in 1962, had only 92000 (38·5% of the active population) in 1968; during the same period the Rhône département as a whole saw its number of resident workers increase by 34000. At Marseilles, urban renovation proper has not progressed as far as at Lyons, but the policy of promotion of higher-level services is in full swing: factories, warehouses, low-order service establishments (businesses whose customers are individuals from the middle and working classes) are leaving the town for localities nearer the Étang de Berre (such as the Vitrolles industrial zone and the Plan de Campagne commercial zone), where site costs are lower than in Marseilles. Marseilles neighbourhoods are ploughed through by motorways and bypasses, and the graph of the rising price of sites reflects the extension of the rapid transport system. As for the renovation undertaken in the centre, it corresponds to the process described by the Nanterre Urban Sociology Group (GSUN, 1970) in the article "Paris 1970: urban reconquest and renovation–deportation": old unmaintained buildings deteriorate; lodgings for North African workers increase there; land values are reduced, as is the ability of the inhabitants to resist expulsion; renovation can then proceed. At Marseilles it is taking place in the rectangle bounded by la Canebière, la Place de la Joliette, and St-Charles station. For the period 1972–1975, renovation was expressed by the construction of 165000 m² of offices, 108000 m² of commercial areas, nearly 9000 parking places, and only 750 dwellings. At some time in the future, the SNCF could, as at Paris-Montparnasse, modernise St-Charles station in the course of a building operation including the construction of 180000 m² of offices.

The whole of the urban policy in Marseilles expressed the interests of the Marseilles bourgeoisie which, with the drying up of colonial profits, has reinvested to a large extent in property and therefore supports all programmes likely to result in rent increases; it also expresses those of the monopolist section of the bourgeoisie, which requires a high-level management and administration centre well served by axial motorways in the neighbourhood of Fos.

The analysis of the urban development policy of high-level services carried out at Marseilles does not, however, cover the full range of interventions made in the promotion of *métropoles d'équilibre*. This, as it was conceived, does not simply imply urban planning operations. It also involves, especially for those centres linked to major zones of industrial activity, ensuring the establishment of a coordinated network of services, communications, and residential complexes at the appropriate scale: the tertiary functions of the *métropole* and its neighbouring productive activities must be able to operate without the danger that sprawling urbanisation, traffic congestion, and serious deficiencies in facilities will harm their competitiveness. The recent creation—as a result of the express will of the government—of the University of Aix–Marseilles III should be analysed in this framework of total redevelopment. The setting up of this university without previous consultation with local university authorities illustrates well the upheavals inflicted on the whole region by the creation of Fos and a *métropole d'équilibre* conceived in terms of the needs of the large industrial enterprises of the area[16].

The object of regional planning intervention is no longer to be an individual conurbation, but the whole of an industrial and urban area— for example, the Marseilles Area, lying within the Marseilles–Aix–Arles–Fos rectangle. This is why regional planning teams with a sphere of intervention covering numerous communes are set up in *métropoles d'équilibre.* OREAM was created in 1966; it prepared the white paper on the Metropolitan Area (OREAM, 1969), and then the development plan for the Marseilles Metropolitan Area (OREAM, 1970). The Étang de Berre development had been set up in 1969, initially with the objective of preparing urban development schemes (SDAUs) for the communes of the Étang de Berre. In 1973, this organisation was radically altered and became a public body both with planning responsibilities and with certain traditionally administrative functions—finance and programming of land reservation and installations.

The implementation of the planning documents for the Marseilles–Fos area was prepared for with relative ease: members of the planning teams such as OREAM and MAEB had the advantage of the extremely favourable combination of a problem to solve—the underindustrialisation and under-utilisation of Marseilles, the Bouches-du-Rhône, and the Mediterranean region—and a plausible solution to it—the project, more tangible as each month went by, of the construction at Fos of one of the most powerful port–industrial complexes in Europe. In the Marseilles Metropolitan Area, the contradiction between the policy of the development of industrial poles (accentuating intraregional inequalities) and the policy of promoting *métropoles d'équilibre* (reducing interregional inequalities) seemed somewhat blurred: the development of the Fos industrial pole and that of the Marseilles *métropole* justified each other.

Although the distance between Marseilles and Fos is only a few dozen kilometres, the contrast remains between the real logic behind the planning of Fos, which is that of direct support to the strongest private enterprises, and the real purpose of the urban development of Marseilles and the metropolitan area, which is first and foremost the reproduction, at least cost, of labour power. At the ideological level at which planning projects are presented, this contrast is concealed by an illusion: between the realisation of the Fos complex and that of the urban development of the metropolitan area, a barrier is lowered at the stages of analysis, of decisions,

[16] The scientific teams which were collected from existing universities at the time of this 'creation', were connected with petrochemicals, metallurgy, and electronics, and are therefore in immediate touch with developments at the Fos port-industrial complex. The opposition raised in the region by the creation has criticised its "authoritarian" and "patronising" character—and has spread beyond the confines of the universities. It has shown that the restructuring of whole sectors of economic activity has brought about a widening of social contradictions, tending to manifest itself on the political scene by an awareness of the extensive overlap of sectoral struggles.

and of realisation, which acts as a sort of two-way mirror. On the Fos side, a central group consisting of DATAR, the large private research offices, the administration of the Port of Marseilles, and, above all, the managers of the big banking, steelmaking, and petroleum firms organise the mode of production quite independently without seeing, and without caring to see, what is happening on the other side of the mirror. On the other side, that of Marseilles and neighbouring towns, first OREAM, then MAEB and local communities organise the mode of consumption trying, each according to their own logic, to take into consideration the upheaval of productive forces seen outlined behind the glass on the Fos side.

The six communes most directly exposed to the Fos 'earthquake', those which from the building of the first factories have had to have the hostels and caravans of the construction workers on their territory, were: Fos-sur-Mer, Port-St-Louis-du-Rhône, Istres, Martigues, St-Mitre-les-Remparts, and Port-de-Bouc. The sharply contrasted political geography of this western zone of the Étang de Berre played a determining role in the particular increase in organisations intervening in the development of the urban environment of the Fos complex. The municipalities of Port-de-Bouc, Martigues, Port-St-Louis-du-Rhône, and St-Mitre have a communist majority; Fos and Istres have an 'apolitical' majority elected by the Right. Although these two groups of municipalities have both asked the state for substantial financial assistance in order to receive the newcomers, their strategies were profoundly different when it came to seeking the satisfaction of these requests.

In September 1971, the state proposed the application of the Boscher law on new towns to the six communes [see Rubenstein (1978, pages 54–62) for a discussion of this law—Editors]. This went against the decision of the General Council of the Bouches-du-Rhône and the coordinating committee of OREAM, which were rejecting the use of the term 'new towns' in connection with the future urban development of the shores of the Étang de Berre. It made financial assistance dependent on setting up not one, but two Syndicats Communautaires d'Aménagement, drawn up according to the political geography of the zone. One of these grouped together the communist towns of Port-de-Bouc, Martigues, and St-Mitre; the other linked the communes of Fos, Istres, and Miramas, this last town being governed by the UDR.

The communist municipalities opposed the application of the Boscher law, declaring that it is unsuitable for an already highly urbanised zone and stressing that it would imply a restriction of their prerogatives, as development operations would be entrusted to a public body whose director is nominated by the prime minister. This position received the support not only of the other communist mayors of the Marseilles Metropolitan Area, but also of numerous socialist elected members, including the mayor of Marseilles. After various negotiations, a Syndicat Communautaire d'Aménagement representing the communes (Fos, Istres, and Miramas) which were favourable to the government's policy was created[17].

As far as urbanisation was concerned, a difference of strategy between the two types of commune can also be established. The communist municipalities, Martigues in particular, which possess relatively large resources, have strong administrative staffs and technical services. Very early on, they called in research organisations (BERIM and ORGECO) to develop their own analyses in opposition to those of the administration. They wished to control their urban growth and avoid excessive tax charges, even at the cost of putting a brake on construction. In June 1971, Martigues thus threatened to prohibit the building of new blocks on its territory. At about the same date, this municipality had a hand in organising a demonstration in front of the prefecture at Marseilles to protest against the fact that certain HLM (low-rent) apartments, largely financed by the citizens of Martigues, were being reserved for SOLMER. Adopting the same policy towards caravan sites, the communist mayors attempted to exclude them from their communes, even going to the extent of personally explaining the situation to the caravan occupants—as the mayor of Port-St-Louis-du-Rhône did. Thus Martigues was awarded a substantial amount of credit for infrastructure at the Interministerial Committee meeting of 7 October 1972.

The other communes seemed much less capable of facing the Fos upheaval. As already noted, three of them accepted strengthened state supervision to the extent that seemed to them to have financial advantages. All of them, however, were subject to the insidious pressure of property developers, behind whom are to be found the big finance groups (the Edmond de Rothschild group, Paris-Bas, Suez, Banque de la Construction et Travaux Publics, for example) which are linked with the Lorraine steel industry.

These developers dealt directly with firms which increased the risks of a segregated environment developing in the zone, and at the same time established privileged relationships with the communes. The way in which the property developers, linked to big banks, exercise economic control over the communes—particularly through ZAC procedures—is now well known, thanks to the establishment of semipublic companies for vast development operations [ZAC procedures are summarised in Rubenstein (1978, pages 102–111)—Editors]. At the stage of *constitution des dossiers* (drafting of plans) the commune, generally lacking competent, well-appointed

[17] The mayor of Fos only agreed to join the syndicate after receiving an assurance that his commune would not be prevented from extension. The overall plan of OREAM, and the subsequent plan of MAEB, anticipated a limit to the growth of this commune, whose area was ill-suited to urbanisation and which also had to put up with pollution not only from the port–industrial zone of Fos, but also from the Istres aircraft testing centre. The promise to construct several thousand dwellings on the outskirts of the commune, which gained the support of the mayor for the Syndicat Communautaire d'Aménagement, is one example of reevaluation of the development plan of the Marseilles Metropolitan Area.

technical services, receives an offer of the services of a private research bureau. When the operation is due to get under way, a management group belonging to the same group as the research bureau then intervenes. It is even possible for a finance organisation, still belonging to the same group, to be present to advance money to the local community. The semipublic company sanctions this type of practice at the legal level. Relative to the representation of local community, the private sector is clearly in the minority within this semipublic company, but it becomes its privileged contractor and can control the placing of very important orders while avoiding the tendering procedure and by investing a symbolic capital (minimum 5% of the total cost of the construction) from which the community's return must also be derived. The local community, generally lacking specialised staff, abandons administrative and technical direction to the private sector. In addition, the local community, as majority participant in the operation, takes on the legal and financial risks. From the beginning of work on the port and industrial zone, the Marseilles Metropolitan Area has witnessed the multiplication of interventions of this type.

The local communities, faced with the alternatives of either not making provision for the reception of temporary populations (thus disguising the shortcomings of the state in this respect), or ruining themselves financially and upsetting existing residents on whom the financial burden would fall, have often seen these private organisations as an unexpected solution to their problems. The property developers were in fact proposing not only to build dwellings but also to provide vital social infrastructure. Only big industrial groups supported by the financial sector can undertake such programmes[18]. Here again we see that the new links being forged between the private and the public sector are directed towards concentration, in this case in the construction sector. The big private and public developers formed an Association of Construction Firms, based on the shores of the Étang de Berre, which was able to deal directly with the administration and which possessed a very important portfolio of land holdings.

The consequences for urban planning of such domination by developers were numerous: within the framework of ZAC procedure, deviation from the provisions of the project became a common practice, if not the rule; this, combined with delays over roads and completion of social infrastructure (schools, hospitals, and so on), increased the anarchic appearance of the zone. While awaiting growth in demand, developers tended to hold up certain building works—in particular those involving nonprofitmaking installations.

Faced with what looked like 'urban anarchy', what was the attitude of the administration? It was fully aware of its own contradictions, the importance of which should certainly not be exaggerated. It did, however, attempt to overcome these by adopting a dual position: when in conflict with local populations, it stressed its own slowness, while systematically

[18] It may be noted that we were able to find only one single important programme in the Fos zone whose promotion was backed by a local family firm.

making short work of the most serious questions which might lead to internal conflict. When the proposal by MAEB that the eastern zone of the Étang de Berre should be declared to be of public utility aroused a public protest by small-scale and medium-scale landowners, the decision could be seen to be blocked in the meanders of administrative channels. Yet as soon as a divergence of views appeared between the Fos central group and the new towns central group over a problem concerning these two organisations, the President of the Republic was swift to act.

At the local level, one could occasionally witness the development of the adoption of contradictory positions by the Prefect of the region[19] (assisted by his regional team), the departmental director of facilities, and MAEB. This led MAEB into several crises. This organisation's technicians, confronted with the realities of the Fos development, went on strike in June 1972. The most obvious reason was overdue wages, but, in fact, as the trade union leaders of the movement informed us[20], the problem was also—and especially—the lack of any perspective surrounding their work.

As we have said, the importance of the effects of these internal divisions should not be exaggerated: even if the MAEB technicians attempted occasionally to oppose certain consequences of the state–steel–developers triple alliance, the very framework of the team is such[21] that it does not allow the whole planning operation to be questioned[22].

[19] The Prefect of the region was the former Prefect of Lorraine, chosen no doubt for the privileged contacts he had been able to establish with the steelmakers during the construction of the SACILOR steelworks in Lorraine.

[20] "This strike was an explosion at a given moment of a certain frustration, ... of a complete lack of agreement between the ideas that one or another of us could have on the objectives of our work. We have come here, from all sorts of backgrounds, with different training. All the same, we came to carry out regional planning, urban development, urban planning in general, both quantitatively and especially qualitatively, and then you realise we haven't the means to do it, nor the power, at least a special type of power to translate what we have studied into facts. That's the first point. Then the second point is, you feel under the pressure of demand, the impetus of development, that what is happening on the ground absolutely contradicts not only our ideas, but in a more general way what we call real planning" (MAEB economist interviewed by us in May 1972, DB and AC).

[21] The fact that the team was headed by a civil engineer, a former colleague of the Prefect of the region, although not necessarily enabling tensions between various local administrative bodies to be eased, at least made it possible to prevent them from appearing at the decisionmaking level.

[22] The same planning organisation was liable to produce, over a two-or-three-year interval, profoundly different development documents: the prospective population and employment figures for the mid-1980s for the western zone of the Étang de Berre, as prepared by OREAM in 1970 in the framework of the development project (approved by the Council of Ministers), correspond to an annual growth rate twice as high as that forecast by the same organisation in a study carried out in 1973 on the development of the same zone. The global population and employment forecasts for the Marseilles Metropolitan Area in 1985 had already been appreciably reduced between the drafting of the white paper of 1969 and the scheme of 1970.

Because of this, the technicians had the impression that the significance of the planning process had eluded them. We can repeat in this connection the comments of Herzog (1971, page 262) regarding planning technicians.

"the *undemocratic* preparation of the monopolist plan isolates technicians in an intellectual ghetto which *aggravates* tendencies to idealistic subjective reflection on social movements, which is normal for intellectuals whose point of view is outside production and, to an even greater extent, outside the political struggle, not only of the working class, but also of capital".

If the planning process seems in this way to elude its practitioners, as it also escapes the majority of local elected representatives, it is, we believe, for two sets of reasons. The first is to do with the setting up of planning organisations which have no real power and are not subject to control by local or regional democratic bodies. The result of this, in spite of 'technocratic' appearances, is a reinforcement of the weight of governmental, and even presidential, decisions on planning, while at the same time developers and major industrialists go from strength to strength in their dealings with the administration. The second set of reasons results from the working of the whole planning apparatus, that is, from the dichotomy between industrial development and confined urban development according to Lojkine and Préteceille (1970), "in closed urban problematics", in the framework of which one tries to resolve problems of housing, traffic, underprovision of services in towns, and inadequacies of collective consumption in general, without ever questioning the state of social relationships of production.

But if the dominated social classes organise to break down the division which separates the spheres of production and consumption; if they point out the responsibilities of the firms establishing their factories at Fos in the organisation of the collective consumption of the workers and therefore in the financing of the urban organisation of the Metropolitan Area; if the municipalities representing these classes refuse to finance investments whose cost, they reckon, cannot be recovered; then a political and economic contradiction begins to threaten the explicit logic of regional planning[23].

The dichotomy between the organisation of production (economic considerations) and the organisation of consumption (social considerations), is attacked, and hence even the supremacy of economic considerations (the search for profit) over social considerations (the satisfaction of social needs) is called in question. Through this questioning, the whole internal coherence of the planning discourse, founded on the separation of industrial

---

[23] One of the favourite protest themes of the working-class municipalities which border the Étang de Berre was "Let the state give us the same financial resources to house incoming workers as the steel industry was offered to settle at Fos". Equally, in June 1973 when the first layoffs of construction workers began, the theme around which strikes and demonstrations were organised was "No layoffs! There's still work for the 'builders of Fos'. We need to build houses and schools for workers and their children".

development and urban development, appears to be of a fundamentally ideological nature.

If this ideological division corresponds to differences in the practice of planning as it has been applied, then it expresses no difference between the nature of the 'economic' and the 'social'. The fundamental unity of the planning process, beyond any distinction between national regional planning and urban development, results from the unity of the real goal of planning: behind its apparent objectives—balanced development of the means of production in regional planning and balanced growth of the means of collective consumption in the sector of urban development— there lies hidden in both sectors the reality of planning and its implicit objective, the greater profit of the large industrial and financial groups. This objective occupies a quantitatively less important position in urban development, for three reasons. Firstly, this is a sector in which the state accepts a certain number of the general costs of capital—those related to the reproduction of labour power. Even these general costs (the case of housing is an example) are, however, liable to serve as the starting point for new profitmaking activities. Secondly, to the extent that the reproduction of labour power really requires a greater and greater extension of collective consumption, the sudden awareness of exploitation establishes the existence of deficiencies in the organisation of that consumption. Because of this, and in spite of the difficulties of organisation they involve, urban struggles (other than wage struggles) for the development of collective consumption make greater and greater progress. The more they are directed against the state, the more they have a directly political character. On the other hand, state intervention in this field is also the product of these protest struggles, whether they originate from the people or through the agency of local elected representatives. In fact local authorities act less and less as a screen between the state and the people, as the growth of their management problems—lack of financial and technical resources, burden of taxation levied by the state, and charges which the state transfers to them—leads them more and more often to proclaim the responsibilities of the state. Thirdly, for a long time the building and public works sector, into whose hands a large part of the urban development credits fall, has undergone a smaller industrial and financial concentration than sectors such as metals production, engineering, and chemicals, which are the principal recipients of industrial credits allocated by the state. But government urban development policy is precisely the instrument whereby large-scale finance capital penetrates the branches of property and public works: by compulsory purchase procedures and joint development zones and by guarantees given by local authorities in private property deals, it removes the obstacles (requisition problems and uncertainties over the profitability of capital invested in property arising from the slowness in the turnover of capital in this sector) which have previously held the banks back from the housing market.

3 Conclusion: the sociological significance of regional planning

Like planning in general, regional planning only appears impotent if the objectives it adopts—growth and harmony in the distribution of productive forces over the territory, satisfaction of the needs of the population, control of urbanisation, and so on—are treated as its real aims. Should one attempt to go beyond this level of immediate representation? Within the framework of a sociological analysis, one is led to ask oneself about the significance of the programme of government intervention as it has been revealed in the national plans or in planning practice.

Three types of sociological responses are possible. The first of these avoids a priori the question of the distinction or lack of distinction between what planning or development could be and what they are. Research is immediately placed in the perspective of a study of the decisionmaking processes of development planning. This is, for example, the orientation adopted by Crozier (1965, page 147): he defines planning as "the rational preparation of growth and economic development". This approach takes the ideology of the plan into account and places itself within the voluntarist and rationalist problematic of the plan. An analysis of this kind, which seems to us to operate only within the constraint of partially regulative mechanisms which may be established at the heart of a given sector of the government institution, has been criticised by Castells (1972, pages 314 and following) in his book *La Question Urbaine*. A second approach to the analysis of planning processes regards planning of development as a form of regulation of certain social *contradictions* and not solely, as the practitioners of planning would make out, the regulation of imbalances of a noncontradictory nature. Planning in general, and 'urban planning' in particular, are therefore defined by their end product: a safeguarding of existing class relationships.

Such a definition presupposes that in the last analysis the political authority would be able to escape the contradictions over which it intervenes, as otherwise it is hard to understand how it could contain, govern, or overcome them. In fact, it implies that one should consider that planning, even though (contrary to its claims) it serves the dominant class, effectively constitutes a form of mastery of social movements, the state intervening where required and with all necessary effectiveness to smother conflicts, or at least channel and limit them, in order to preserve bourgeois domination. Thus the state becomes a sort of tutelary genius of capital, detecting and defusing, by means of the plan, the minefields which lie in the path of bourgeois society. In short, one can state that the products of planning are not those set out in a plan, but they are unacknowledgeable because of their class character; nevertheless planning does indeed exist, and the economy is planned. Here there is, in our opinion, a kind of consecration by sociological argument of the effectiveness which that planning claims. This, if it exists, must appear to be the product of sociological analysis and not be admitted a priori by a definition of planning as a phenomenon of regulation. On analysis, the opposite seems to be the case; and here there appears a third orientation, which we believe to be the most fertile—that the 'planned' intervention by the state sometimes corrects certain contradictions, but sometimes engenders or deepens them.

As far as the principal contradiction at the heart of the capitalist social structure is concerned (that between the development of the productive forces and the private appropriation of the means of production), the main effect of these interventions is to aggravate it, and not to limit it. In fact, no division exists between the general political interests of the dominant class, which are represented by the state as the effective guarantor of unity of the social structure, and its economic interests, which develop in civil society at the risk of threatening its integration. As Herzog (1971, page 38) shows:

"Behind the apparent and false division of functions between the political and the economic, the state best serves (insofar as it is able to intervene) the economic interests of the dominant fraction, bearing in mind the degree of political development of the economic contradictions. The state does not stand outside the capital–labour relationship like a regulator in the mechanical sense of the term, perhaps as that outside a boiler which it prevents from overheating; for example: as the problems of the dominant class arising from the investment of their capital get worse, because of the broadening of the fundamental contradiction which at the heart of the economic base opposes the private ownership of the means of production and the social employment of productive forces, the state more and more directly supports accumulation and capitalist markets; it differentiates its support to an increasing extent in favour of the dominant section represented at the heart of the capitalist class by the most concentrated industrial and financial groups; thus it accentuates inequalities of development at the heart of the whole range of productive forces, and it reinforces the fundamental contradiction of the mode of production, as it strengthens both industrial and financial concentration and the socialisation of productive forces".

The establishment of the port–industrial complex of Fos-sur-Mer is a perfect example of this: at the level of productive forces, it meant the development of the cooperation of thousands of workers on a scale rarely attained; on the level of ownership of this social unit of production, the association of several of the biggest European steel firms to set up the Fos works could represent a step towards the constitution of a group which would control almost the entire French output. Without the massive and many-sided support of the state, neither the socialisation of the apparatus of production nor the concentration of ownership of that apparatus would have reached such a high degree.

In this respect, the role of the state is exactly the reverse of a regulator.

It is true that sociologists who define planning according to its regulatory effects make analyses of urban planning in isolation, divorced from regional development: its immediate object is seen not as the location of big industrial enterprises, but as the organisation of consumption on an urban scale (housing, commerce, public utilities, and movement between these elements). This is what Castells (1972) shows in particular, when he defines *urban planning* as "the intervention of politics on the specific interconnection of different elements of a social structure *at the heart of a collective unit of reproduction of labour power*". It could therefore be conceived that the general field of planning can be subdivided into two sectors, each obeying a different logic: on the one hand, industrial policy and regional development, insofar as the determination of the location of principal industrial units and large-scale means of distribution and exchange are factors in the increased reproduction of the means of production; on the other hand, town planning and the development of metropolitan areas (territorial development in connection with urban planning), which are factors in the increased reproduction of labour power. The sector of the reproduction of the means of production corresponds to an *economic* policy of state contribution to the formation of capital, whereas the sector of the reproduction of labour power corresponds to a state regulatory policy of a *social* nature created by sacrifices on the part of capital. The divisions which ensue within institutions taking part in urban and regional planning seem to confirm the existence of a division between economic planning—the planning of production—and social planning—the planning of consumption. In the Fos-sur-Mer operation, as we have seen, the organisations intervening in the establishment of the Fos industrial complex (Groupe Central de Fos, Port Autonome de Marseille), and those which prepare development and planning papers relating to the Metropolitan Area adjacent to Fos (Groupe Central de Planification Urbaine, OREAM, and MAEB), operate separately from each other, the first group of organisations pursuing a policy apparently independent of that of the second group.

Such a division between the economic and social, inherent in the institutions and practices of regional planning, seems to us to arise from the ideological aspects of state intervention. These disguise the reality of the social relationship of exploitation and the role played by the state in the extension of this relationship. In fact, the real wages of workers are made up to a large extent by a number of collective services which therefore contribute to the value of labour power. When the state increases fiscal pressure (on local authorities) while limiting the quantity and quality of collective consumption, there is an increase in the global mass of surplus value. In this respect, state intervention represents a new form, established on the scale of the entire social structure, of extraction and distribution of surplus value.

This is why analyses of planning in terms of regulatory processes, which disregard the involvement of the state in socioeconomic relationships as an active force against any decrease in the rate of profit, and which acknowledge the abilities of the state as set out in the ideology of regional and national planning—following the tradition of the ideas of Hegel, Weber, and Crozier—regard the state as an entity capable of voluntary action. It seems to us, on the contrary, that regional planning be regarded only as an *attempt* at social regulation, and that it introduces coherence only insofar as it allows a moment of overall reflection on the programming of public intervention, the effects of which are only likely to broaden the contradictory nature of the social relationships of production.

References

Boccara P, 1966 "Le capitalisme monopoliste d'État" *Économie et Politique* (143-144)

Castells M, 1972 *La Question Urbaine* (Maspéro, Paris) [translated as *The Urban Question* (Edward Arnold, Maidenhead, Berks)]

Claude H, 1969 *Histoire, Réalité et Destin d'un Monopole, la Banque de Paris et des Pays-Bas et son Groupe (1872-1968)* (Éditions Sociales, Paris)

Crozier M, 1965 "Pour une analyse sociologique de la planification française" *Revue Française de Sociologie* 6

Damette F, 1970 "Fos résoudra-t-il la crise de Marseille et de sa région?" *Économie et Politique* 195 29-42

DATAR, 1964 *Rapport de la Commission Nationale d'Aménagement du Territoire* (La Documentation Française, Paris)

DATAR, 1968 "Industrialisation et aménagement du territoire" in *Notes et Études Documentaires* (La Documentation Française, Paris)

DATAR, 1969 "Métropoles d'équilibre et aires métropolitaines" *Notes et Études Documentaires* number 3633 (La Documentation Française, Paris)

DATAR, 1970 *Rapport de la Commission «Aménagement du Territoire» sur les Orientations du VIème Plan* (La Documentation Française, Paris)

Gruson C, 1968 *Origines et Espoirs de la Planification Française* (Dunod, Paris)

GSUN, 1970 "Paris 1970, reconquête urbaine et rénovation-déportation" *Sociologie du Travail* 12 488-514

Guichard O, 1965 *Aménager la France* (Laffont-Gonthier, Paris)

Herzog P, 1971 *Politique Économique et Planification en Régime Capitaliste* (Éditions Sociales, Paris)

Joly J, 1971 "Perspectives industrielles à Fos-sur-mer" *Aménagement du Territoire et Développement Régional* 4 391-419

Labasse J, 1966 *L'Organisation de l'Espace* (Hermann, Paris)

Laffont P, 1971 "Les entreprises sidérurgiques depuis cinq ans" *Économie et Statistique* 10

Lojkine J, Préteceille E, 1970 "Politique urbaine et stratégie de classe" *Espaces et Sociétés* (1)

Massé P, 1968 *Le Plan ou l'Anti-Hasard* (Gallimard, Paris)

Ministère de la Construction et Urbanisme, 1950 *Plan d'Aménagement du Territoire* (Imprimerie Nationale, Paris)

Ministère de la Planification, 1970 "Rapport sur les principales options qui commandent la préparation du VIème Plan" *Journaux Officiels de la République Française* 70-109

OREAM, 1969 *Perspectives d'Aménagement de l'Aire Métropolitaine Marseillaise* (Organisation pour les Études d'Aménagement de l'Aire Métropolitaine, Marseilles)

OREAM, 1970 *Schéma d'Aménagement de l'Aire Métropolitaine Marseillaise*
  (Organisation pour les Études d'Aménagement de l'Aire Métropolitaine, Marseilles)
SEDES, 1965 *Étude Socio-économique de l'Aménagement du Golfe de Fos* [4 volumes]
  (Société d'Études pour le Développement Économique et Social, Paris)
SEMA-SETEC, 1965 *Développement Économique et Social du Golfe de Fos*
  [19 volumes] (Société d'Économie et de Mathématiques Appliquées-Société
  d'Études Techniques Économiques, Paris)
Rubenstein J, 1978 *The French New Towns* (Johns Hopkins University Press,
  Baltimore, Md)

The development of Fos-sur-Mer: a footnote

R HUDSON, J R LEWIS
University of Durham

Since the original publication of Bleitrach and Chenu's classic study of the origins and early development of Fos-sur-Mer (Bleitrach and Chenu, 1975), there have been a number of other studies which deal with its subsequent development: for example, Beau et al (1978), which contains an extensive bibliography of material in French; Kinsey (1978; 1979); Tarrow (1978). Drawing on these and other sources, we intend here to summarise briefly the history of Fos in the 1970s, paying particular attention to the relationship between actual developments and the regional planning objectives originally specified.

Undoubtedly there has been some industrial growth, in terms both of investment and of employment' at Fos (see figures 1 and 2, and table 1). However, this must be assessed in relation to planned targets for output and employment and to the intention of producing an integrated manufacturing complex at Fos. In terms of output, perhaps the most significant figures relate to SOLMER: by 1978 annual steel output was only 2·5 million tonnes, considerably below the target of 7·0 million tonnes for that year, the ultimate target of 20·0 million tonnes, and indeed, even below that of 3·5 million tonnes for 1973; moreover, in 1978 SOLMER was only working at 60% capacity. One consequence of this low level of capacity utilisation and the below-target growth of output was the postponement

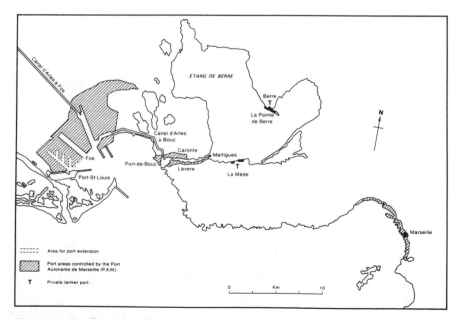

Figure 1. The Fos–Marseilles area.

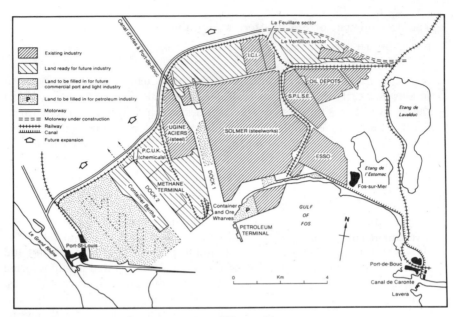

Figure 2. The port-industrial complex of Fos-sur-Mer.

Table 1. Employment growth at Fos-sur-Mer industrial zone, 1970-1977. Source: Kinsey (1978, page 261).

Year [a]	Number employed							
	SOLMER	Ugine-Aciers [b]	ICI [c]	CFEM [d]	PAM [e]	Esso [f]	others [g]	total
1970	–	–	–	–	47	196	140	383
1971	300	2	20	1	47	225	169	764
1972	980	82	170	138	85	294	236	1985
1973	3432	722	181	232	97	298	266	5228
1974	6082	722	198	308	97	298	266	7971
1975	6082	1186	198	308	113	298	266	8451
1977	6700	1200	260	260	350	300	900 [h]	9970

[a] Figures are for December.

[b] Special steels plant, began operating in 1973.

[c] Imperial Chemical Industries polyethylene plant; annual capacity 700000 tonnes.

[d] La Compagnie Française d'Entreprises Métalliques (metal structures plant).

[e] Port Autonome de Marseille.

[f] Oil refinery, established in 1965.

[g] Includes regasification (from liquid natural gas imported from Algeria) plant of Gaz de France, and Air Liquide oxygen and nitrogen plant.

[h] Given as 9000 in Kinsey (1978); Beau et al (1978, page 41) quote a total employment figure of 9034 for Fos in 1977.

of the second phase of the steel plant, initially to 1980–1981 (Kinsey, 1978, pages 253–257). The failure of the steel industry to grow as planned at Fos can be related to worldwide overcapacity and the overproduction crisis in steel, following the ending of the steel boom in 1974 (Mandel, 1978, page 56). This was acutely felt in France, as there had been tremendous expansion in the steel industry in the preceding years, with annual French crude steel output rising from 17·3 million tonnes in 1960 to 27·0 million tonnes in 1974 and subsequently fluctuating between 21·5 million tonnes and 23·5 million tonnes between 1975 and 1979 (Commission of the European Communities, 1980, page 91). In these circumstances, the planned expansion at Fos was not attained, and further savage cuts in employment in the Nord and Lorraine regions were enforced (Carney et al, 1980).

Not only was the growth of output less than anticipated but the expected integrated manufacturing complex, with the output of one plant forming the input to another, also failed to materialise. The SOLMER iron and steel plant has not acted as a propulsive industry and has failed to attract electrometallurgical, mechanical and electrical engineering, and motor vehicle assembly plants as originally intended; indeed, its links with other plants at Fos are relatively minor ones, such as the rolling of some special steels for Ugine-Aciers, and most of its output is exported, for example to the Nord and to West Germany. Nor have major interplant links developed between the oil and chemical companies, with the exception of an exchange of commodities between the Air Liquide and Gaz de France plants, and even this is on a smaller scale than originally anticipated; ICI, for example, set up its plant specifically to export to the North African market (Kinsey, 1979, page 282). Rather than forming a highly interlinked, technically advanced manufacturing complex, the various new plants have formed one link in national and international corporate structures of production, elements in a newly emergent international division of labour (see Kinsey, 1979, for an attempt to analyse the logic of these corporate location decisions). Nor have they become linked with existing small manufacturing firms; instead, a dual structure has emerged of new, modern, capital-intensive, export-oriented branch plants and small traditional, labour-intensive local manufacturing firms. Insofar as a relationship has developed between the two types of manufacturing, it has been an indirect and deleterious one, as the new large plants have forced up regional wage rates thereby forcing small local firms to close (Kinsey, 1979, page 282).

The third dimension on which the development of Fos has diverged from original intentions is that of employment. OREAM forecast that by 1985 the Fos scheme would provide 155000 new jobs—30000 directly, 50000 indirectly, and 75000 induced (Kinsey, 1978, page 252; see also Beau et al, 1978, page 41). Such targets will not be attained; the continuing crisis in bulk steel and petrochemicals production will mean that direct employment will fall far short of 30000, and the combination of smaller-than-anticipated multiplier effects and interfirm linkages will reduce the

numbers of jobs indirectly created and induced to substantially below
125 000. Furthermore, there is evidence that many of the currently existing
jobs have been filled by in-migrants to the area, so that unemployment
there has not been reduced as was intended; for example, in 1974 only
one-third of SOLMER's work force (itself 75% of all employment at Fos,
as shown in table 1) had been recruited in the immediate vicinity (the
départements of Bouches-du-Rhône, Var, and Gard), whereas one-third
had been recruited from Lorraine and one-third from elsewhere, both
inside and outside France (Kinsey, 1978, page 259; see also Poncet and
Damette, 1980). Indeed, the reduction of construction employment from
a peak of 17 000 in 1973 to 150 at the end of 1975 with the completion
of the first phase of the Fos scheme led to a rise in unemployment in the
area (even though over one-half of the construction work force was foreign).

There is, therefore, considerable evidence to suggest that the industrial
growth pole at Fos has not been successful in attaining the regional
planning objectives specified for it. Equally, the related central-area and
more general urban redevelopment intended to transform Marseilles into a
high-level service centre able to compete with Paris has also largely failed
in this respect. For although a certain amount of new office development
has occurred as part of the Centre Directionnel complex, this is mainly
occupied by transport, commerce, and public administration rather than
serving as major headquarters and accommodating high-level decisionmaking
functions. Although declining in relative terms as Fos expands, Marseilles
continues to function as a port rather than a métropole with financial and
decisionmaking autonomy (Kinsey, 1978, page 261).

In conclusion, then, the developments at Fos have had a limited degree
of success in terms of promoting internationally competitive branches of
basic industry within France, but have manifestly failed in terms of
meeting the economic, environmental, and social objectives concerned with
the development of the Marseilles region. This gap between intentions
and outcomes, in what can be regarded as a classic example of the
implementation of the 1960s orthodoxies of regional planning in relation
to promoting the development of peripheral regions, raises serious questions
as to the continuing appropriateness of these principles, and about
alternatives for the 1980s.

References

Beau J-P, Ferrier J-P, Girard N, Richez J, 1978 "Fos-sur-Mer: un espace-clé pour la
  compréhension des changements de la société française?" *Méditerranée* **4** 27–44
Bleitrach D, Chenu A, 1975 "L'aménagement: régulation ou approfondissement des
  contradictions sociales? Un exemple: Fos-sur-mer et l'aire métropolitaine
  marseillaise" *Environment and Planning A* **7** 367–391
Carney J, Hudson R, Lewis J R (Eds), 1980 *Regions in Crisis: New Perspectives in
  European Regional Theory* (Croom Helm, London)
Commission of the European Communities, 1980 *Basic Statistics of the Community*
  (Eurostat, Luxemburg)

Kinsey J, 1978 "The application of growth pole theory in the Aire Métropolitaine Marseillaise" *Geoforum* **9** 245-267

Kinsey J, 1979 "Industrial location and industrial development in the Aire Métropolitaine Marseillaise" *Tijdschrift voor Economische en Sociale Geografie* **70** 272-285

Mandel E, 1978 *The Second Slump* (New Left Books, London)

Poncet E, Damette F, 1980 "Global crisis and regional crises" in *Regions in Crisis: New Perspectives in European Regional Theory* Eds J Carney, R Hudson, J R Lewis (Croom Helm, London) pp 93-116

Tarrow S, 1978 "Regional policy, ideology and peripheral defense: the case of Fos-sur-Mer" in *Territorial Politics in Industrial Nations* Eds S Tarrow, P J Katzenstein, L Graziano (Praeger, New York) pp 97-122

The Limits of Economism: Towards a Political Approach to Regional Development and Planning

C WEAVER
University of British Columbia

1 Introduction

Recent critical approaches to regional theory provide a framework for analyzing the political economy of uneven development. Escalating local and regional economic problems in industrialized countries are explained as an outcome of the redeployment of capital. The main actors in this scenario are the multinational corporation and the class-based capitalist state. The contemporary logic of corporate decisionmaking is aimed at increasing the surplus value extracted from labour and expediting its realization through the circulation of capital. Among the results of this process are deindustrialization in traditional manufacturing areas, dependent branch-plant development in the periphery, resource exploitation and 'boomtownism' in various regions, and tertiarization of the metropolis. Through a new geographic specialization of economic activities by production stage, monopoly capital gains expanding control over the global economy, and territorial communities must suffer the consequences. The contradictory role of government under these circumstances—forced to encourage the rationalization of industry, but also to legitimate the resulting dislocations—has shifted regional problems squarely into the political sphere. Regional grievances have become politicized, adding to the growing crisis of the capitalist state.

Radical analyses offer a more satisfying explanation of regional problems than the empirical generalizations of inherited regional science. The mystery of lagging regions and stagnant growth poles is lessened by a structural understanding of capitalist economic relations and their transformations. The essential political and ideological factors in uneven development have also been recognized, but here, despite a continuing debate, much is left unanswered. Some of the more important problems yet to be settled include the relationships between superstructure and base, the limits of economic determinism, the power of monopoly forces vis-à-vis regional and class alliances, and the political alternatives to continued dependency and underdevelopment.

In this paper, I will suggest an approach to these issues in the context of regional planning, focusing on two questions which appear to be of paramount concern in any reconsideration of regional development theory. First, what is the relationship between the production of economic value, regional specialization, and exports? Second, what are the roles of politics and ideology in the local accumulation of wealth and development?

2 The sources of economic wealth or value

Figure 1 portrays the sources of economic wealth or value in a space economy. *Labour power*, *physical resources*, and *capital*, of course, represent the primary factors of economic production; use value and exchange value are the outcomes of that process. A region may employ its own labour (LP), resources (PR), and capital (C), or these can be brought in from outside the area (denoted LP′, PR′, and C′). *Use value* (UV), meaning goods and services created for the benefit of their producers, is normally site specific, typically being utilized in situ. Likewise, *potential exchange value* (PEV), commodities produced for sale in the market economy, is initially an attribute of economic activities which occur at specific geographic locations. It is only when its value is realized through sale, that is, as *realized exchange value*, either within the region of origin itself (REV) or somewhere else (REV′), that it enters the capital circuit and can be enumerated.

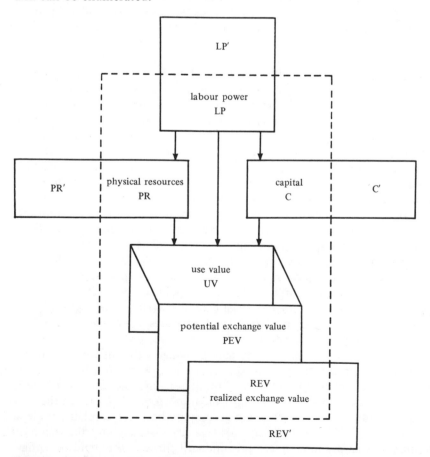

Figure 1. The sources of economic wealth or value.

Although these fundamental concepts are quite familiar, their implications within the regional setting have seldom really been explored. Theoretically fixed boundaries have limited the view of regional wealth creation to a narrow range of alternatives. This reductionism has then been accorded scientific legitimacy and political sanction, built into the institutional structure of government, and made the linchpin of economic policy—as well as the target of radical criticism. It is disseminated through the schools and media, and we are hard put to think outside its terms of reference. I will argue here, however, that such a particularistic viewpoint has identifiable historic origins and serves explicit ideological purposes (Myrdal, 1969). Furthermore, in order to achieve substantial change under contemporary circumstances, it may be necessary to adopt an entirely different perspective, based on broader definitions of economic value creation and a strategy of political education and grass roots organization.

We must begin with the question of economic value. Classical economists in the eighteenth and nineteenth centuries were anxious to identify the origins of wealth in a national economy. Their search began with analysis of the mechanisms which determine the 'natural' price of commodities, and carried them to formulation of the labour theory of value (Marx, 1967; Ricardo, 1953; Smith, 1970). In this context, it was only a short step to the identification of the general benefits of encouraging comparative advantage through the division of labour and economic specialization (Ricardo, 1953). In fact, as writers in the classical tradition from Smith to Marx pointed out, primitive accumulation and the foundations of capitalist production were dependent on specialized labour and exchange (Heilbroner, 1953; Barber, 1967; Deane, 1978). Even more fundamental than the question of economic efficiency was the imperative to develop a wider spectrum of needs which must be met through trade. Only then could true commodity relations be established, and only then could significant amounts of surplus value be realized, creating in middleman profits the first free form of capital (Bookchin, 1974). The political creation of wage labour through such devices as the Enclosure Acts and the Poor Law in England allowed this process to be pushed back a step further, to the extraction of potential surplus value at the point of production itself; they thus laid the basis for industrial capitalism (Hobsbawm, 1962).

Although it was recognized that the first widespread division of labour probably took place between town and countryside (Merrington, 1975), the local geography of production and exchange was a matter of minor concern. Mercantilism and industrial capitalism, were both based on national class alliances between the bourgeoisie and the aspiring absolutist monarchy. The national market provided an economic basis for the modern nation-state, as well as the geographic basis for capitalist trade and accumulation. The liberal battle for free trade throughout the nineteenth century was an attempt by the predominant powers to extend potential markets, and thus capital circuits, over even wider geographic areas.

Protectionism on the part of newly industrializing countries such as the United States and Germany was an extremely telling precaution, for although capital might be brought in from outside, the realization of surplus value added by manufacture had to be limited as far as possible to entrepreneurs within the national economy if local accumulation was to occur.

We can trace historical developments and the arguments of the theorists with the aid of figure 1. Realized exchange value, in the lower right-hand corner of the diagram, was recognized to be the source of capitalist accumulation (C). Profit gained through selling commodities in the market was the major circuit of such accumulation under merchant capitalism; the amount accumulated was a determinant of market size and selling price. Theorists traced the question of price to the potential exchange value of a commodity, and ultimately to the labour power necessary for its production. Market size rested upon the geographic area opened to trade, typically an artifact of political boundaries, represented in figure 1 by the broken line, and upon the sphere of economic life which could be directed away from use value and simple commodity production and refocused around market transactions (Bookchin, 1974). In Europe both these matters were in part, if not predominantly, political issues; they rested on the breakdown of guild monopolies and price-fixing, the establishment of larger polities, and the replacement of feudal obligations with money payments[1]. The economist's doctrine of free trade was an attempt to push market boundaries beyond the frontiers of the nation-state (that is, to produce REV'), a political device with profound economic implications that could only work themselves out with industrialization.

Merchant capitalism had been a mechanism for organizing, expanding, and exploiting the *distribution* side of the economy; the genius of industrial capitalism was that it controlled and developed *production* as well. The factors of production themselves became commodities which could be controlled by capital and organized systematically for the creation of potential exchange value. This new efficiency, aided by political demands of the rising middle class, and eventually the policies of liberal governments, allowed capitalist manufacturing to displace most use-value and simple commodity production. The possibilities for creating and realizing surplus value were multiplied manyfold, and reinvestment of surplus value in productive capital established new capital circuits which endowed the entire process with a revolutionary dynamism. As manufacturing grew and destroyed the guild system of production it was able to move into the towns, through its expansive energies and various legal contrivances, creating the vast proletarian conurbations of the nineteenth and early twentieth centuries (Bookchin, 1974; Merrington, 1975).

---

[1] The well-known political demands of the bourgeoisie throughout the age of revolution were based on this very programme; see, for example, Hobsbawm (1962) and Rudé (1964).

Within the nation-state, productive forces became highly mobile, concentrating in established industrial centres: people, resources, and capital (LP', PR', C') could be brought together from various regions according to the capitalists' ability to realize exchange value (REV, REV') and pay for them. A monopoly over techniques, a head start in accumulation, and direct access to political power gave ascendent metropolitan entrepreneurs an overwhelming advantage. If the structure of figure 1 is taken within the context of subnational regions, capital from the metropolis (C') was able to buy up local productive forces (LP, PR, C) and redirect them towards its own ends (PEV), selling some of the commodities inside the region itself (REV) and some outside the area (REV'). Production factors could also be purchased and then transformed and sold in other regions. In either case, capital circuits were redirected to centre on the metropolis, and a kind of regional specialization was established, if only by attrition in peripheral areas. Based to some extent on the peculiarities of history and physical geography, some places (the metropolises) built up an increasing fund of capital and productive capabilities, whereas others found themselves with less and less wealth (UV, REV, REV') and with fewer and fewer things to do (UV, PEV).

Moving back to the national scale, the concept of free trade advocated creating these same circumstances between countries. Commodity markets would be expanded (REV'), as would factor markets (LP', PR', C'). Of course countries exporting resources (PR') would typically be different from those exporting capital and labour (C', LP'). And it would be the countries which controlled capital circuits and determined the nature of production which would be the most likely to benefit. Without this power, any increase of potential exchange value brought in from outside the country and realized in the local economy would only mean fewer possibilities for local production and accumulation[2]. Countries which came into control of modern productive forces experienced economic expansion, and their middle classes flourished; countries that supplied mainly raw materials (PR) and created little indigenous potential exchange value (PEV) became, at least relatively, poorer and increasingly dependent.

[2] Rudé (1964, pages 59–60) observed this uneven relationship between England and France at the beginning of the industrial revolution: "Pitt, the Prime Minister, who had read Adam Smith and been convinced by many of the arguments of the new school of political economy, set about the work of peaceful reconstruction in vigorous style: he increased the annual revenue, reduced the national debt, kept public expenditure on a tight string, and even signed a highly advantageous 'Free Trade' agreement (the Eden–Vergennes Treaty of 1786) with the French: thus manufactures prospered". This was only in England, however. Writing of the economic crisis of 1787–1789 in France, Rudé (1964, pages 73–74) noted: "From agriculture it [the crisis] spread to industry; and unemployment, already developing from the 'Free Trade' treaty of 1786 with England, reached disastrous proportions in Paris and the textile centres of Lille, Lyons, Troyes, Sedan, Rouen and Rheims".

In spite of the repeated use of protectionism to foster national industrialization wherever circumstances allowed, the traditional liberal doctrine of *laissez-faire*, under the mantle of free trade theory, has remained the centrepiece of economic thinking up to the present day (see, for example, Heller, 1968). Emanating first primarily from Great Britain and then the United States, free trade has been enforced whenever possible, on others, as the basis of international relations. Exchange value realized through exports (REV') has become almost the only acknowledged source of wealth. Concepts such as comparative advantage and the benefits of geographic specialization became handmaidens to this idea. Their origins in the apologetics of the classical theorists and modern ideological purpose—with multinational capital expanding exchange value at every stage of production—are clear. We must now turn to regional economics to appreciate their place in regional development and planning.

3 Economic value and the regions
Trade theory and the economics of location were the foundation stones of regional science (Meyer, 1963), which in turn has provided the conceptual framework for planning over the last twenty years[3] (Friedmann and Weaver, 1979). Free trade within the national economy presumably could be taken for granted, and the ideas of comparative advantage and geographic specialization became the main components of regional science arguments. In the sparsely settled environment of North America, Innis (1930) had identified *staple exports* as the basis of capital accumulation and eventual industrialization. North (1955) adapted this *export base* concept as the primary explanation for regional economic development, and Perloff et al (1960) used it as the key to their classic empirical analysis of *Regions, Resources and Economic Growth*. Whatever the historical reality—and there can be no doubt that resource exploitation for the market has played a formative role in North American life—economic base theory became the *idée fixe* of regional science. Regional growth models from that of North (1955), through that of Borts and Stein (1962), to that of Richardson (1973) have rested on arguments concerning comparative advantage, specialization, interregional factor flows, and eventual diversification. Interpretations of input–output models and such techniques as industrial complex analysis have all been directly dependent upon this singular view of economic value creation. And regional planning strategies both of the *areal development* school (Klaassen, 1965) and of the *growth centres* school (see, for example, Kuklinski, 1972; Kuklinski and Petrella, 1972) have been explicitly dedicated to encouraging specialization as the royal road to development.

Again with reference to figure 1, the logic of such constructs was quite simple. If the area bounded by the broken line represents a region, inside its borders will be found some combination of labour power, physical

[3] For example, Walter Isard, the father of regional science, began his career as an international trade theorist.

resources, and capital. Development was said to be dependent upon putting together a mixture of factors which could produce a specific commodity (PEV) at a competitive price which could be sold on the national or international market, realizing exchange value (REV'). All else would flow from this beginning. If additional productive forces were necessary, they would be brought in from the outside. Typically this meant bringing in exogenous capital (C'), but resources (PR') or labour (LP') could also be supplied if the other inputs seemed attractive enough. Exchange value gained through export (REV') could then be used to make complementary local investments which build up the regional economic base, this process leading to a Rostowian world of sustained economic growth (Rostow, 1960).

The success, in Western countries, of regional policies founded on such thinking has been problematic. Even liberal commentators give them doubtful marks (for example, Richardson, 1978), and a burgeoning school of critical analysts point to their fundamental structural fallacies and ideological motivation (for example, Holland, 1976; Lipietz, 1977; Editorial Collective, 1978; Carney et al, 1980). The two major variants of this radical critique can also be outlined fairly clearly in terms of figure 1.

Underdevelopment/dependency theory (UDT) had its origins in the disillusionment of Third World intellectuals with the outcomes of capitalist development (Frank, 1967). Its fundamental indictment of neocolonialism and the multinational corporation has also come to be used to explain regional problems in industrialized countries (Hechter, 1975; Holland, 1976; Phillips, 1978; Marchak, 1979). UDT begins with the observation that direct investment by the multinational corporation, or meso-sector (C'), gives corporate decisionmakers the capability of organizing other regional production inputs (ie LP, PR) to suit their own specialized purposes, thus controlling the region's potential exchange value and internalizing the exchange value realized through 'domestic' sales and exports (REV, REV'). This decreases the sphere of use-value production as well as the potential exchange value which can be produced by existing capital (C). Local capital accumulation is short-circuited, and specialized production for export imposes significant opportunity costs on the regional economy.

The outcome of this process, as portrayed by some writers on UDT (Lafont, 1971; Hechter, 1975), is a cultural division of labour: internal colonialism. Without the attributes of sovereignty, peripheral regions are unable to promote local accumulation (C) and the development of a well-rounded local economy. Dependent institutions lay them open to a continuing cycle of economic specialization and underdevelopment at the hands of national and multinational capital (C'). Producing only the most limited range of regionally-oriented commodities (PEV), little exchange value can be realized locally (REV) and corporate decisionmakers can choose at any time to cut off the slim exogenous sources of regional livelihood (REV'). Indeed, despite their attempts at negotiation and

appeasement, many nation-states today find themselves in a similar
position. Group solidarity and regionalist activism in Brittany and Wales,
for example, are perhaps inevitable sequels in this chain of events, striking
at the dependent institutions which restrict more effective forms of
political action.

The second strand of radical regional science takes its roots in Marxist
economic theory, and provides a more generalized analysis of uneven
development under monopoly capitalism (see, for example, Mandel, 1978).
The health of a regional economy can be explained by an understanding
of *capital circuits* (Palloix, 1977) and the contemporary *geographic
organization of production* (Massey, 1976). For the sake of simplicity,
figure 1 shows only the simple production (PEV) and realization of exchange
value (REV, REV') through commodity sales. In fact, the self-expansion of
capital occurs in all three capital circuits: commodity, finance, and
productive. Today, in the framework of the multinational corporation,
self-expansion takes place on a world scale, and the predominant capital
circuit is the sphere of production itself (Palloix, 1977). Not only do the
multinationals increase their holdings by monopoly control of globalized
markets and by autofinancing, but each new export platform scattered
across the world periphery increases their internalized stock of productive
capital (C') and potential exchange value (PEV). While monopoly capital
benefits at each step along the way, regional populations gain few rewards
in terms of economic 'rent' from export sales (REV'), interest, and equity
shares from finance (C), or from increased productive capacity (C) and
inventories (PEV).

This 'divide and conquer' strategy is implemented through the global
organization of geographic specialization by production stage (Massey,
1976). Each region is allocated one specific operation to accomplish, the
products of which are then duly passed on within the corporate structure
to some other location for further assembly and processing. Few branch
plants produce commodities for final demand; they typically deal in
components. There is frequently no local exchange value that could even
be realized from their activities (REV), only an accounting entry forwarded
to the corporate headquarters, as are all other forms of capital expansion
which take place within the corporate structure.

The class-based capitalist state is obliged to aid and abet monopoly
capital in the rationalization of the geographic pattern of production.
Analysis of the role of the state in uneven development has become a
central focus of debate among critical regional scientists (see, for example,
Bleitrach, 1977; Carney et al, 1980; Dunford et al, 1980; Geddes, 1979;
Hudson, 1980; Jensen, 1980; Morgan, 1979; 1980). At a general level,
two fundamental questions have been raised:
(1) What is the relative autonomy of state activity?
(2) What are the inherent contradictions involved in state intervention?

Answers have been sought by examining the instruments of state power: administration, arbitration, regulation, monetary and fiscal control, direct action, and urban and regional planning.

It is found that these instruments of governmental power are used to further two general class-based objectives: (a) the production and reproduction of capital; and (b) reproduction of the social formation. The first of these entails encouraging in every way possible the more efficient extraction of surplus value from labour (LP, LP′), increased production or commodities (PEV), more rapid circulation of capital (in the form of REV, REV′, for example), and further accumulation of capital (C, C′). On the other hand, reproduction of the social formation means guaranteeing continued reproduction of the relations of production, assuring the replacement of labour power (LP, LP′), and providing for maintenance of the superstructure. Under the logic of capitalism, maintenance of the social formation is *essential* for, but *auxiliary* to, commodity production (PEV) and the accumulation of capital. Ultimately, continued survival of the state depends on its promotion of efficient self-expansion capital, which today requires the state to form alliances with multinational interests against regional entrepreneurs and workers (Dulong, 1976; 1978). The obvious contradictions involved in the active government promotion of uneven development create a crisis in the political sphere (Habermas, 1973; Poulantzas, 1976). As with the UDT scenario, once again we are faced with regions in crisis (Carney et al, 1980) and with festering political unrest (Nairn, 1977).

4 The possibilities of political action

Contemporary regional problems can hardly be ignored when combined with the growing contagion of regional unrest and political activism. Radical political economy, I believe, provides a useful explanation of the causes of regional problems, but stops short of suggesting systematic regional solutions. Running throughout the skein of underdevelopment/ dependency theory and Marxist regional science is a focus on the explosion of commodity relations, exchange value, and capital circuits to the global scale. This is an accurate reflection of dominant forces in the contemporary economy. It provides critical analysis with poignant insights. Concomitantly, however, it typically assigns the idea of *positive* political action below the national scale to the dustbins of utopianism or reaction. Like the liberal regional scientists and the classical economists, radicals have built a theoretical framework based almost exclusively on the assumption of production for exchange and export. But what is the necessity of such an assumption, and what strategies might an alternative view suggest?

These questions must be approached with two basic observations. First, whereas the interests of monopoly capital and the capitalist state may be served in varying degrees by global rationalization, those of most regional populations clearly are not. Many organized regional groups display a growing awareness that increasing specialization, dependence, and outside control lead to structural emaciation and instability, not development. Modern technology notwithstanding, much of the formerly humanized landscape in Western countries has become socioeconomically uninhabitable over the last generation. And how many today would argue that the megalopolis is a viable replacement? Commodity relations penetrate the most intimate dimensions of life; living standards are eroded; work for most people, when available, verges on the senseless; and the lack of community—the moral void—is all but overpowering.

Second, as shown in figure 1, the sources of economic value in a territorial community simply are not limited to exchange value realized through exports. The emerging middle class under mercantile capitalism did indeed owe its position to such wealth, as does the multinational corporation. But this cannot be allowed to circumscribe our field of vision. Nor can public ownership merely be substituted for private, leaving unchanged the regional structures of production and exchange. A more fundamental change is needed, and the roadblocks are apparently not primarily economic; they are political and ideological.

Figure 2 suggests some of the political leverage points in the space economy. Traditionally, concern has been focused on the upper part of the diagram. Classical economists were concerned to establish an ideology which would sanction extension of the market economy and promote capital accumulation; this was a truly radical doctrine under the *ancien régime*. Political struggles during the age of revolution eventually saw the bourgeoisie in control of government, and *laissez-faire*, at least nominally, the constitutional basis of society. In Europe and North America this led to the creation of metropolitan-dominated industrial economies linked together by finance capital and commodity exchange. Private monopolies and global economic cycles brought on a new series of political struggles during the first half of the twentieth century, which have redefined the ideology of state–capital relations and legitimized the concepts of demand management, state subsidies, and limited government ownership. The 1970s found governments absorbed in coping with the multinational invasion, simultaneously promoting it and attempting to protect the scope and interests of national capital.

For fifty years there have been sporadic attempts by the capitalist state to intervene in the process of geographic rationalization. Whatever else may have been accomplished, however, interventionist doctrines at the national level have done little to even out the developmental map, and today multinationalism is taking much effective power out of the hands of national decisionmakers, who might be responsive to territorial politics. Recent theoretical discussions of politics, ideology, and the capitalist state have tended to focus on the macroissues touched upon above (see, for example, Clark, 1980), but local development and planning may require that we concentrate our attention towards the bottom of figure 2, on national–regional relations and local politics (Friedmann, 1980; Dear, 1981; Dear and Clark, 1981).

Regions are tied into the broader political economy by the flows and linkages shown in the lower half of figure 2, and these structural relationships are fixed and mediated at the interface by politics. Seen from one perspective, then, regional development, at the outset, is a political struggle to readjust these structures so as to favour regional wealth creation and local accumulation. Table 1 specifies some of the more important aspects of this struggle in terms of the national–regional interrelationships suggested in figure 2; the leverage points illustrated in this figure are described below.

(1) *Regional social formations* The first steps toward development *must* take place within the regions themselves; the problem is to enhance regional political awareness and organization without falling back on

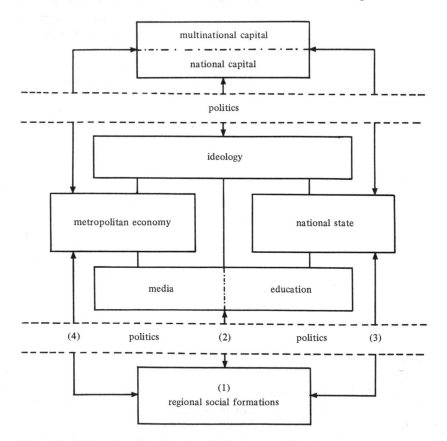

Figure 2. Political leverage points in the space economy.

reactionary status-group solidarity (Hechter, 1975). Geographically uneven development in Western countries today is an outcome of production relations under multinational capitalism (Soja, 1980); typically, it can only be reversed by progressive class alliances. In many instances, regional capitalists have largely been displaced by national and multinational interests. Here, regional struggle becomes almost purely class struggle; elsewhere, local politics retain a more traditional form, serious internal conflict remains, but uniting the producing classes holds the key to victory at the ballot box.

Progressive class alliances and electoral control of local institutions depend directly on elaboration of a regional ideology and on construction of a 'corporative' regional economy [see (2) and (4) below]. A possible building block both for political organization and for economic production along these lines is the *syndicalist community*: an association of inter-penetrating labour unions, community action groups, progressive clubs, and local political parties. Their goals centre on creating a self-managed regional economy—a corporate economy in the true sense—in which use-value production plays an increasingly important role, and where the reduced sphere of market transactions becomes a predominantly regional affair. Unlike the current situation, where multinational capital plays countries and regions off one against the other (Goodman, 1979), self-reliant development is not a 'zero sum' game. Communities organized to meet any of their own needs share much in common, and their mutual interests set the groundwork for productive interregional alliances: a kind of *integral federalism*, both economic and political (Bancal, 1973; Voyenne, 1973).

Table 1. Political struggle and national–regional relations.

Domain	Components	Objectives
(1) Regional social formations	Labour power; local capital; the regional market; the local state.	Regional and interregional class alliances; region-serving productive relations and institutions [see (4) below].
(2) Ideology and communications	Political and economic philosophy; the press, media, and education.	Regional consciousness and ideology; locally directed education; opposition in the press and media.
(3) Ties with the national state	Laws; regulations; policy; taxes and transfer payments.	Minimization of outside control and dependence.
(4) Ties with the metropolitan economy	Factor flows; realization of surplus value; commodity movements.	Expansion of use-value and regional-exchange-value creation; control of local capital circuits.

(2) *Ideology and communications* The ideology of multinational
capitalism makes itself felt in local social formations primarily through the
communications media and through public education. The metropolitan
economy and national state act, with fluctuating enthusiasm, as
intermediaries in this process, and a substantial residue of contradictory
values tints most regional thinking. Besides the explicit doctrines of
free trade, specialization, and production for export, a universalizing
consumer culture permeates the press and airways, and textbooks from
elementary school to university present history as a *fait accompli*
culminating in the present state of affairs. Not a unique prejudice,
perhaps, as Toynbee (1948) has pointed out, but it seems clear that if
development at the regional level requires increasing self-awareness and
further evolution then this way of thinking must be changed. The cultural
basis for such a reawakening might be what Professor Hou Renzhi has called
"The principle of *critical inheritance*": an appreciation and transformation
of past accomplishments within the context of contemporary struggle[4].

At the macroscopic level, ideology tends to be created through political
manoeuvering between capital and the national state; at the regional level
today, predominantly, it is imposed from above. A political confrontation
between the regions and the national state, such as that currently taking
place across Western Europe and North America, may serve as the bellows
for forging an alternative regionalist ideology. This, in turn, finds its own
countervailing voice through locally inspired media and education.
Newspapers, radio, and television operated by the national government
or owned by various segments of capital probably cannot perform this
function. Nor is it likely to be furthered by school systems using nationally
structured curricula and educational materials. The success of many
progressive locally run schools suggests that other options are available,
however, as do some community-controlled television stations and
newspapers (see, for example, Kopkind, 1979). Writing of community
power and self-management at the neighbourhood level, Morris and Hess
(1975, pages 24–25) have observed in practice that:
> "Communication links are established, first on a haphazard basis
> (passers through bring news of new developments), then in a more
> formal network (WATS lines, newsletters, labour exchanges), and
> ideology and rootedness mix together to produce a new concept of
> neighbourhood and territory and politics".

(3) *Ties with the national state* Forward-looking political organization and
construction of a progressive regionalist ideology require some measure of
disengagement from the policies, regulations, laws, and purse strings of the
national state. The ease with which this can be done obviously varies

---

[4] Professor Hou, Head of the Geography Department at Beijing University, explained
the concept of *critical inheritance* as the ideological motivation of the new city plan of
Beijing, in a guest lecture at the University of British Columbia, 7 March 1980.

from country to country. Further devolution in Canada, for example, could provide the institutional structure for a genuine confederation; this would be significantly more difficult in the United States, with federal ownership of untapped natural resources and effective centralized control over most administrative functions. In industrial Europe, the mixed outcomes of devolution campaigns in the United Kingdom and Belgium underline the importance of differing constitutions, histories, and political cultures. Centralized France—the crèche of modern regionalism—has operated under a Jacobin system, despite the often violent efforts of Corsicans and Bretons, until the modest reforms of the current socialist government.

National policies are perhaps the easiest of these centralist ties to break, requiring mainly unity of purpose, organization, and traditional territorial politics (Tarrow, 1977; Tarrow et al, 1978). Central government regulations pose a more difficult problem, because they go hand in hand with transfer payments and other accoutrements of the welfare state that depressed regions, especially, have come to depend upon. It might be hoped that the current post-Keynesian retrenchment from social democracy in many countries can act as a positive incentive to more self-reliant behaviour. Changing legal forms to favour local initiatives presents arguably the most heroic task, for gaining the indispensable measure of regional sovereignty, upon which development probably rests, demands a real devolution of power. This is particularly critical in the area of taxation, as independent local government action requires local access to local wealth, and the national state is understandably loath to give up any of its revenues during a time of fiscal crisis (O'Connor, 1973; Poulantzas, 1976).

The idea here, however, is not merely to gain control of the local state apparatus and then to do battle with London, Washington, or Paris. The greatest regional strength in such a struggle is that political power at the local level can be reabsorbed into civil society, and this transformation rests largely in the organization of economic production.

(4) *Ties with the metropolitan economy* Civil society in the regions can wield substantial decisionmaking power through social control of the means of production. Peripheral economies—both in the private sector and in the public sector—are typically run from the metropolis. Whereas many sophisticated products and services depend on high technology, scale-economies, and global markets, the vast majority of things in material life require no such thresholds. Outside capital, political control, and dumping are the secrets of the monopolists. Historically, forced migration of regional labour power and the geographic transfer of surplus value have reinforced this outside hegemony. Today, market control, capturing wealth through exchange value, and forced savings transfers, primarily pension funds and insurance (Rifkin and Barber, 1978; Holland, 1979), are the main channels of exploitation. The path to development bypasses these detours, internalizing local economic needs and locally created wealth.

At the regional level in some countries, it may be possible to employ a limited range of traditional protectionist measures. Examples include the local state monopoly of liquor sales in British Columbia which safeguards provincial wine production, or California's strict control of imported fruits and vegetables. But the options here are relatively limited, and the dangers of controls leading to business as usual under local state capitalism are ever present. A positive alternative structure needs to be built which cannot be co-opted from the metropolis or the legislative assembly hall.

Pragmatically, commodities will obviously continue to be produced for the local market, earning local exchange value, and some specialized production for export will also continue in order to buy things which simply cannot be made within the region. But these activities cannot be the main thrust of development strategies; they provide only the most limited self-reliance and subsequent political leverage. The tasks of regional planning are expanding the sphere of use-value production and helping to implement new, protected capital circuits.

The idea of use-value production on the part of individuals and domestic living units has limited applicability as a development strategy, although contemporary life undeniably offers many positive opportunities for a 'retreat to subsistence'. Use-value creation for regional development can most effectively be centred around the syndicalist communities mentioned earlier; these put ownership and management of the means of production in the hands of the producer/consumers. Depending on the specific regional setting, a wide range of 'wage goods' and personal services can be made available in this fashion, including locally produced foods, clothing, and child care, for example. Consumer durables, such as construction materials and even housing, can be produced in this manner as well. And some part of regional exchange-value production, a kind of simple commodity production, can also take place within this syndicalist structure, by using *labour unit credits* and modern computerized accounting methods in place of the standard credit cards, cheques, and currency. This latter provision would allow modern production outside the cash economy; it would simultaneously provide a practicable medium of exchange while protecting locally created wealth from the leakages so typical of regional economies.

Conceivably, a regional *labour-exchange bank* can also supply financing for further regional development, although more conventional financial circuits play the lead role in this area, at least in the beginning. These are accessible and can be controlled. Local legislative powers can ensure that locally collected taxes are deposited in a local development fund which can only be used for local investments. Efficiency arguments recommending a global search for profitable investments completely overlook the quintessential structural importance of interindustrial linkages and multipliers. Regional perspectives should similarly be applied in the creation of *mutualist insurance programmes* of all sorts, which establish through private contracts and public law a matrix of channels for capital accumulation at the heart of the syndicalist community.

Corporate pension funds are said to represent one of the largest contemporary sources of investment capital (Rifkin and Barber, 1978). Labour unions and regional government, working within the syndicalist structure, must see that these great reservoirs of surplus value are put to work in the place that they are created, until such time as export production can be more fully integrated into the fabric of regional society. The profound temptation to become overly entangled in export production for short-term gain, however, is vividly illustrated in many regions, where petroleum development and other resource exploitation have made provincial government policies the most immediate stumbling blocks to self-reliant development. Long-term stability and equity can only be created by working from the bottom up, investing the primary structures of civil society with political and economic competence.

5 Conclusion

It has long been proscribed to emphasize the political side of political economy. For regional planners, politics are typically anathema: at best a nuisance, at worst a dangerous foray into the realm of power and the irrational. Conversely, market exchange, the specialization of labour, and free trade have achieved canonical status, associated almost uncritically with progress and modernity. Any serious suggestion of their curtailment is suspect. And yet commodity relations, specialization, and metropolitan dominance coincide precisely in recent Western history with regional decay and the ascent of national power. There are signs of change abroad once again, however. Multinational influence, economic crisis, and political activism point to the possible transformation of many established relationships. One of these portents is the increasing ferment in the industrial periphery, as regional activists rediscover the politics of development and the perennial strength of cooperative economy. Significant practical experience and research is needed to identify the real intervention points and limits. There can be no doubt that the road is long and wearisome—and often unsuccessful. But relevant regional science and planning will be deeply involved in this struggle.

Acknowledgements. I would like to express my appreciation to Jim Carney, Michael Dear, William Goldsmith, Torsten Hägerstrand, Michael Hebbert, Ray Hudson, and Ernst Weissmann for their detailed comments and criticisms of an earlier draft of this article. Its many remaining faults, of course, are my own responsibility.

References
Bancal J, 1973 "L'anarchisme et l'autogestion de Proudhon" *Anarchisme et Fédéralisme* (163/64) 15–38
Barber W J, 1967 *A History of Economic Thought* (Penguin Books, Harmondsworth, Middx)

Bleitrach D, 1977 "Région métropolitaine et appareils hégémoniques locaux" *Espaces et Sociétés* 47-55

Bookchin M, 1974 *The Limits of the City* (Harper Colophon Books, New York)

Borts G H, Stein J L, 1962 *Economic Growth in a Free Economy* (Columbia University Press, New York)

Carney J G, Hudson R, Lewis J R (Eds), 1980 *Regions in Crisis: New Perspectives in European Regional Theory* (Croom Helm, London)

Clark G L, 1980 "Capitalism and regional inequality" *Annals of the Association of American Geographers* **70** 226-237

Deane P, 1978 *The Evolution of Economic Ideas* (Cambridge University Press, Cambridge)

Dear M, 1981 "A theory of the local state" in *Political Studies from Spatial Perspective* Eds A D Burnett, P J Taylor (John Wiley, Chichester, Sussex) pp 183-200

Dear M, Clark G L, 1981 "Dimensions of local state autonomy" *Environment and Planning A* **13** 1277-1294

Dulong R, 1976 "La crise du rapport état/société locale vue au travers de la politique régionale" in *La Crise de l'État* Ed. N Poulantzas (Presses Universitaires de France, Paris) pp 209-232

Dulong R, 1978 *Les Régions, l'État et la Société Locale* (Presses Universitaires de France, Paris)

Dunford M, Geddes M, Perrons D, 1980 "Working notes on the crisis and regional policy" paper presented to the CES Regionalism Conference, April

Editorial Collective (Eds), 1978 "Special issue on uneven regional development" *Review of Radical Political Economics* **10** (3) (Fall)

Frank A G, 1967 *Capitalism and Underdevelopment in Latin America* (Monthly Review Press, New York)

Friedmann J, 1980 "Urban communes, self-management, and the reconstruction of the local state" School of Architecture and Urban Planning, University of California, Los Angeles, Calif.

Friedmann J, Weaver C, 1979 *Territory and Function: The Evolution of Regional Planning* (Edward Arnold, Maidenhead, Berks)

Geddes M, 1979 "Uneven development and the Scottish Highlands" Urban and Regional Studies Working Paper 17, University of Sussex, Brighton, England

Goodman R, 1979 *The Last Entrepreneurs* (Simon and Schuster, New York)

Habermas J, 1973 *The Legitimation Crisis* (Beacon Press, Boston, Mass)

Hechter M, 1975 *Internal Colonialism: The Celtic Fringe in British National Development, 1536-1966* (Routledge and Kegan Paul, Henley-on-Thames, Oxon)

Heilbroner R L, 1953 *The Worldly Philosophers* (Simon and Schuster, New York)

Heller H R, 1968 *International Trade: Theory and Empirical Evidence* (Prentice-Hall, Englewood Cliffs, NJ)

Hobsbawm E J, 1962 *The Age of Revolution, 1789-1848* (Mentor Books, London)

Holland S, 1976 *Capital Versus the Regions* (Macmillan, London)

Holland S, 1979 "Capital, labour and the regions: aspects of economic, social and political inequality in regional theory and policy" in *Spatial Inequalities and Regional Development* Eds H Folmer, J Oosterhaven (Martinus Nijhoff, The Hague) pp 185-218

Hudson R, 1980 "Capital accumulation and regional problems: a study of North East England" unpublished manuscript, Department of Geography, University of Durham, Durham, England

Innis H A, 1930 *The Fur Trade in Canada* (University of Toronto Press, Toronto, Ontario)

Jensen H T, 1980 "The role of the state in regional development planning and management" Dunelm Translations 5, Department of Geography, University of Durham, Durham, England

Klaassen L, 1965 *Area Economic and Social Redevelopment. Guidelines and Programmes* (OECD, Paris)
Kopkind A, 1979 " 'Sea-level' media: up from underground" in *Co-ops, Communes and Collectives: Experiments in Social Change in the 1960s and 1970s* Eds J Case, R Taylor (Pantheon Books, New York) pp 66-88
Kuklinski A (Ed.), 1972 *Growth Poles and Growth Centres in Regional Planning* (Mouton, Paris)
Kuklinski A, Petrella A (Eds), 1972 *Growth Poles and Regional Policies* (Mouton, Paris)
Lafont R, 1971 *Décoloniser en France* (Gallimard, Paris)
Lipietz A, 1977 *Le Capital et son Espace* (Maspero, Paris)
Mandel E, 1978 *Late Capitalism* (Verso, London)
Marchak P, 1979 *In Whose Interest: An Essay on Multinational Corporations in a Canadian Context* (McClelland and Stewart, Toronto)
Marx K, 1967 *Das Kapital* Ed. F Engels, volume 1 (International Publishers, New York)
Massey D, 1976 "Restructuring and regionalism: some spatial effects of the crisis" CES Working Note 479, Centre for Environmental Studies, London
Merrington J, 1975 "Town and country in the transition to capitalism" *New Left Review* 93 71-92
Meyer J R, 1963 "Regional economics: a survey" *American Economic Review* 53 19-54
Morgan K, 1979 "State regional interventions and industrial reconstruction in post-war Britain: the case of Wales" Urban and Regional Studies Working Paper 16, University of Sussex, Brighton, England
Morgan K, 1980 "The reformulation of the regional question, regional policy and the British state" Urban and Regional Studies Working Paper 18, University of Sussex, Brighton, England
Morris D, Hess K, 1975 *Neighborhood Power: The New Localism* (Beacon Press, Boston, Mass)
Myrdal G, 1969 *The Political Element in the Development of Economic Theory* translated by P Streeten (Simon and Schuster, New York)
Nairn T, 1977 *The Break-up of Britain* (New Left Books, London)
North D C, 1955 "Location theory and regional economic growth" *Journal of Political Economy* 63 243-258
O'Connor J, 1973 *The Fiscal Crisis of the State* (St Martin's Press, New York)
Palloix C, 1977 "The self-expansion of capital on a world scale" *Review of Radical Political Economics* 9 1-29
Perloff H S, Dunn E S Jr, Lampard E E, Muth R F, 1960 *Regions, Resources and Economic Growth* (Johns Hopkins University Press, Baltimore, Md)
Phillips P, 1978 *Regional Disparities* (James Lorimer, Toronto)
Poulantzas N (Ed.), 1976 *La Crise de l'État* (Presses Universitaires de France, Paris)
Ricardo D, 1953 *Principles of Political Economy and Taxation* (Cambridge University Press, Cambridge)
Richardson H W, 1973 *Regional Growth Theory* (John Wiley, New York)
Richardson H W, 1978 *Regional and Urban Economics* (Penguin Books, Harmondsworth, Middx)
Rifkin J, Barber R, 1978 *The North Will Rise Again* (Beacon Press, Boston, Mass)
Rostow W W, 1960 *The Stages of Economic Growth: A Non-Communist Manifesto* (Cambridge University Press, Cambridge)
Rudé G, 1964 *Revolutionary Europe, 1783-1815* (Meridan Press, Elnora, NY)
Smith A, 1970, in *The Wealth of Nations* Ed. A Skinner (Penguin Books, Harmondsworth, Middx) pp 157-166

Soja E, 1980 "The socio-spatial dialectic" *Annals of the Association of American Geographers* **70** 207-225

Tarrow S, 1977 *Between Centre and Periphery: Grassroots Politicians in Italy and France* (Yale University Press, New Haven, Conn.)

Tarrow S, Katzenstein P J, Graziano L (Eds), 1978 *Territorial Politics in Industrial Nations* (Praeger, New York)

Toynbee A J, 1948 *Civilization on Trial* (Oxford University Press, London)

Voyenne B, 1973 *Le Fédéralisme de P. J. Proudhon* (Presses d'Europe, Paris)

Previous volumes in the series

Volume 1

Spatial Data and Time Series Analysis *C W J Granger*

The Problem of Spatial Autocorrelation *A D Cliff, J K Ord*

On the Optimal Partitioning of Spatially Distributed Point Sets *A J Scott*

Reducing the Travel Time in a Transport Network *T M Ridley*

The Integration of Accounting and Location Theory Frameworks in Urban Modelling *A G Wilson*

Alternate Urban Population Density Models: An Analytical Comparison of Their Validity Range *E Casetti*

Some Factors Influencing the Income Distribution of Households within a City Region *M J H Mogridge*

Regional Econometric Models: A Case Study of Nova Scotia *S Czamanski*

International and Interregional Economic Co-operation and Planning by Linked Computers *T O M Kronsjö*

Two-stage Planning in the Irish Context *M Ross*

Volume 2

Consumer Behaviour and the Tertiary Activity System *H F Andrews*

A Systemic Approach to the Study of Interdependence in Urban Systems *O Wärneryd*

Changes in Production and Technology and Their Spatial Effects *L Nordström*

Transportation and Urbanization *A Ekström, M Williamson*

Service and Spatial Change *B Ohlsson*

Decision-making and Spatial Changes *L Andersson*

A Model of Activity Interrelation and Location *P Terris*

A Model of Interregional Transportation Demand *P Rochefort*

Geographical Specialisation and Trade *L Curry*

The Metropolitan Plan-making Process: Its Theory and Practical Complexities *D E Boyce*

Optimal Goal Achievement in the Development of Outdoor Recreation Facilities *M Hill, M Shechter*

Generalising the Lowry Model *A G Wilson*

The Development of a Model of a Town: Some Considerations *M Echenique, D Crowther, W Lindsay*

Urban Systems: A Generalized Distribution Function *L March*

The Use of Probability Distributions for Comparing the Turnover of Families in a Residential Area *M L Marshall*

Some Theoretical Aspects of Developing Networks *D Fine, P Cowan*

Some Lines of Urban Research in Progress *G Mercadal*

Volume 3

Social Energy: A Relevant New Concept for Regional Science? *W Isard, P Liossatos*

An Econometric Export Base Model of Regional Growth: A Departure from Conventional Techniques *V K Mathur, H S Rosen*

Dynamic Simulation of an Urban System *M Batty*

Static and Dynamic Characteristics of the Negative Exponential Model of Urban Population Distributions *R Bussière*

The Empirical Development of a Disaggregated Residential Location Model: Some Preliminary Results *E L Cripps, Erlet A Cater*

A Comparative Study of Transportation in Major Cities: Some Preliminary Results *Sandra Kensall, B G Redding, R B Smyth*

The Distribution of Social Groups within Cities: Models and Accounts *P H Rees*

Multi-regional Models of Population Structure and Some Implications for a Dynamic Residential Location Model *A G Wilson*

Inter-sectoral Contact Flows and Office Location in Central London *L L H Baker, J B Goddard*

The Structure of Activity Patterns *I Cullen, Vida Godson, Sandra Major*

The Objectives and Methodology of Transport Assessment *J M Clark*

Land Use Planning in Urban Growth Areas: Evaluation—a Compromise *A Metcalf, B Pilgrim*

Some Remarks on People's Evaluation of Environments *P Stringer*

Volume 4

Transport Rate and Pollution as Basic Variables in Space-Time Development *W Isard, P Liossatos*

Space Through Time: A Case Study with New Zealand Airlines *P C Forer*

Two Disequilibrium Models of Regional Growth *H W Richardson*

A Gravity Flows Approach to an Interregional Input-Output Model for the UK *I R Gordon*

An Area-stratified Regional Econometric Model *N J Glickman*

Equilibrium and Catastrophic Modes of Urban Growth *J C Amson*

Spatial Equilibrium in an Ideal Urban Setting with Continuously Distributed Incomes *E Casetti*

Disaggregated Residential Location Models: Some Tests and Further Theoretical Developments *M L Senior, A G Wilson*

On the Feasibility of Simulating the Relationship Between Regional Imbalance and City Growth *M Cordey-Hayes*

Space Allocation Methods in the Design Process *B Harris*

The Development of an Activity-Commodity Representation of Urban Systems as a Potential Framework for Evaluation *R Barras, T A Broadbent*

Volume 5

Trading Behaviour (Transport), Macro and Micro, in an Optimal Space–Time Development Model *W Isard, P Liossatos*

The Problem of Externalities in a Spatial Economy *R A Jackman*

Distributional Bias in the Welfare Pricing of Public Transport Service *N Sakashita*

The Determinants of Urban Manufacturing Location—A Simple Model
G Cameron, J Firn, Mary Latham, D Maclennan

A Model of Air Quality Impact on Industrial Land-use Allocation
D Shefer, J M Guldmann

Approaches to Industrial Location Theory: A Possible Spatial Framework
Doreen Massey

Interregional Programming Models for Economic Development *S R Hashim, P N Mathur*

A Method for Estimating the Spatial Demand for Air Travel: A New England Case Study *C L Choguill*

Learning and Control Mechanisms for Urban Modelling *A G Wilson*

The Construction of Residential Price Indices Incorporating Qualitative and Regional Variation *G J Davies*

The Design of Zoning Systems for Interaction Models *I Masser, P W J Batey, P J B Brown*

Spatial Decomposition and Partitions in Urban Modelling *M Batty, I Masser*

Volume 6

Some Directions for the Extension of Dynamic Spatial Analysis *W Isard*

Regional Underdevelopment in Late Capitalism: A Study of the Northeast of England
J Carney, R Hudson, G Ive, J Lewis

Urban Growth, Rent, and Quasi-rent *G R Walter*

Retailers' Profits and Consumers' Welfare in a Spatial Interaction Shopping Model
A G Wilson

Analysing Multiple Connectivities *R H Atkin*

Heuristic Methods for Solving Combinatorial Problems *T B Boffey*

A Maximum Likelihood Model for Econometric Estimation with Spatial Series
L W Hepple

Constrained Random Simulation: The North Sea Oil Province *K E Rosing, P R Odell*

Urban Commodity Flows and the Environmental Balance *S M Macgill*

Government Action and Manufacturing Employment in the Northern Region
1952–1971 *M E Frost*

Volume 7

The Regional Effects of the Crisis on the Forms of Organisation of Production and Location of Industry in the Mediterranean Basin
J-P Laurençin, J-C Monateri, C Palloix, R Tiberghien, P Vernet

Regional Relations and Economic Structure in the EEC *R Lee*

Central and Peripheral Regions in a Process of Economic Development: The Italian Case
B Secchi

Coal Combines and Interregional Uneven Development in the UK
J Carney, J Lewis, R Hudson

Multinationals, Spatial Inequalities, and Workers' Control *Oonagh McDonald*

An Impact Analysis of Environmental Attraction Profiles and Spatial Mobility
P Nijkamp

Calibrating a Disaggregated Residental Allocation Model—DRAM *S H Putman*

On Hierarchical Dynamics *W Isard*

Urban Simulation—The Vancouver Experience *M Goldberg*

Spatial Externalities and Locational Conflict *M Dear*

Volume 8

Demometrics of Migration and Settlement *A Rogers*

An Alternative Model of the Central-place System *J B Parr*

The Potential of the Microbehavioural Approach to Regional Analysis *R Leigh, D J North*

Accumulation, the Regional Problem, and Nationalism *J Carney, J Lewis* (Editors)

The Politics of Epistemology in Regional Science *J Lewis, B Melville*

On the Stability of a Spatial Classification of Census Enumeration District Data
S Openshaw, A A Gillard

The Merseyside Input–Output Study and its Application in Structure Planning
J de Kanter, W I Morrison

Policy-oriented Housing Models: Some Tentative Applications
P Holm, F Snickars, J R Gustafsson, B Hårsman

Assisted Labour Mobility Policy in Britain: An Assessment of Performance
P B Beaumont

Volume 9

The New Social Science: Toward a Mandala of Thought-and-Action *G Olsson*

Generative and Cognitive Models of Biological Pattern Formation *B C Goodwin*

Efficient Calibration of an Urban Model with Dynamic Solution Properties *M Batty*

Life Cycle Factors and Housing Choice in the Private Sector: A Temporal Economic Study using Path Analytic Approaches *D Bonnar*

The Functional Form of Migration Relations *C P A Bartels, H ter Welle*

Labour Market Dynamics: A Stochastic Analysis of Labour Turnover by Occupation *D Palmer, D Gleave*

Attitude and Social Meaning—A Proper Study for Regional Scientists *M Benwell*

Approaches to Multiple-objective Decision Making with Ranked Objectives *A D Pearman*

Conflicting Social Priorities and Compromise Social Decisions *P Nijkamp, P Rietveld*

The Generation and Evaluation of Structure Plans using a Decision Optimizing Technique (DOT$_2$) *S Openshaw, P Whitehead*

Information Competition and Complementation in Hierarchical Impact Assessment *P Kaniss*

British Colliery Closure Programmes in the North East: from Paradox to Contradiction *J Krieger*

Volume 10

Some Illustrations of Catastrophe Theory Applied to Urban Retailing Structures *A G Wilson, M Clarke*

A Mathematical-programming Framework for the Optimal Location of Spatially Interacting Activities: Theory and Algorithms *G Leonardi*

A Locational-surplus Maximisation Model of Land-use Plan Design *J D Coelho*

A Variable-elasticity-of-substitution Production Function and Urban Land Use: A Theoretical and Empirical Investigation *J B Kau, C F Sirmans, C-F Lee*

Quantification of Gains in Manufacturing Imports of Interregional Cooperation among Developing Countries *P N Mathur, S R Hashim*

Labour Market Turnover: An Industrial Analysis of the Effects of Vacancies, Unemployment, and Firm Size *D Gleave, D Palmer*

A Time-series Analysis of Population and Employment Change in the West Midlands *D Booth, G Hyman*

Externalities for Manufacturing Industry in British Subregions *P M Townroe*

The Standard Metropolitan Labour Area Concept Revisited *M G Coombes, J S Dixon, J B Goddard, S Openshaw, P J Taylor*

The Standard Metropolitan Labour Area Concept Revisited: Comment *M W Smart*